D1447835

THE HANDS OF THE TONGUE
ESSAYS ON DEVIANT SPEECH

Edited by
Edwin D. Craun

STUDIES IN MEDIEVAL CULTURE XLVII

Medieval Institute Publications
Kalamazoo, Michigan

Library of Congress Cataloging-in-Publication Data

The hands of the tongue : essays on deviant speech / edited by Edwin
    D. Craun.
      p. cm. -- (Studies in medieval culture ; 47)
    Includes bibliographical references and index.
    ISBN-13: 978-1-58044-114-8 (casebound : alk. paper)
    ISBN-13: 978-1-58044-115-5 (paperbound : alk. paper)
    1. English language--Middle English, 1100-1500--History.
 2. Language and culture--Great Britain--History--To 1500.
 3. English language--Social aspects--Great Britain. 4. English
 language--Psychological aspects. 5. Blasphemy--Great Britain--History.
 6. Language and languages--Religious aspects. I. Craun, Edwin D.
 PE525.H36 2006
 427'.02--dc22
                                          2006029033

Printed in the United States of America

    1   2   3   4   5   C   P   5   4   3   2   1

Contents

DEVIANT SPEECH AND GENDER

Acknowledgments

I mapped out and began editing this collection of essays at the National Humanities Center, supported by a Jessie Ball duPont Fellowship, made possible by the Jessie Ball duPont Religious, Charitable, and Educational Trust. Supplemented by the Duke Endowment, that fellowship enabled me to work for an academic year at the Center, assisted by its marvelous staff and encouraged by other fellows, especially Helen Solterer. The following fall I edited the essays and wrote the introduction while holding a Fellowship for College Teachers from the National Endowment for the Humanities.

Patricia Quattrin suggested collecting essays on deviant speech from sessions I had organized at the International Congress on Medieval Studies (Kalamazoo, MI) over three years, and all of the essays have profited from the erudition and critical rigor of the anonymous reader for Medieval Institute Publications. Patricia Hollahan has been a dream of an editor, witty and quick to lay out reasonable ways of proceeding, while Julie Scrivener and Juleen Eichinger moved things along resourcefully. Sandy O'Connell performed hitherto unknown feats in revising files in all sorts of word processing formats.

Among the essays, Sandy Bardsley's, written for this collection, became the fourth chapter of her *Venomous Tongues: Speech and Gender in Late Medieval England* (2006); it is printed here, in its original form, with the permission of the University of Pennsylvania Press.

Introduction
Marking Out Deviant Speech

Edwin D. Craun

"Mors et vita in manibus linguae" [Life and death are in the hands of the tongue] (Prov. 18:21).[1] To attribute hands to the tongue is to ascribe power to the instrument of speech, and through it to speech itself. Like the sword and fire, two central sapiential and biblical figures for the tongue recast endlessly in medieval texts, especially *pastoralia* and sermons, this metaphor conveys the tongue's power to destroy life as well as to preserve it.[2] The hands also insist upon the corporeality of the tongue as the instrument of speech and so upon its capacity to act: its words are deeds with consequences for speakers and listeners. This insistent corporeality is manifested in some of the punishments for destructive speech that Elizabeth Ewan's and Miriam Gill's essays present below: the tongues of the damned pierced, nailed, or set afire by demons; the tongue addressed by Scottish malefactors with the prescribed formula "Tongue, you lied."

What destructive powers did the tongue and its speech have for medievals? It could damn humans through blasphemy (Gill essay). It could occlude penitential knowledge of the self, especially of the misdirected will, by generating excuses for what the medieval clergy regarded as sin (Craun essay). It could disrupt monastic disciplines of meditation or distract parishioners during sermons (essays by Scott and Phillips). It could turn good repute to ill repute, destroying a woman's chances for marriage, a man's masculine self, a merchant's credit, or a defendant's status (a plaintiff's, too) in a court of law (essays by Bardsley and Neal). However, speech, in court or other public places, also could maintain or restore credit, status, and masculinity—if not always a woman's marriage prospects. And it could preserve a knight's honor as justiciar and liege or a woman's honor as a faithful feudal wife (Schroeder's essay on Lancelot's equivocations in *Le Morte Darthur*).

What institutions—and what social groups enmeshed in them—determined that certain types of speech were destructive in medieval culture? What institutionally sanctioned social, religious, and political norms and practices demanded that some speech acts be judged as deviant, as departing ("de via") from beneficial forms of living? And who policed speech, promulgating norms and punishing deviant acts? Finally, how were these norms and disciplinary actions contested, insofar as the written and visual record discloses that?

Let me begin with the general institution that generated the most explicit, full, and sustained taxonomizing of speech. The western Church constructed the Sins of the Tongue from Jewish and Christian scripture, Greek and Roman moral philosophy (usually filtered through the Latin Fathers), patristic texts, and contemporary social life. Early monasticism (Benedictine, Cluniac) had its lingual *bêtes noires,* as Scott Bruce explains below: blasphemy, slander, and especially idle talk, forbidden by its rules, by glosses on them, and by customaries. Sermons within monastic communities cited scriptural prohibitions. *Exempla* drawn from monastic life illustrated how these forms of speech eroded the integrity of individual and corporate religious life, violating obedience to the example of Jesus, disrupting prayer and attention to Scripture, involving the vowed in life beyond the walls. The deviant forms of speech guarded against by monastic regulators and by abbots were multiplied and developed much more fully in the movement of pastoral reform that was born in eleventh-century Gregorian reform. This movement was enabled by the constitutions of the Fourth Lateran Council of 1215 and the provincial and diocesan legislation that followed, and it was carried out in parishes by preaching, directing confessions, catechizing, admonishing, and excommunicating.

The higher clergy, often educated in the growing universities (many of them new), directed this movement not only by legislation and visitation but also by its writing of *pastoralia.* As I have argued in *Lies, Slander, and Obscenity*, an Augustinian semiotic undergirded pastoral texts—and their offspring of sermons, confessional dialogues, and the give-and-take of catechesis. It defined speech as the messenger ("nuntius") of reason, designed by God and early human communities to make the speaker's thoughts manifest to others and so to build trustworthy human institutions: courts of law, political assemblies, religious teaching, marriages. Such a semiotic, grounded in Christian scripture and partially built from Aristotelian and Stoic philosophy, prized certain types of speech such as prayer, praise, and preaching. More broadly, it sanctioned all forms of teaching and learning, all forms of communicating thought, except, of course, for what contravened Scripture.[3] When speakers deviated from this general norm, according to pastoral writers, they were moved by a malicious will that generated intentions to deceive or to injure others. Like the moral theologians on whom they drew, these pastoral writers analyzed intentions, states of will, and, to a lesser extent, the truth of statements, to differentiate twenty-four common verbal sins, most of which are thoroughly set forth by Carla Casagrande and Silvana Vecchio's study of theological and pastoral literature from the 1180s to the fifteenth century, *I peccati della lingua*. Like monastic *regulae*, pastoral texts also prized silence, stigmatizing as deviant excessive speaking and idle speaking (see Phillips' essay below). These texts also generated a rhetoric of figures, *exempla*, horrifying consequences, and authoritative sayings designed, especially in preaching and in admonition (in and out of auricular confession), to create revulsion against specific types of deviant speech.[4]

While the long life of the most widespread pastoral texts on the Sins of the Tongue, such as the ninth tractate in Guillelmus Peraldus's *Summa de vitiis*, and the sheer quantity of *pastoralia* ensured that this clerical typology and rhetoric reigned even beyond medieval culture, it was neither ossified nor uncontested. Types could be employed more loosely by ecclesiastical officials when they combated perceived threats to doctrine and practice or, more generally, when a religious community was scandalized by religious difference, as David Lawton has demonstrated in the case of blasphemy.[5] And casuistical theologians could relax some hard-and-fast distinctions, permitting some types of equivocation that become central to Peter Schroeder's reading of Lancelot's speeches defending Queen Guinevere (and himself).[6] Other pastoral categories, such as idle talk, scurrility, and base speech, loosely constructed even in scholastically derived texts, became even more plastic as they passed into the hands of lay listeners and of those (clerical and lay) who wrote extended narratives, lyrics, and plays. (See, for example, the essays edited by Ziolkowski in *Obscenity*.) Moreover, in the more playful discursive space of fiction, pastoral discourse on deviant speech could be countered, parodied, and rejected by fictional figures, such as Geoffrey Chaucer's Wife of Bath in my essay below. Authors built such deviant speakers into longer texts—and also disciplinary or teaching clerics (or quasi-clerics), such as Chaucer's Parson, John Gower's Genius, and Jean de Meun's Raison—in order to explore the claims of pastoral discourse, evaluating its norms, probing and modifying its arguments, gutting or validating its rhetoric.[7] As Susan Phillips argues below, the clergy was particularly worried that *exempla*, unmoored from the context of preaching, would be transformed and used for different purposes by lay auditors and readers.

Speech acts that might be construed as deviant according to pastoral moral theology were policed, in the first rank, by priests at every level of the Church. Their schools enforced lingual discipline. Their sermons, confessional dialogues, and admonitions, the commissioned wall paintings, stained glass, and misericords in their churches all dwelt on eternal consequences of sinning by word (as well as, in the ancient tripartite formula, by thought and deed), using *exempla* in which God's lightning strikes blaspheming knights and merchants who swear falsely in court, causing them to immediately fall into convulsions and die, grotesquely disfigured. Writers who adopted clerical rhetoric did much the same. Recall Dante's blaspheming Capanaeus or flattering Thais. The clergy, of course, disciplined verbal sinners by imposing penances, usually private, but public when they judged that the community was threatened. Blasphemers, who might draw divine wrath on a city or country, performed penances in front of the church, and, at times, kings (Louis IX of France, for example) or civic authorities promulgated laws mandating ritual public punishments for blasphemers. Ecclesiastical courts heard cases involving some deviant speech, such as defamation (Neal's essay below), defined (in England at least) more narrowly than the pastoral movement's slander as maliciously and falsely imparting a crime to someone.[8] The higher clergy policed the speech of the parish clergy, especially during visitations, where bishops, as Sandy Bardsley explains below, heard lay complaints against their priests' slander and gossip. However, *pastoralia*, narrative literature, plays, and legal records indicate that deviant speakers were notorious for impudently persisting in their habits, flaunting their resistance to clerical acculturation. Repeat offenders, of course, sometimes were excommunicated. And heretics turned imputations of blasphemy against their clerical inquisitors, accusing them of the same (John Wyclif's *De blasfemia*, for example).

The most prudential strains of pastoral discourse often were drawn by compilers into works on good governance in the overlapping spheres of the individual, the household, the city, and the kingdom. School texts (such as the *Disticha Catonis*) and parental admonitions in prose or verse were designed to inculcate verbal self-control within the disciplinary structures of the school and the household. Constructing the deviant in terms of the dangers that ungoverned speech could pose to domestic life, reputation, livelihood, and life itself, this advice literature took particular aim at loquacity, slander, and lying. To speak deviantly is to violate your own self-interest. How-to manuals for adults, like the legal counselor and civil servant Albertano da Brescia's *Ars loquendi et tacendi* (1245), promoted disciplined speech in courts of law and political assemblies, casting the normative and the deviant in terms of what promoted or what damaged the speaker's reputation and, sometimes, his political community (the commune, in Albertano's case).[9] However, some works on good counsel, whether solely discursive, like Brunetto Latini's *Li livres dou tresor* (ca. 1265), or mixedly discursive and fictive, like the English *Mum and the Soothsegger* (after 1409) and Book VII of John Gower's *Confessio Amantis* (late fourteenth century), grounded norms for speech in the ruler's knowledge of himself and of his subjects' needs. These texts, James Simpson argues, are often somewhat Aristotelian, privileging politics over ethics. In them, political advisors were exhorted to be truth-tellers (albeit often tactful ones), shunning self-promoting flattery and lies out of loyalty to the king's welfare and the common good.[10]

Less prudential and more prescriptive, courtesy books drew their norms for speech from the more expansive monastic customaries of the twelfth century and from courtly life. Read in mercantile as well as noble households, they promoted verbal self-control and proscribed lying and oath breaking as contrary to truth, in the ethical sense of the word: contrary to personal integrity and loyalty to those to whom one is bound. That is, fidelity to self and others matters to them as much as, or more than, reputation. The same types of speech, of course, were branded as deviant by the chivalric romances shaped by courtesy books and by the social practices of chivalry, as clerics developed them to restrain and channel the violence of the warrior class.[11] Also consumed by the same classes, the literature of *fin amor*, in its many forms, features authority figures, like Amour in the *Roman de la Rose* or Gower's Genius, who issue commandments to male lovers, framed so that they will gain reputations as men worthy of being loved by women. (Do not gossip. Do not defame rivals.) In chivalric romance, there are those who reject the speech norms of homosocial life and of love, the *médisants* and the oath-breakers whose transgressive speech is contained by the narrative as they are exposed and defeated.

The previous two paragraphs are littered with the pronoun "his." In judging acts of speech, perhaps even more than in other areas of medieval life and writing, gender comes to the fore. Men often were associated with violent types of speech, speech that assaulted God or others, like great oaths (a form of blasphemy, as Gill explains below) and insults (Bardsley's essay). Women were associated with transgressive forms of garrulousness, on the grounds of Greek and Roman philosophy and misogynist literature, of the wisdom books in Jewish scripture, and of patristic writing. As developed in twelfth-century satire, this misogynist strain in medieval texts singled out as deviant those types of speech which threatened to betray male secrets or damage male reputations in the largely or wholly homosocial worlds of formal education, trade, and ecclesiastical offices: revealing secrets, loquacity, lies, slander. It also defined the deviant in terms of female speech—insults, badgering, and deceptive sweet talk—that threatened male dominion, especially in the household.[12] Groups of female speakers were perceived as particularly potent agents of such threatening speech. *Exempla* featuring deviant female speakers passed from pastoral texts into conduct literature for women, often a form of education in middle-class as well as noble households. Offering advice on how to maintain families' reputations and social standings, texts such as the widely read *Le livre du Chevalier de la Tour Landry* cautioned women against chiding or reproving men (especially in public places), against slandering men or women, and against divulging their husbands' counsel (read "secrets").[13] However, accusations of slander also could be defensive weapons in the hands of women whose reputations were assaulted by sexual slurs, or whose character and capacities were diminished by misogynist speakers hellbent on mastery. At least in fifteenth-century France, writers such as Christine de Pizan, who combated verbal injury to themselves and women in general, could situate their writing in a Roman tradition that sought to curb slander as a threat to the commonwealth.[14]

Late medieval civic officials also considered slander a threat to public order, as well as to their own authority and reputations. As a crime against society in a highly verbal culture, slander not only injured reputations and so legal, social, and economic standing, but it also provoked violent retaliation, threatening social stability.[15] So, slander cases were tried in English and Scottish manorial and borough courts, and ritual punishments, as Elizabeth Ewan analyzes them below, were designed to satisfy the injured community, as well as those slandered. English and Scottish courts, at least, showed particular concern for the verbal abuse of community officials and disruptive speech in the courts, prosecuting both extensively (Bardsley below). These local courts also targeted as scolds a "new" type of deviant speaker, viz., those whose insults posed dangers to local overlapping social, economic, and governing elites. Suits for scolding and slander often were directed against economic competitors, especially women and outsiders. In such suits, Sandy Bardsley has argued elsewhere, pastoral discourse on deviant speech was appropriated by the laity in late medieval England to "reinscribe traditional social hierarchies and discourage disruptive and inflammatory speech."[16]

The sheer range of medieval institutions and social groups that evolved norms for deviant, as for sanctioned, speech demands that this collection of essays be multidisciplinary. We are social historians, literary historians and critics, historians of religion, and an art historian. Many of our essays bridge disciplines, with social historians adducing evidence from lyrics, narrative poetry, and plays, or literary historians working from moral theology and biblical exegesis. Some of our essays also bridge the even greater chasm—in many medievalists' minds at least—between text and practice, examining both prescriptive literature, such as *pastoralia,* and court records. Certainly the whole set of essays works to remind medievalists that any aspect of medieval culture worth studying must be explored collectively. A collective enterprise generated the collection. All but two of its essays were read, in an early form, at four sessions labeled Sins of the Tongue/Transgressive Speech, at that high fair of the crossroads, the International Congress on Medieval Studies. Together they present a clear picture of what we know about deviant speech in medieval culture, a picture that has begun to achieve the depth and richness of scholarship on slander in the early modern period, exploring what speech acts can tell us about gender, crime and punishment, agency, ethics, and literary craftsmanship.[17]

NOTES

1. Although modern editions of the Vulgate read "in manu," pastoral texts on the Sins of the Tongue pluralize the noun (e.g., *Speculum morale,* col. 866, and Guillelmus Peraldus, *Summa,* fol. F1r).

2. Casagrande and Vecchio present the central metaphors for the tongue, as developed in moral theology and pastoral discourse, in "Le métafore."

3. Craun, *Lies,* 25–37. Colish discusses Augustinian sign theory in *Mirror* and "Stoic Theory"; Jackson, in "Signs"; Markus, in "St. Augustine." Myles examines signification, will, and intentionality in medieval theories of language, then reads in detail those Canterbury tales centered on acts of cursing and slander (*Chaucerian Realism*). Some moral theologians and pastoral writers also define deviant types in terms of what violates the virtues of charity and justice. See Johnston's brief discussion of Thomas Aquinas in "Treatment," 29–31.

4. Craun, *Lies,* 56–72.

5. Lawton, *Blasphemy,* 43–109.

6. These casuistical writers were anticipated by some patristic and twelfth-century writers, who, Colish recently has shown ("Rethinking Lying"), countenanced certain lies that harm no one and benefit some and "pious frauds," such as those of Judith or Jacob. I am grateful to Marcia Colish for sending me page proofs of this essay.

7. Other examples from Middle English literature: Chaucer's Pardoner (Patterson's *Chaucer*, 367–421), his Manciple and the *Patience*-poet's Jonah (my *Lies*, 187–212 and 73–112), and enemies of Christ and the vices in Middle English plays (Forest-Hill, *Transgressive Language*).

8. *Select Cases*, ed. Helmholz, xiv–xl.

9. Powell develops the civic context of Albertano's rhetoric in *Albertanus of Brescia*.

10. Simpson, *Reform*, 201–29. Barr examines the rhetoric of good counsel in *Mum and the Soothsegger* ("Spekyng" and *Signes and Sothe*, 51–94).

11. Nicholls surveys western European courtesy books in *Matter of Courtesy*, 7–76.

12. Burns, *Bodytalk*, especially ch. 1; Lochrie, *Margery Kempe*; Cox, *Gender and Language*; Blamires, ed., *Women Defamed*.

13. Ashley and Dronzek have researched recently the readership and educative uses of conduct books ("*Miroir*" and "Gendered Theories"). Christine de Pizan also advises her female readers to hew to these norms for women's speech, just as she defends women on the grounds that they fulfill them (for example, women keep men's secrets better than men themselves in the *Le livre de la cité des dames*). However, she defends these norms and advises against deviating from them on religious and ethical, as well as on prudential and familial, grounds: divine commandments, loyalty, fidelity to oaths, reciprocity (*Le livre des trois vertus* 2.6–8). Fenster explores Christine's acute sense of the risks of defining the self in terms of reputation in "La Fama."

14. Solterer, "Fiction," and *Master*, 97–216; Walters, "Constructing Reputations."

15. Lindahl takes his London cases from the *Calendar of Pleas and Memoranda Rolls*, from Letter Books, and from guild records (*Earnest Games*, 73–86).

16. Bardsley, "Sin," 146; Jones and Zell, "Bad Conversation"; McIntosh, *Controlling Misbehavior*, throughout, but especially 57–62. Always loosely defined, scolding, McIntosh demonstrates, came to include spreading lies that damaged others' reputations.

17. For example, Kaplan's *The Culture of Slander*; Gowing's *Domestic Dangers*; Jardine's "'Why should he call her whore?'"; Sharpe's *Defamation*.

WORKS CITED

PRIMARY SOURCES

Guillelmus Peraldus. *Summa de vitiis*. Cologne: Quentell, 1479.

Speculum morale. In Vincent of Beauvais, *Speculum maius*. Vol. 3. Douai: Belleri, 1625; repr. Graz: Academische Druch, 1964.

SECONDARY SOURCES

Ashley, Kathleen. "The *Miroir des bonnes femmes*." In *Medieval Conduct*, ed. Kathleen Ashley and Robert L. A. Clark, 86–105. Minneapolis: University of Minnesota Press, 2001.

Bardsley, Sandy. "Sin, Speech and Scolding in Late Medieval England." In *"Fama": The Politics of Talk and Reputation in Medieval Europe,* ed. Daniel Smail and Thelma Fenster, 145–64. Ithaca: Cornell University Press, 2003.

Barr, Helen. *Signes and Sothe: Language in the "Piers Plowman" Tradition.* Cambridge: D. S. Brewer, 1994.

———. "'Spekyng for one's sustenance': The Rhetoric of Counsel in *Mum and the Sothsegger,* Skelton's *Bowge of Court,* and Elyot's *Pasquil the Playne.*" In *The Long Fifteenth Century: Essays for Douglas Gray,* ed. Helen Cooper and Sally Mapstone, 249–72. Oxford: Clarendon, 1997.

Blamires, Alcuin, ed. *Women Defamed and Women Defended: An Anthology of Medieval Texts.* Oxford: Clarendon, 1992.

Burns, E. Jane. *Bodytalk: When Women Speak in Old French Literature.* Philadelphia: University of Pennsylvania Press, 1993.

Casagrande, Carla, and Silvana Vecchio. "Le métafore della lingua (secoli XII e XIII)." In *Oralità: Cultura, letteratura, discorso,* 635–62. Rome: Edizioni dell'Ateneo, 1985.

———. *I peccati della lingua: Disciplina ed etica della parola nella cultura medievale.* Rome: Istituto della Enciclopedia italiana, 1987. (*Les péchés de la langue: Discipline et éthique de la parole dans la culture médiévale.* Trans. Philippe Baillet. Paris: Cerf, 1991.)

Colish, Marcia L. *The Mirror of Language: A Study in the Medieval Theory of Knowledge.* Rev. ed. Lincoln: University of Nebraska Press, 1983.

———. "Rethinking Lying in the Twelfth Century." In *Virtue and Ethics in the Twelfth Century,* ed. Richard Newhauser, 155–73. Leiden: Brill, 2005.

———. "The Stoic Theory of Verbal Signification and the Problem of Lies and False Statements from Antiquity to Saint Anselm." In *Archéologie du signe,* ed. Lucie Brind'Amour and Eugene Vance, 17–44. Toronto: Pontifical Institute for Mediaeval Studies, 1983.

Cox, Catherine. *Gender and Language in Chaucer.* Gainesville: University of Florida Press, 1997.

Craun, Edwin. *Lies, Slander and Obscenity in Medieval English Literature: Pastoral Rhetoric and the Deviant Speaker.* Cambridge: Cambridge University Press, 1997.

Dronzek, Anna. "Gendered Theories of Education in Fifteenth-Century Conduct Books." In *Medieval Conduct,* ed. Kathleen Ashley and Robert L. A. Clark, 135–59. Minneapolis: University of Minnesota Press, 2001.

Fenster, Thelma. "La Fama, la femme, et La Dame de la Tour: Christina de Pizan et la médisance." In *Au Champ des scriptures: IIIe Colloque international sur Christine de Pizan,* ed. Eric Hicks, 461–77. Paris: Honoré Champion, 2000.

Forest-Hill, Lynn. *Transgressive Language in Medieval English Drama: Signs of Challenge and Change.* Aldershot: Ashgate, 2000.

Gowing, Laura. *Domestic Dangers: Women, Words, and Sex in Early Modern England.* Oxford: Clarendon, 1996.

Jackson, R. Darrell. "The Theory of Signs in *De doctrina Christiana.*" In *Augustine: A Collection of Critical Essays,* ed. R. A. Markus, 92–147. New York: Doubleday, 1972.

Jardine, Lisa. "'Why should he call her whore?': Defamation and Desdemona's Case." In *Addressing Frank Kermode,* ed. Margaret Tudeau-Clayton and Martin Warner, 124–53. Urbana: University of Illinois Press, 1991.

Johnston, Mark. "The Treatment of Speech in Medieval Ethical and Courtesy Literature." *Rhetorica* 4 (1986), 21–46.

Jones, Karen, and Michael Zell. "Bad Conversation? Gender and Social Control in a Kentish Borough, c. 1450–1570." *Continuity and Change* 13 (1998), 11–31.

Kaplan, M. Lindsay. *The Culture of Slander in Early Modern England.* Cambridge: Cambridge University Press, 1997.

Lawton, David. *Blasphemy.* Philadelphia: University of Pennsylvania Press, 1993.

Lindahl, Carl. *Earnest Games: Folkloric Patterns in the "Canterbury Tales."* Bloomington: Indiana University Press, 1987.

Lochrie, Karma. *Margery Kempe and the Translations of the Flesh.* Philadelphia: University of Pennsylvania Press, 1997.

Markus, R. A. "St. Augustine on Signs." In *Augustine: A Collection of Critical Essays,* ed. Markus, 61–91. New York: Doubleday, 1972.

McIntosh, Majorie Keniston. *Controlling Misbehavior in England, 1370–1600.* New York: 1998.

Myles, Robert. *Chaucerian Realism.* Woodbridge: Boydell and Brewer, 1994.

Nicholls, Jonathan. *The Matter of Courtesy: Medieval Courtesy Books and the Gawain-Poet.* Cambridge: D. S. Brewer, 1985.

Patterson, Lee. *Chaucer and the Subject of History.* Madison: University of Wisconsin Press, 1991.

Powell, James M. *Albertanus of Brescia: The Pursuit of Happiness in the Early Thirteenth Century.* Philadelphia: University of Pennsylvania Press, 1992.

Select Cases on Defamation to 1600. Ed. Richard Helmholz. London: Seldon Society, 1985.

Sharpe, J. A. *Defamation and Sexual Slander in Early Modern England.* Borthwick Papers 58. York: Borthwick Institute, 1980.

Simpson, James. *Reform and Cultural Revolution. The Oxford English Literary History,* vol. 2, 1350–1547. Oxford: Oxford University Press, 2002.

Solterer, Helen. *The Master and Minerva: Disputing Women in French Medieval Culture.* Berkeley: University of California Press, 1995.

———. "Fiction vs. Defamation: The Quarrel over the *Romance of the Rose.*" *The Medieval History Journal* 2:1 (1999), 111–41.

Walters, Lori. "Constructing Reputations: *Fama* and Memory in Christine de Pizan's *Charles V* and *L'Advision Christine.*" In *"Fama": The Politics of Talk and Reputation in Medieval Europe,* ed. Daniel Smail and Thelma Fenster, 118–42. Ithaca: Cornell University Press, 2003.

Ziolkowski, Jan, ed. *Obscenity: Social Control and Artistic Creation in the European Middle Ages.* Leiden: Brill, 1998.

Sins of the Tongue

The Tongue Is a Fire
The Discipline of Silence in
Early Medieval Monasticism (400–1100)

Scott G. Bruce

Early medieval abbeys were alive with sound. The glorification of God through the celebration of the divine office was the primary activity of cloistered men and women, who intoned the psalms for the benefit of their souls and for the spiritual well-being of the entire Christian community. Like heavenly bees in their hives, monks were not silent in their industry. Their lips were always busy with the buzzing of prayer and praise.[1] Yet in the sonorous environment of early medieval abbeys, monks also esteemed silence as a saving virtue. Apart from their participation in devotional activities such as the divine office, it often was forbidden for them to utter a sound. Monastic silence did not entail the complete suppression of human speech, however, as the term *silence* implies in its modern sense. Rather, it involved the regulation of the desire to utter words that were harmful to the disciplined development of the individual monk and the prayerful purpose of the entire *coenobium*.

This study has two goals: first, to examine the general principles of monastic silence through an investigation of the rules and rationales for the cultivation of this virtue in early coenobitic communities; and second, to highlight the unique contribution of the monks of the Burgundian abbey of Cluny (founded in 910) to the understanding and expression of this custom. The first principle of Christian asceticism was the renunciation of the world in anticipation of the Last Judgment.[2] In accordance with this, early medieval monks renounced any spoken words that mired their thoughts in the world and distracted their attention from God. Rules of personal conduct and literary models of virtuous behavior written for monks in this period shared a general concern with the avoidance of sinful speech. As a result, in the early Middle Ages, the cultivation of silence emerged as an important aspect of monastic discipline, defined here as the practices through which individuals formed and directed their moral disposition in pursuit of Christian virtue.[3]

Silence was an important instrument of monastic conduct, but in the early tenth century, the translation of this discipline into practice became an issue of contention. At a time when civil wars, foreign invasions, and the lay appropriation of abbeys caused standards of observance to languish in many cloistered communities in the Frankish heartlands, the abbots of Cluny espoused an ideal of personal silence that was much more rigorous and comprehensive than the customs of other communities. They amplified traditional precepts against speaking to such an extent that their contemporaries accused them of novelty and innovation. The Cluniac response to these criticisms articulated an understanding of the discipline of silence freighted with moral significance and eschatological expectation. Their standards of discipline were in fact so rigorous that they developed an unprecedented form of non-verbal communication—a language of hand signs—to encourage and enforce the practice of silence in their communities. In their effort to emulate the conduct of the angels in anticipation of joining their ranks in heaven at the end of time, the monks of Cluny fostered a celestial silence that challenged and threatened the received traditions of their contemporaries.

Set a Watchman to My Mouth

Early monastic authors were not effusive cataloguers of sins of the tongue. Evidence for their attitudes towards idle conversation is relatively scant, especially when compared to the rich and ordered taxonomies of harmful speech and its consequences that survive in scholastic and pastoral literature from the later Middle Ages.[4] Nonetheless, currents of concern for the danger of careless words are discernable in many monastic sources written between the fourth and sixth centuries.[5] They are especially prevalent in normative rulings of conduct, such as the sixth-century *Rule of Benedict*, which became the most influential touchstone of monastic legislation in the Middle Ages.[6] The authors of these rules lived with a strong sense of history and tradition. For them the instruments of monastic virtue were preserved in a body of literature by and about the ancient monks of the eastern deserts, particularly the *Sayings of the Desert Fathers* and the *Rule of Saint Basil.*[7] Among these works were translations of Greek texts on monastic life as well as the original compositions of displaced eastern ascetics, such as

John Cassian, who wrote for Latin-speaking audiences. The words and deeds of the earliest hermits provided templates of discipline and practice for the abbeys of early medieval Italy and Gaul.

The first Christian monks led harsh lives of self-deprivation and devotion on the fringes of urban societies throughout Egypt and the Near East in late antiquity.[8] The desert, the measureless setting of their struggles, was an ambivalent image in early monastic literature. It was depicted both as a flowering paradise inhabited by angels and as a sweltering landscape of terrifying vastness, abounding in monstrous creatures.[9] For the monks themselves, the desert was a crucible of discipline, where they tempered their carnal passions through sexual abstinence, extreme fasts, sleepless nights, and ceaseless prayers. The aim of their devotion was intensely personal. Through rigorous mortifications, the desert fathers strived to strip away all vestiges of their individual will and surrender themselves completely to God. They sought nothing less than a return to the condition of Adam in the Garden of Eden, before his willful disobedience caused the Fall of Man. In the words of Peter Brown:

> Once they had faced out the terrible risks involved in remaining human in a nonhuman environment, the men of the desert were thought capable of recovering, in the hushed silence of that dead landscape, a touch of the unimaginable glory of Adam's first state.[10]

The "hushed silence of that dead landscape" was broken routinely by the voices of the hermits. Verbal exchange was an essential feature of the relationship between ascetic masters and their disciples. The desert was home to many great old men, spiritual fathers whose purity of heart lent their words an unassailable authority.[11] These men attracted a steady stream of aspirants and visitors, who clamored to hear their advice: "Abba, speak a word to me."[12] The *Sayings of the Desert Fathers* depicted with extraordinary vividness a series of intimate and anxious consultations between masters and disciples about the doubts that assailed aspiring monks in the desert: "How should we live? Why is my heart hard and why do I not fear God? Tell me, what must I do to be saved?"[13] The responses of the desert fathers provided their listeners with spiritual direction, but they also reinforced the norms and behaviors of the community of disciples. Taken together, first as an oral tradition and later as a body of texts, these sayings created a shared context of moral understanding for the correct practice of ascetic discipline.[14]

Not all verbal utterances were beneficial, however; some threatened the integrity of monastic communities and the souls of their inhabitants. Early rules of conduct for cloistered men and women made a sharp distinction between words used for holy purposes, such as the instruction of disciples and the praise of God, and those that were useless and potentially harmful.[15] Generally speaking, idle words were those which did not pertain to the edification of the faith.[16] The sins of slander and murmuring merited special attention in early monastic literature. Slander was perilous for monks because it countermanded the teachings of Christ on one of the most important commandments: to love your neighbor as yourself (Matt. 22:36–40). Envious disparagement pitted the brethren against one another and created discord within the community.[17] In the words of one desert father: "It is better to eat meat and to drink wine, than to eat the flesh of the brothers in slander."[18] Preachers in early medieval Gaul also warned their monastic audiences that such talk eroded the spiritual benefits of their vocation.[19] Monks who spoke evil of others were especially vulnerable to the "poisoned blades of their own tongues."[20] Slanderous words wounded the object of their malice as well. According to Bishop Valerian of Cimiez, the tongue had an evil all its own: the power to pierce the secret recesses of the human heart. Once inflicted, these wounds lasted a lifetime. Only death could free the stricken organ from the spite of evil speech.[21]

Unlike slander, which eroded lateral relationships in the abbey, the sin of murmuring was an act of disobedience, an expression of discontent against one's superiors that undermined the vertical hierarchy of the monastic community. Many ancient rulings advised monks to complete their assigned tasks without verbal complaint.[22] Murmurers should live in fear of Paul's foreboding advice to the Christian community at Corinth (1 Cor. 10:10): "Do not grumble, as some of them did and perished at the hands of the Destroyer."[23] Like the ancient Hebrews who murmured against Moses and Aaron in the wilderness (Num. 14:1–37), rebellious and disgruntled monks made their complaint in the hearing of the Lord and risked kindling the fire of divine wrath. If some among the people of God perished in the desert because of the sin of murmuring, asked Alcuin, how much more deserving of punishment is a cloistered monk, if he does not fear to sow evil grumblings in his mind?[24]

Early monastic authors also condemned the unbridled expression of foolish mirth.[25] There was no place for laughter in the tortured landscape of the desert. The great old men despaired to hear their disciples express levity. Upon overhearing someone laugh, a hermit was said to ask in an ominous tone: "We have to render an account of our whole life before heaven and earth and you can laugh?"[26] The saints of early monasticism were ever mindful of the terrible reckoning of sinful words and deeds that confronted every soul at the end of time.[27] Their constant reflection on the coming judgment meant that the spirit of penitence followed them like a shadow.[28] It was more fitting for the desert hermits to weep in this world and thereby earn laughter in the world to come (Luke 6:21). Some of their western emulators, such as Martin of Tours, never were seen to laugh.[29] On the whole, however, Latin authors tempered the harsh penitential spirit of the desert with respect to the expression of mirth. Their rulings tended to treat laughter like any other verbal utterance: it only became a sinful and dangerous practice when it was excessive and disruptive.[30]

Like an embankment that wards off a destructive tide, the cultivation of silence deflected the dangerous erosion of sinful words. Early medieval precepts on monastic conduct promoted silence at all times. Rulings for cloistered communities forbade talking specifically in the church, the refectory, and the dormitory. Personal conversation was strictly prohibited in the church because the celebration of the divine office demanded the full attention of monks.[31] Even brethren who came there to pray in solitude were encouraged to do so in silence, esteeming tears and the fervor of the heart over a clamorous voice.[32] Garrulous monks distracted the devout from their attentive worship. Likewise, personal silence in the refectory ensured that the brethren applied their minds to the lessons of the texts read aloud during meals.[33] Bishop Aurelian of Arles (d. 551) instructed monks to attend to the reader without conversing so that they could be nourished outwardly by the food and inwardly by the Word of God.[34] Lastly, talking at night always was expressly forbidden.[35] The fifth-century *Rule of the Master* discouraged its readers from speaking once they had completed Compline, the last office of the day. They were instructed to keep so profound a silence throughout the night that no one would believe that any monks were in the abbey at all.[36] In the seventh century, a monk named Waldebert advised the cloistered women of Faremoutiers not to sleep facing each other in the same bed because it may incite the desire to talk together in the dark.[37]

Early medieval hagiographers made clear to their monastic audiences the dreadful consequences of idle speech. In the *Life of Benedict*, Pope Gregory the Great (d. 604) related how the holy abbot warned two religious women to curb their tongues and refrain from unguarded conversation under threat of excommunication. A few days later, both women died without changing their ways and were buried in the church. So powerful and binding was Benedict's admonition that, during the celebration of the mass, whenever the deacon called out "Whoever is not in communion, let him leave this place," the dead women rose from their tombs and shambled from the church.[38] An offering to God from the saint restored the women's souls to communion, but the message of the episode was plain to Gregory's audience: sins of the tongue had the power to exclude Christians from the community of the faithful, both in this life and in the life to come. When speech was pregnant with danger, silence offered the greatest protection.

The discipline of silence was more than a safeguard against the perils of wayward speech; it was also a positive practice in its own right. In the vastness of the desert, where spoken words could resound with unearthly force, the early hermits taught that the cultivation of silence was essential both as a means of achieving a heightened awareness of the presence of God and as a necessary preparation for the utterance of good and useful words.[39] The hermit Agathon allegedly kept a stone in his mouth for three years to learn how to remain silent.[40] The reward for such diligence was enlightened discernment: "If the soul keeps far away from all discourse and words, the Spirit of God will come to her and she who was barren will be fruitful."[41] Consequently, hermits were not hasty to answer the questions of their disciples. It was not uncommon for them to sit in silence for many days, ignoring the pleas of their followers until the spirit moved them to speak.[42]

Monastic rules from Gaul and Italy emphasized that the abnegation of the desire to converse was a virtue intimately related to humility and obedience. Cassian warned that the sin of pride clouded monastic discernment with respect to the tongue.[43] Individuals who were puffed up with self-importance were usually far too eager to engage in idle conversation and only seemed to cultivate silence when nursing rancorous thoughts about others. Monks of this kind were no friends of silence ("nec umquam taciturnitatis amica"). The sixth-century *Rule of Benedict* devoted an entire chapter to the moral benefits of this virtue (Ch. 6: *De taciturnitate*), commencing with verses from the Book of Psalms that united silence and humility: "I have set a watchman to my mouth. I was mute and was humbled and I remained silent from good things" (Ps. 38:2–3).[44] Silence was also an expression of obedience, a virtue closely related to humility.[45] Early medieval monks emulated the example of Christ, who was obedient unto death. Through fear of hell or in expectation of eternal life, they hastened to obey the command of a superior as though it was a command from God.[46] The *Rule* enjoined them never to speak without permission:

> Therefore, because of the grave importance of silence, let the permission
> to speak be granted only rarely to observant disciples, even though it be
> for good and holy and edifying words, because it is written: 'In speaking
> profusely you will not escape sin' (Prov. 10:19). And elsewhere: 'Death and
> life are in the power of the tongue' (Prov. 18:21).[47]

Monks were required to seek permission to speak from a superior with the
utmost humility and respectful submission.[48] This privilege was granted only
to individuals who could be trusted to shun worldly topics and temper their
words with modesty and restraint.[49] Important monastic officials, such as
the abbot, the cellarer, and the porter, also were allowed to converse in accordance with the demands of their offices.[50] Without permission to speak,
however, the obedient monk was expected to remain silent.

In the economy of personal salvation that characterized early monasticism, the discipline of silence had a dual function: it safeguarded the monk's
soul from the perils of sinful speech, and it fostered the virtues of humility
and obedience. It would be misleading to conclude, however, that early
medieval monks abandoned the need for speaking altogether. From Egypt
to Gaul, the spoken word was the medium of divine service, humble teaching, and official duties. The tongue was always a dangerous instrument,
liable at any time to succumb to the pleasures of idle conversation and
immoderate laughter, but the discerning monk knew the boundaries of its
proper use: "To speak and to remain silent, each is a perfection. The case of
each consists in holding to the proper measure of words. Silence is great and
speech is great, but the wise man sets a measure upon them both."[51]

Nourisher of Virtues, Guardian of Souls

In the Carolingian age, the internal life of abbeys underwent significant
changes that posed direct challenges to traditional standards of personal
conduct, including the discipline of silence. By the eighth century, monastic
communities had spread and flourished throughout the new kingdoms of
the West.[52] Inspired by the hardships of the first hermits, the monks of
northern Europe sought the remoteness of impenetrable swamps, high
mountain tops, and other uninviting locales that recalled the hostile and
otherworldly landscape of the desert. Like the early fathers, their goal was
personal salvation. They strived for perfection in this world and deliverance
in the next through a penitential life dedicated to the praise of God and the
cultivation of virtue. Due to a steady increase in monastic vocations

throughout this period, however, many abbeys expanded from quiet settlements to bustling communities that resembled small towns.[53] The custom of oblation, the act of consecrating a child to God's service in an abbey, became a common practice by the eighth century and may account for the growth of some monasteries.[54] In communities such as Fulda, Corbie, and Aniane, the liturgical celebration of the brethren competed with the noise of resident artisans and the multitude of servants and livestock necessary to sustain the material needs of expanding monastic complexes. This new dynamic within the walls of Carolingian abbeys marked a departure from the ideals of seclusion that had characterized ancient monasticism, raising concerns about the disruptive effect of idle conversations among the brethren.[55]

At the same time, the Carolingians were taking an active interest in controlling religious life in their kingdom in ways that influenced regulations concerning the avoidance of sinful words.[56] There was no uniformity of monastic custom in this period. Every community employed its own amalgam of rulings ("regulae mixtae") culled from oral tradition and from written customs circulated under the names of great abbots such as Benedict and Columbanus.[57] The Carolingian rulers and their advisors believed that the military success and spiritual well-being of the political community depended on the prayerful intervention of monks.[58] As a result, in the early ninth century, Emperor Louis the Pious (814–40) undertook a sweeping reform of monastic life, with the goal of standardizing the customs of the abbeys in his realm. The emperor wanted abbots to promote and enforce a uniform standard of discipline to ensure the efficacy of monastic prayers for the kingdom. Two councils of religious officials convened at the royal palace in Aachen in 816 and 817, where they endorsed the precepts of the *Rule of Benedict* as the model for this unprecedented reform.[59] In the three centuries since its composition, the *Rule* had established itself as a trusted and balanced guide for monastic life, but it was only one voice in a chorus of received tradition. Some ancient communities resisted the imperial policies of monastic reform, but many responded by introducing new rules of conduct, including regulations intended to prevent idle speech.

Beginning in the eighth century, abbots adopted measures to ensure that the close proximity of secular servants and visitors did not disturb the brethren. Carolingian monks inhabited an enclosed network of rooms and corridors known collectively as the *claustrum*. This precinct comprised the cloister, the dormitory, the refectory, the chapter hall, and various service chambers.[60] A doorway in the choir of the abbey church provided entry to the cloister, but access was forbidden to all but the monks. Guesthouses were built at a distance from the monastic precinct to prevent the activities of secular guests from distracting the brethren. The *Plan of Saint Gall,* a ninth-century schematic layout for a large abbey, portrayed separate hospices for visitors, pilgrims, and dignitaries with their retinues, all of which were well removed from the dormitory of the resident monks.[61] According to Hildemar of Corbie, a *magister* who gave expository lectures on the *Rule of Benedict* in Civate around 845, the segregation of monks and laymen was especially important at night because it was expected that laymen would stay up late talking and laughing. Monks, in contrast, should pass the night in silence and prayer.[62] Nonetheless, the steady drone of human discourse surrounded the brethren in their cloister. Large Carolingian abbeys were the nexus of oral information, where a constant influx of travelers exchanged news of the outside world. Monks whose duties took them beyond the monastic precinct were forbidden from speaking about their outings, but even the best precautions could not prevent them from overhearing rumors of war and diplomacy, portents and weather, murder and miracles.[63] As a ward against such distractions, Hildemar urged his students to build a spiritual *claustrum* within themselves and therein protect their souls from the onslaught of the relentless din that echoed around them.[64]

New rulings on silence also governed personal interaction among the monks themselves. The earliest Carolingian customaries reiterated the *Rule of Benedict*'s precepts on the observation of silence in the refectory, the oratory, and the dormitory, but they also gave voice to new concerns.[65] Many attempted to curb wayward speech in situations that had not troubled the sixth-century author of the *Rule.* Carolingian abbots were especially worried about brethren who spoke needlessly while they worked, whether inside the monastic precinct or on the grounds of the abbey. Beginning in this period, monks were instructed to perform their appointed tasks either in silence or with the singing of psalms.[66] The continuous recitation of the Psalter served the same purpose as silence for laboring monks: it kept them from engaging in idle conversation. Unlike silent contemplation, however, which was private and knowable only to God, the voices of monks intoning the psalms assured their superiors that their minds were directed toward heaven as they worked.[67]

Other venues for harmful speech occupied the attention of Carolingian abbots as well. At Corbie, monks required the permission of a superior or the reason of necessity to speak in the warming room when they gathered by the fire in the winter months.[68] The ritual of foot washing also provided an occasion for them to engage in illicit conversation. The *Rule of Benedict* gave no specific directives for the conduct of monks during this weekly activity, but Carolingian abbots felt it necessary to restrict their interaction.[69] The Aachen decrees ordered that foot washing be accompanied by the singing of antiphons, but in some ninth-century abbeys it was customary to perform the ritual without uttering a word.[70] Lastly, while the *Rule* had set aside certain parts of the abbey and times of the day for personal silence, by the late eighth century a striking inversion had occurred. Unease about the detrimental effects of idle talk concerned abbots so much that for the first time they felt it necessary to set aside specific parts of the monastery and regulated times of the day for supervised conversation.[71] From this point onward, in many abbeys, monks could speak with their fellows only for a short period of time, under the watchful eyes of their superiors. These rulings further limited and controlled opportunities for idle speech among the brethren. With them, silence gained new territory in Carolingian abbeys.

Monks were not alone in their struggle against the desire to speak. One of the salient features of Carolingian monasticism was the penetration of its ideals into the highest levels of secular society. During the ninth century, Frankish emperors donning the mantle of kingship shouldered with it the expectation that they would govern their personal will as well as their kingdoms. Books of counsel composed by abbots and church prelates provided rulers with moral compasses for the exercise of imperial justice and mediated to them the monastic value of self-mastery in matters of personal comportment.[72] Works written to promote the reign of Emperor Louis the Pious are the most conspicuous exponents of monastic kingship in the Carolingian period.[73] An episode in Thegan's account of the emperor's life written in 836 stressed his studious detachment from frivolity in terms reminiscent of contemporary monastic precepts against the expression of unbridled mirth.[74] When actors and jesters delighted his court with their antics, Louis remained unmoved. Even though his entourage showed proper moderation in their laughter, the emperor set himself apart by expressing no emotion at all.[75] His controlled countenance was a public declaration of a mastery of the will that legitimized his right to rule.[76]

The discipline of silence acquired new meanings in the crowded halls of Carolingian abbeys. The Aachen assemblies assured the primacy of the *Rule of Benedict* in most ninth-century houses, but they were unable to impose a uniform interpretation of its customs. As a result, intense scrutiny surrounded the text. The *Rule* devoted considerable attention to the custom of silence, but the ambiguity of some passages puzzled Carolingian commentators. Particularly vexing was its author's tendency to modify the word *silence* ("silentium") with adjectives such as *utmost* ("summum") and *total* ("omne").[77] Hildemar of Corbie attempted to reconcile these distinctions for his students. His commentary on the *Rule* thus provides one of the clearest articulations of the character of monastic silence in Carolingian thought. When bolstered by a superlative or totalizing adjective, he explained, the word *silentium* carried the weight of absolute silence. This meaning was context specific, however. It applied only to the refectory, during the time set aside for private reading, and to the oratory at the close of the liturgy.[78] In all other instances, the word *silentium* did not signal a prohibition against verbal utterances. The *Rule* encouraged the cultivation of silence at all times, especially at night.[79] According to Hildemar, this precept meant that monks could converse with discretion, but only with suppressed voices ("sub silentio"), that is, in whispers.[80] In Carolingian monastic thought, the goal of the discipline of silence was not the complete cessation of human sound but the fostering of a hushed and reverential tone among the brethren that pervaded every aspect of their cloistered lives.[81]

This expectation challenged even the most stalwart individuals. Hildemar understood the abnegation of the desire to speak freely as a kind of mortification because it was a denial of the will.[82] His contemporary, Smaragdus of Saint Mihiel, stressed the salvific benefits of this discipline in vivid metaphors that underscored the graveness of his concern for sins involving speech. The tongue was a fire that devoured the forest of virtues by speaking badly.[83] Both prohibitive and unifying, silence was among the monks' strongest allies. By moderating discerning speech and preventing sinful utterances, it was the nourisher of virtues and the guardian of souls.[84] It also bound the brethren together in their common purpose. The denial of carnal needs, like the desire to speak, distinguished monks from the rest of humanity. Like the celebration of the liturgy, it was a shared and harmonious experience in a world of individual and discordant voices. Shrouded in personal silence, Carolingian monks transcended the cacophony of the earthly sounds that surrounded them.

SILENCE CONTESTED: THE CASE OF CLUNY

The appropriate measure of the custom of silence became a contested issue in post-Carolingian monasticism. Although the decrees of the Aachen councils of 816 and 817 succeeded in establishing the *Rule of Benedict* as the authoritative guide for cloistered communities throughout the Frankish realms, the reformers did not achieve their objective of enforcing a uniform interpretation of its precepts.[85] Owing to the influence of Benedict's *Rule*, the avoidance of sinful speech remained a cornerstone of personal discipline in most abbeys, even though monastic legislation from this period suggests that there was considerable variation in the understanding and implementation of this practice.[86] In the early tenth century, monastic reformers at Cluny and other communities in its orbit of influence emerged as the most direct heirs of the concern for monastic silence that manifested itself so strongly in Carolingian thought.[87] Founded in 910, the abbey of Cluny grew over the course of the next two centuries to become one of the most prestigious and influential religious houses in Europe.[88] The earliest evidence for the custom of silence at Cluny shows that its regulations against speaking were much stricter than those observed in other abbeys in this period. Contemporaries marked these differences as well. They criticized the Cluniacs for tampering with time-honored precepts on silence and dismissed their customs as modern novelties with no precedent in the monastic tradition.[89] Around 944, John of Salerno, an early proponent of Cluniac monasticism, responded to these criticisms in his account of the holy life of Odo, the second abbot of Cluny (926–42). He based his defense of Cluniac regulations on scriptural precedents and articulated a new understanding of the avoidance of human discourse in moral and eschatological terms.

According to John of Salerno's *Life of Odo*, monks of Cluny never spoke at unsuitable hours, that is, when the *Rule of Benedict* forbade talking altogether. In addition, no conversation was permitted on days when the brethren celebrated a twelve-lesson office. Moreover, during the week-long octaves of Christmas and Easter, complete silence reigned day and night throughout the entire abbey.[90] These practices were elaborated and codified in the great books of customs produced at Cluny in the late eleventh century.[91] According to the customary of Bernard, no one was allowed to speak anywhere in the monastery during the celebration of the divine office, an activity that took place during most hours of the day. The monk in charge of the infirmary was the only exception to this rule. If he had the need, he could speak to the sick monks when they gathered for their common meal.[92] Ulrich of Zell (d. 1093) rehearsed the list of traditional places in the abbey where monks never were allowed to talk in the customary that he compiled for the monks of Hirsau, but his readers already were familiar with these long-established customs and desired to know more about the times when speech was permissible. Ulrich explained that there were only two periods set aside for supervised conversation at Cluny: after the prayers that followed the chapter meeting, and again in the afternoon after the office of

Sext.[93] The length of these recesses is unknown, but Ulrich cautioned his readers to keep them very brief ("brevissimus").[94] Otherwise, monks should avoid human discourse at all costs to protect themselves from the dangers of idle speech.

The cultivation of a profound silence was so important to the monks of Cluny that they invented a medium of non-verbal communication to exchange essential information without the need for spoken words. John of Salerno's *Life of Odo* described how they employed a silent language of hand signs to safeguard the discipline of silence:

> Whenever it was necessary for them to ask for something, they made it known to each other through various signs, which I think grammarians would call *notas* of fingers and eyes. This practice had developed to such an extent among them that I believe, if they lost the use of their tongues, these signs would suffice to signify everything necessary.[95]

While it is tempting to cast a cynical eye on this practice as a way to cheat the rules against speaking, evidence for the linguistic character of this silent language suggests that monks considered the garrulous use of hand signs to be as dangerous as an unbridled tongue, particularly for novices. Collections of customs from eleventh-century Cluny preserved copies of a descriptive lexicon of sign-forms that novices were required to put to memory before their formal profession as monks.[96] The sign vocabulary of the novices was limited to 118 signs, primarily for nouns. Moreover, the Cluniac sign language had no formal grammar or syntax, which further restricted its application as a vehicle for illicit conversation. The monks learned a sufficient number of signs to communicate their essential needs and to understand instruction and reprimand when speaking was forbidden, but they lacked the linguistic tools to express more complex thoughts. By replacing spoken words with a system of silent signs, the monks of Cluny further avoided most opportunities for verbal exchange and thereby achieved a new ideal of personal silence in their abbey.

In John of Salerno's view, the denial of the desire to speak freely set the Cluniacs apart from other ascetics of their time.[97] To counter contemporary claims that their rules of conduct were unprecedented in the monastic tradition, John compiled a genealogy of sacred silence to establish a continuity of practice between the monks of Cluny and the saints of antiquity.[98] The Hebrew prophets attested to the centrality of silence in their proclamations that it accompanied hope, strength, and goodness (Isa. 30:15 and Lam. 3:26–28). King David also confirmed the importance of the custom in a psalm favored by early monastic authors on the avoidance of sinful utterances (Ps. 38).[99] The life of Christ provided even more compelling evidence in support of monastic silence, because monks were encouraged first and foremost to emulate the virtues he displayed during his earthly ministry. From the Gospel accounts of Christ's life, John listed several instances of Jesus retiring alone to spend entire nights praying on a mountain (Matt. 14:22–23; Mark 6:45–46; Luke 6:12 and 21:36–37; and John 8:1–2). Although there is no explicit reference to silence in these narratives, John clearly understood the solitude of Christ to mean that he passed the night in silent prayer. The profound silence of the Cluniacs thus could be understood as an imitative expression of Christ's holy conduct. Furthermore, John argued that the lives of the holy abbots Paul, Anthony, Hilarion, John Cassian, and Benedict—the very founders of the monastic tradition—provided abundant examples of personal silence as a virtuous practice and forged the final link in the continuity of a tradition stretching from the Hebrew prophets, through the Gospels and the saints, to the monks of Cluny.

Throughout the *Life of Odo,* John of Salerno expressed the consequences of idle speech in an uncompromising tone. Without silence, he maintained, the monastic life was fruitless and barren. When a monk lost his ability to bridle his speech, whatever he believed that he could do virtuously or well would come to nothing, according to the teachings of the Fathers.[100] John populated his narrative of Odo's life with exemplary monks who cultivated silence when others would have been tempted to speak. A disciple of Odo preferred to lose a horse to a thief rather than raise the alarm during the night, when speech was forbidden.[101] Another monk who had received instructions from Saint Benedict in a dream duly waited for the period of silence to end before he informed his brethren what the saint had said.[102] Two monks captured by Norsemen refused to speak, even when threatened with death.[103] Bound and beaten, they remained silent in imitation of Christ, as he was prefigured in the Book of Isaiah: "Like a lamb that is led to the slaughter and like a sheep that before its shearers is dumb, so he opened not his mouth" (Isa. 54:7). John encouraged his readers to consider how reprehensible it would be for monks to transgress the tenets of the rule by breaking their silence when they acted of their own free will. Their conduct, he assured them, would be compared to that of the captive monks by God at the Last Judgment. He left his audience to consider the terrible outcome of this comparison.[104]

The Cluniacs cultivated an expectant, all-embracing silence as part of a program of moral reform that directed them to live in consonance with their angelic counterparts in heaven. By the tenth century, the favorable comparison of monks and angels was an old one.[105] Odo of Cluny and his followers were the first, however, to emphasize this similitude repeatedly and emphatically as a defining aspect of their monastic vocation and as a rationale for their rigorous standards of personal asceticism. For Odo, cloistered life was nothing less than the conduct of angels ("coelestis disciplina") embodied in human practice.[106] The saints were those who perfected in this life the otherworldly demeanor of the heavenly host. Odo's biographer described him as equal parts angel and mortal ("angelicus videlicet et humanus").[107] One hundred years later, this appellation was being applied to the Cluniac community as a whole. In the eleventh century, Peter Damian addressed Abbot Hugh the Great (1049–1109) as an archangel of monks who fostered the celestial life among his brethren.[108] The identification of the Cluniacs with angels was more than empty self-promotion. In early Cluniac thought, it enunciated a way of life that had eschatological consequences. Odo defined them succinctly in his *Life of Count Gerald of Aurillac:* "If monks are perfect, they are like blessed angels, but if they return to the desire of the world they are rightly compared to apostate angels, who by their apostasy did not keep to their home."[109] Living in the perfect likeness of God's servants, the brethren of Cluny could expect to join their company at the end of time. If any monk chose to abandon this way of life, however, he would be cast down into the darkness to await the final judgment with the rebel angels.

Avoiding all human discourse, the monks of Cluny conformed their behavior to an angelic ideal that actualized in this life their future participation in the eternal silence of God. John of Salerno justified the strict week-long periods of reverential silence observed by the Cluniacs during the octaves of Christmas and Easter in direct reference to this eschatological anticipation.[110] This teaching was an echo of a precept of Gregory the Great in his *Exposition on the Book of Job.*[111] Pope Gregory taught that God could not communicate the divine majesty directly to the frailness of human faculties in this life. Instead, he used the voices of his apostles and preachers. After the resurrection of the saved, however, there would be no need for God to communicate through spoken words because his Word would fill everyone and penetrate their minds with the power of its innermost light.[112] Shrouded in silence, the Cluniacs foreshadowed their experience of the silent omnipresence of God.

John of Salerno's *Life of Odo* was an eloquent defense of Cluniac silence, but the need for such a response tells us a great deal about prevailing values in the monastic world of early medieval Europe. The strictness of the precepts against speaking enforced at Cluny evoked strong criticism among contemporaries precisely because these individuals esteemed their received traditions and wanted to protect them from the introduction of novel practices. The *Life of Odo* is a partisan voice in a one-sided debate about authority, tradition, and the threat of innovation in cloistered communities. While the exact contours of this debate will remain elusive until the emergence of further evidence, it is clear from the tone and content of John's work that monks were ready to defend their claims on the virtue of silence. Their outspoken willingness to do so underscores the importance of this ancient, yet contested, custom in the western monastic tradition.

Conclusion

From the beginnings of monasticism in the fourth century, the discipline of silence was a distinct and important idiom in the language of Christian virtue. The desert fathers cultivated silence as a preparation for good and useful speech and as a safeguard against the sins of slander and murmuring. In emulation of these saints, monks in the earliest coenobitic communities abstained from idle conversation to cultivate the virtues of humility and obedience and to attend to the celebration of the divine office. As monastic vocations increased and abbeys grew to accommodate hundreds of monks in the Carolingian period, the dangers of sinful speech multiplied. At the same time, the virtuous conduct of the brethren came to be understood in direct relation to the efficacy of monastic prayers for the spiritual well-being of the Carolingian emperors and the entire Christian community. By the early ninth century, imperial reforms of monastic life reinforced and extended traditional precepts on silence to meet the new expectations placed on the standards of discipline in religious houses by abbots and kings. As a result, there were fewer and fewer opportunities for personal discourse in early medieval abbeys.

In the decades around the year 1000, the monks of Cluny stood apart from their contemporaries by amplifying these traditions even further and by enriching them with explicit moral and eschatological associations. In emulation of the heavenly host, they avoided uttering mundane sounds in order to actualize in their cloister the eternal silence that they anticipated would accompany the resurrection of the elect at the end of time. To safeguard their tongues, they employed a silent language of hand signs that permitted them to communicate basic information without the need for human speech. Responding to criticism that the Cluniacs introduced novelties to the monastic tradition with these restrictions, John of Salerno's *Life of Odo* argued that the custom of keeping silent was an ancient and worthy practice attested by the Hebrew prophets, the earthly ministry of Christ, and the deeds of monastic saints. For the monks of Cluny, the denial of the desire to speak, like the avoidance of other worldly pleasures, was an essential characteristic of their deliberate self-fashioning on the model of angelic conduct. It was an expression of their hopeful expectation that in the world to come they would experience the silent majesty of God.

NOTES

This paper has benefitted from the generous and insightful comments of audiences at the Thirty-Fifth International Congress on Medieval Studies at Western Michigan University (May 2000) and the Institute for the Humanities at the University of Colorado at Boulder (April 2003). My thanks to Ed Craun and Jeffrey Cox, who provided the opportunity for me to present this work on those occasions; to Lisa K. Bailey for sharing with me her expertise on early medieval sermons; and to Anne E. Lester for her careful reading of the final draft. All translations are my own unless otherwise noted. All remaining errors of fact or judgment are mine alone.

1. Many medieval authors compared monks and bees. For examples from early monastic texts, see Gindele, "Bienen-, Waben- und Honigvergleiche"; Taylor, "Mother Bee."

2. Leclercq, *Life of Perfection*, 27: "All forms of asceticism—mortification, chastity, obedience, poverty—derive from this first idea of the total renunciation of everything that is not from God and to prepare for the total adherence, in the glory to come, of the soul and body of the redeemed to the one all-sufficient God."

3. I am indebted throughout this study to Asad's discussion of monastic discipline in *Genealogies of Religion*, 125–67 (Ch. 4: "On Discipline and Humility in Medieval Christian Monasticism"), esp. 135–39.

4. Casagrande and Vecchio, *Les péchés*; Craun, *Lies*; Bardsley, "Sin, Speech, and Scolding."

5. Wathen, *Silence*, remains a reliable guide to the study of this topic and covers a broader range of material than its title implies. See also RB, ed. de Vogüé, 227–80; Fuchs, "Die Weltflucht der Mönche"; and, more generally, Gehl, "*Competens Silentium*."

6. The date of the RB and its relationship to the anonymous RM have inspired some debate in recent years. See Dunn, "Mastering Benedict"; de Vogüé, "The Master and St. Benedict: A Reply"; and Dunn, "The Master and St. Benedict: A Rejoinder." I am most persuaded by the traditional sixth-century dating of the RB. For

a complete list of the earliest surviving monastic rules from Gaul and Italy, see de Vogüé, *Les règles monastiques anciennes (400–700)*, 53–60.

7. "Aut quis liber sanctorum catholicorum Patrum hoc non resonat ut recto cursu perueniamus ad creatorem nostrum? Necnon et Collationes Patrum et Instituta et Vitas eorum, sed et Regula sancti Patris Basilii, quid aliud sunt nisi bene uiuentium et oboedientium monachorum instrumenta uirtutum?" (RB 73.4–6, 672–74). On the reception of Basil of Caesarea's work in western abbeys, see de Vogüé, "Influence de sainte Basile." More generally on the transmission of eastern ascetic ideals to the West in this period, see Lorenz, "Die Anfänge."

8. Chitty, *The Desert a City*; Rousseau, *Ascetics, Authority, and the Church*; idem, *Pachomius*; Brown, *The Body and Society*, esp. 213–40; Burton-Christie, *The Word in the Desert*, esp. 76–103 and 134–77; Gould, *The Desert Fathers on Monastic Community*; Goehring, *Ascetics, Society, and the Desert*; Dunn, *The Emergence of Monasticism*, 1–81; Leyser, *Authority and Asceticism*; de Vogüé, *Regards sur le monachisme*.

9. For examples of these images in the writings of Jerome and other early monastic authors, see Guillaumont, "La conception du désert"; Miller, "Jerome's Centaur"; and Goehring, "The Dark Side of the Landscape."

10. Brown, *Body and Society*, 220.

11. Rousseau, *Ascetics, Authority, and the Church*, 19–32; Burton-Christie, *The Word in the Desert*, 76–103; Gould, *The Desert Fathers on Monastic Community*, 26–87.

12. "Dic mihi aliquod verbum" (*Vitae patrum* 5.3.2, 5.3.25, and 5.6.12, PL 73, cols. 860c, 864b, and 890d; trans. Ward, *Desert Fathers*, 5, 17, and 140).

13. "Quomodo debet homo conversari? Unde est, abba, cor meum durum et non timeo dominum? Dic mihi, quid faciam ut salvari possim" (*Vitae patrum* 5.1.13, 5.3.22, and 5.14.2, PL 73, cols. 856c, 864a, and 947d; trans. Ward, *Desert Fathers*, 5, 17, and 140).

14. Burton-Christie, *The Word in the Desert*, 150–77; Gleason, "Visiting and News," 502–03.

15. See, for example, Basil of Caesarea, *Regula* 40 and 86, ed. Zelzer, 85–86 and 165–66; Augustine of Hippo, *Ordo monasterii* 5 and 9, ed. Lawless, 74 and 76; *Regula orientalis* 17.9 and 17.16, ed. de Vogüé, 2: 472; RM 9.51, 1: 416; RB 4.53 and 6.8, 460 and 472; and Columbanus, *Regula monachorum* 2, ed. Walker, 124.

16. Basil of Caesarea, *Regula* 40, ed. Zelzer, 85–86.

17. Burton-Christie, *The Word in the Desert*, 138–43; Gould, *The Desert Fathers on Monastic Community*, 121–23.

18. Hyperechius, *Sentences* 4, cited by Gould, *The Desert Fathers on Monastic Community*, 121.

19. "Quid enim prodest afflictio corporalis, si linguam nequitiis et obtrectationibus polluamus?" (*Eusebius 'Gallicanus,'* Homilia 39 [Ad monachos 4], ed. Leroy and Glorie, 2: 459–60).

20. "Hic sumus, et tuti non sumus. Aut enim cordis cogitationibus uariis et improbis atque inhonestis agitamur aut uenenatis linguae gladiis uulneramur, pro minimis et paruissimis rebus scandalizantes" (*Eusebius 'Gallicanus,'* Homilia 40.6 [Ad monachos 5], ed. Leroy and Glorie, 2: 480). Early medieval warnings about the

dangers of monastic slander were not limited to Gaul. See McDougall and McDougall, "Evil Tongues."

21. "Singulare autem malum est lingua . . . Enumerari non potest quantis sit lingua jaculis accincta verborum, quibus satis promptum est etiam quae sunt animae secretiora percutere. Quamcumque autem aures injuriam suscipiunt illico ad cordis secreta transmittunt: ubi si semel introierit, sine mortis exitu non recedit" (Valerian of Cimiez, *Homilia* 5.2–3, PL 52, cols. 706c and 707c). Further on Valerian, see Weiss, "Le statut du prédicateur."

22. See, for example, Augustine, *Ordo monasterii* 5, ed. Lawless, 74; *Statuta patrum* 26, ed. de Vogüé, 1: 278; RM 2.44 and 5.7, 1: 368 and 378; and RB 35.13, 568. Cloistered women also were warned against the sin of murmuring. See Caesarius, *Regula virginum* 17.1–2, ed. Courreau and de Vogüé, 1: 192.

23. "Timere debent illud dictum terribile: Nolite murmurare, sicut quidam eorum murmurauerunt et ab exterminatore perierunt" (*Regula sanctorum patrum* 3.13, ed. de Vogüé, 1: 194).

24. "Si aliqui ex populo Dei in heremo propter murmurationis perierunt peccatum, quanto magis monachus monasterii spirtuali plectatu vindicta, si murmurationis malo mentem inolescere non metuit" (Alcuin, *Epistola* 168, ed. Dümmler, 276).

25. Steidle, "Das Lachen"; Alexander, "La prohibición"; Schmitz, "Quod rident homo," 3–15; Resnick, "Risus monasticus"; Le Goff, "Le rire."

26. "Vidit senex quemdam ridentem, et dicit ei: Coram coeli et terrae Domino rationem totius vitae nostrae reddituri sumus, et tu rides?" (*Vitae patrum* 5.3.23, PL 73, col. 864b; trans. Ward, *Desert Fathers,* 17).

27. *Vitae patrum* 5.11.10, PL 73, col. 934b.

28. *Vitae patrum* 5.3.24, PL 73, col. 864b.

29. "Nemo umquam illum vidit iratum, nemo commotum, nemo maerentem, nemo ridentem" (Sulpicius Severus, *Vita sancti Martini* 27, ed. Fontaine, 1: 314). The *Life of Martin* exerted a strong influence on ideals of saintly comportment throughout the early medieval period. See Rosenwein, "St. Odo's St. Martin"; and Smith, "The Problem of Female Sanctity," 14–16.

30. See, for example, "risus leuis ac fatuus, effrenata atqua indisciplinata cordis elatio" (John Cassian, *De coenobiorum institutis* 12.27.6, ed. Guy, 492); RM 9.51, 1: 416; RB 4.53–54, 6.8, 7.59–60, 460, 472, and 486–88; Defensor of Ligugé, *Liber scintillarum* 2.55, ed. Rochais, 2: 142–46; Columbanus, *Regula coenobialis fratrum* 4, ed. Walker, 148; Donatus, *Regula ad virgines* 17, ed. de Vogüé, 262; and *Regula Pauli et Stephani* 37, ed. Villanova, 122–23.

31. John Cassian reported this practice among the monks of Egypt in *De coenobiorum institutis* 2.10.1, ed. Guy, 74. See also *Statuta Patrum* 39, ed. de Vogüé, 2: 282.

32. RB 52.1–4, 610.

33. The custom of silence *ad mensam* first was attested in Egyptian monasteries as well: John Cassian, *De coenobiorum institutis* 4.17, ed. Guy, 144. See also "Et summum fiat silentium, ut nullius musitatio uel uox nisi solius legentis ibi audiatur" (RB 38.5, 574).

34. Aurelianus, *Regula ad monachos* 49, PL 68, col. 393a. The same rule applied to cloistered women. For example, "Sedentes ad mensam taceant, et animum lectioni intedant" (Caesarius, *Regula virginum* 18.2, ed. Courreau and de Vogüé, 1: 192).

35. For example, "Nemo alteri loquatur in tenebris" (*Regula orientalis* 44, ed. de Vogüé, 2: 494).

36. RM 30.12–13, 2: 164.

37. Waldebertus, *Regula ad virgines* 14, PL 88, col. 1065b.

38. Gregory the Great, *Libri dialogorum* 2.23.1–4, ed. de Vogüé, 2: 204–08. Excommunication usually was reserved as punishment for chronic lapses in discipline. See RB 23, 542.

39. Burton-Christie, *The Word in the Desert,* 146–50; Holze, "Schweigen und Gotteserfahrung."

40. *Vitae patrum* 5.4.7, PL 73, col. 865b.

41. *Apophthegmata patrum* (Poemen 18), ed. Guy, 31; Burton-Christie, *The Word in the Desert,* 147.

42. See, for example, *Apophthegmata patrum* (De abbate Pambo 2), PG 65, col. 368cd.

43. For what follows, see John Cassian, *De coenobiorum institutis* 12.27, ed. Guy, 488–92.

44. "Posui ori meo custodiam. Obmutui et humiliatus sum et silui a bonis" (RB 6.1, 470). According to the *Rule,* monks achieved the ninth step of humility when they remained silent and spoke only when asked a question (RB 7.56, 486).

45. Prompt obedience was the first step of humility (RB 5.1 and 7.10–30, 464 and 474–80). Further on monastic obedience, see Leclercq, "Religious Obedience"; de Vogüé, "Obéissance et autorité"; and Hildebrand, "*Oboedientia* and *oboedire*."

46. RB 5.3–4 and 7.34, 464 and 480.

47. "Ergo, quamuis de bonis et sanctis et aedificationum eloquiis, perfectis discipulis, propter taciturnitatis gravitatem rara loquendi concedatur licentia, quia scriptum est: In multiloquio non effugies peccatum. Et alibi: Mors et vita in manibus linguae" (RB 6.3–6, 470).

48. RB 6.7, 470–72.

49. See, for example, Caesarius, *Regula virginum* 19.1–5, ed. Courreau and de Vogüé, 1: 192–94; and RB 6.7, 7.60, 22.8, 42.11 and 47.4, 470–72, 486–88, 542, 586, and 598.

50. RB 2.4–25, 6.6, and 64.2, 442–46, 470, and 648 (abbot); RB 31.13–14, 558 (cellarer); RB 66.1–4, 658–60 (porter).

51. "Ita et loqui et tacere perfectio est. Est autem utriusque partis causa verborum tenuisse mensuram. Magnum est tacere, magnum est loqui; sed sapientis est utrumque moderari" (Valerian, *Homilia* 5.7, PL 52, col. 709b [trans. Ganss, 334–35, slightly modified]).

52. Prinz, *Frühes Mönchtum.*

53. On the great numbers of monks reported in Carolingian abbeys, see Berlière, "Le nombre des moines," 242–43.

54. De Jong, *In Samuel's Image.*

55. On this point, see Oexle, "Les moines d'occident et la vie politique et sociale dans le haut Moyen Âge"; and Sullivan, "What Was Carolingian Monasticism?"

56. For the impact of the Carolingians on monastic life, see Semmler, "Karl der Grosse," 2: 255–89; idem, "Pippin III"; idem, "Mönche und Kanoniker"; and McKitterick, *The Frankish Kingdoms*, 106–39.

57. Moyse, "Monachisme et réglementation monastique."

58. The *Notitia de servitio monasteriorum*, composed in 828, delineated the services demanded from royal monasteries by the crown. Many provided revenues and produce as gifts ("dona"). Others provided men from their lands for military service ("militia"). Most abbeys offered prayers for the health and success of the emperor and the stability of his kingdom ("orationes pro salute imperatoris vel filiorum eius et stabilitate imperii"). See the edition of Becker, 493–99.

59. De Jong, "Carolingian Monasticism," 630–31.

60. On the boundaries of the *claustrum* and the fear of secular intrusion into monastic space, see de Jong, "Carolingian Monasticism," 636–40.

61. Horn and Born, *The Plan of Saint Gall*, 1: 249–53, and 2: 139–53.

62. Hildemar, *Expositio* 65, ed. Mittermüller, 611–12.

63. On the prohibition against speaking for monks returning to the abbey, see RB 67.5, 662; and Hildemar, *Expositio* 67, ed. Mittermüller, 612–13.

64. Hildemar, *Expositio* 67, ed. Mittermüller, 613.

65. See, for example, Theodomar, *Epistula ad Theodoricum* 24, ed. Winandy and Hallinger; and *Ordo Casinensis I* 1, ed. Leccisotti, 101.

66. Ardo, *Vita Benedicti* 38, ed. Waitz, 216.

67. This precept may have been an echo of Ambrose of Milan's discussion of the psalms as agents of silence. See Ambrose, *Enarrationes* (PL 14, col. 925b), prol.: "Cum psalmus legitur, ipse sibi est effector silentii. Omnes loquuntur, et nullus obstrepit."

68. Hildemar, *Expositio* 6, ed. Mittermüller, 203.

69. RB 35.9, 566.

70. *Synodi primae decreta authentica* 21, ed. Semmler, 463; *Epistola* 10, ed. Frank, 336; Hildemar, *Expositio* 42, ed. Mittermüller, 454–55.

71. See, for example, *Ordo Casinensis I* 6, ed. Leccisotti, 102; *Consuetudines Corbeienses* (Capitulorum fragmenta 2), ed. Semmler, 418; and *Memoriale qualiter II* 8, ed. Morgand, 271–72.

72. Further on the marriage of moral and political ideologies in the Carolingian age, see Anton, *Fürstenspiegel*; and Smith, "Gender and Ideology."

73. Noble, "The Monastic Ideal"; idem, "Louis the Pious"; de Jong, "Power and Humility."

74. See, for example, Benedict of Aniane, *Concordia regularum* 20, PL 103, cols. 861–62; and Smaragdus, *Expositio* 2.7.59, ed. Spannagel, 188. Both abbots had the ear of the young emperor.

75. Thegan, *Gesta Hludovici imperatoris* 19, ed. Tremp, 200–04.

76. For a compelling analysis of this episode, see Innes, "He Never Even Allowed His White Teeth to Be Bared in Laughter."

77. RB 38.5 ("summum fiat silentium"), 48.5 ("cum omni silentio"), and 52.2 ("cum summo silentio"), 574, 600, and 610.

78. This precept did not imply, however, that monks read silently. Rather, it was intended to dissuade them from making any noise that would be disruptive to those reading aloud in groups or reading quietly by themselves. Reading aloud was not contrary to the rule of silence. In the words of Paul Saenger, in early medieval abbeys "oral group reading and composition were in practice no more considered a breach of silence than were confession or the recitation of prayers." See Saenger, "Silent Reading," 383. Further on the act of reading in this period, see Carruthers, *The Book of Memory*, 170–73.

79. "Omni tempore silentium debent studere monachi, maxime tamen nocturnis horis" (RB 42.1, 584).

80. "Hoc enim notandum est, quia, ubi B. Benedictus dicit silentium cum adjectione *summum*, sicuti in hoc loco facit, et ubi dicit *maxime nocturnis horis*, et iterum *nulla sit denique cuiquam loqui licentia*, et ubi dicit cum omni silentio, vult, ut nullatenus loquatur; ubi vero dicit solummodo *silentio* sine adjectione aliqua, de suppressa voce dicit, sicut legitur in evangelio, ubi legitur mortuo Lazaro Martha silentio dixisse Mariae sorori suae: 'Magister adest et vocat te.' Ibi enim, sicut dicit B. Augustinus, silentio de suppressa voce intelligendum est" (Hildemar, *Expositio* 38, ed. Mittermüller, 424 [see also 453 and 456–57]). For the source of this allusion, see Augustine, *In Johannis evangelium tractatus cxxiv* 49.16, ed. Willems, 428.

81. Hildemar, *Expositio* 7, ed. Mittermüller, 262–64.

82. "Et hoc etiam sciendum est, quia sicut laborat erga voluntatem propriam, ita etiam erga silentium, quia silentium mortificationem significat" (Hildemar, *Expositio* 43, ed. Mittermüller, 457).

83. "Ignis est lingua, quia virtutum silvam male loquendo devorat" (Smaragdus, *Expositio* 6.5, ed. Spannagel, 159). Smaragdus was the abbot of Saint Mihiel in Lotharingia in the early ninth century.

84. "Nutrix virtutum et custos est animarum" (Smaragdus, *Expositio* 6.1, ed. Spannagel, 159).

85. Semmler, "Benedictus II."

86. On the variety of regulations against the use of idle words in tenth- and eleventh-century abbeys, most of which follow the precepts of the RB, see Hallinger, *Gorze-Kluny*, 925–28.

87. The influence of the Carolingian reforms on the monks of Cluny is plain from the tenth-century *Life of Odo*, which stated that Berno, the first abbot of Cluny, was the follower of a "certain Euticus," that is, Benedict of Aniane, the abbot who directed the religious reforms of Emperor Louis the Pious. See John of Salerno, *Vita Odonis* 1.22, PL 133, col. 53cd. Further on this issue, see Bredero, "Cluny et le monachisme carolingien."

88. On the early history of Cluny, see Wollasch, *Cluny, Licht der Welt*; Constable, "Cluny in the Monastic World."

89. "Diximus ista de antiquis vatibus, ut nullus arbitretur hoc silentium modernis temporibus fuisse inventum, sicut quidam male suspicantes fatentur" (John of Salerno,

Vita Odonis 2.12, PL 133, col. 68b). On "die von Kluny geübte Steigerung des altmonastischen Ideals vom Schweigen," see Hallinger, *Gorze-Kluny*, 925–26.

90. John of Salerno, *Vita Odonis* 1.32, PL 133, col. 57ab.

91. On the customaries attributed to Bernard of Cluny and Ulrich of Zell, see the articles collected in *From Dead of Night to End of Day*, ed. Boynton and Cochelin. On the dates of these customaries and their relationship to one another, see Wollasch, "Zur Verschriftlichung," 317–49.

92. Bernard of Cluny, *Ordo Cluniacensis* 1.74.33, ed. Herrgott, 273.

93. Ulrich of Zell, *Constitutiones Cluniacensis* 1.12, PL 149, col. 658d.

94. Ulrich of Zell, *Constitutiones Cluniacensis* 1.40, PL 149, col. 686a.

95. "Nam, quoties necessarias ad exposcendum res instabant, toties diversa in invicem fiebant ad perficiendum signa, quas puto grammatici digitorum et oculorum notas vocare voluerunt. Adeo nempe inter eos excreverat ordo iste, ut puto si sine officio linguae essent, ad omnia necessaria significanda sufficere possent signa ipsa" (John of Salerno, *Vita Odonis* 1.32, PL 133, col. 57ab). The term *nota* means "marks" or "characters." It was a more precise qualification than the ambiguous *signum*, because it implied that each sign carried a specific value or meaning. See du Cange, *Glossarium mediae*, 5: 609–10, s.v. *nota*.

96. For a modern critical edition of this sign lexicon, see Jarecki, *Signa Loquendi*, 121–42. Further on the history of monastic sign language, see Bruce, *Silence and Sign Language*.

97. "Est et alius inter eos taciturnitatis modus" (John of Salerno, *Vita Odonis* 1.32, PL 133, col. 57a). Although John was describing the customs of Baume-les-Moines, where Odo made his profession, it is likely that these descriptions reflected contemporary practice at Cluny as well, because Berno was the abbot of both houses at that time.

98. For what follows, see John of Salerno, *Vita Odonis* 2.12–13, PL 133, cols. 68a–69a.

99. See n. 45 above.

100. John of Salerno, *Vita Odonis* 2.11, PL 133, cols. 67a.

101. John of Salerno, *Vita Odonis* 2.10, PL 133, cols. 66cd.

102. John of Salerno, *Vita Odonis* 3.11, PL 133, cols. 83a.

103. John of Salerno, *Vita Odonis* 2.12, PL 133, cols. 67b.

104. John of Salerno, *Vita Odonis* 2.12–13, PL 133, cols. 68a–69a.

105. Leclercq, *The Life of Perfection*, 15–42.

106. Odo of Cluny, *Sermo* 3 ("De sancto Benedicto abbate"), PL 133, col. 722a. I have borrowed the phrase "embodied in human practice" from Asad, *Genealogies of Religion*, 137.

107. John of Salerno, *Vita Odonis* 2.5, PL 133, cols. 63c.

108. Peter Damian, *Epistola* 6.4, PL 144, col. 374ab.

109. "Si, inquit, monachi perfecti sunt, beatis angelis assimilantur; sin vero ad saeculum desiderium revertuntur, apostaticis angelis, qui suum domicilium non servaverunt, per suam utique apostasiam, jure comparantur" (Odo of Cluny, *Vita Geraldi* 2.8, PL 133, col. 675b; trans. Sitwell, 331).

110. "Octava enim Natalis Domini et ejus Resurrectionis summum silentium die noctuque fiebat in illis. Brevissimum quippe istud, illud significare fatebantur aeternum silentium" (John of Salerno, *Vita Odonis* 1.32, PL 133, col. 57ab).

111. For the inference that Gregory the Great's work informed the monks of Cluny in their practice of silence, see Hallinger, "Zur geistigen Welt," 427–29. An epitome of the *Moralium in Job* attributed to Odo appeared in a later library catalogue from Cluny. Further on this work, see Braga, "Problemi di autenticità per Oddone di Cluny."

112. Gregory the Great, *Moralium libri* 30.4.17, PL 76, col. 533ab.

Works Cited

Abbreviations

CCM   Corpus consuetudinum monasticarum. Ed. Kassius Hallinger. Siegburg: Respublica Verlag Franz Schmitt, 1963–.

MGH Epistolae Monumenta Germaniae historica inde ab anno Christi quingentesimo usque ad annum millesimum et quingentesimum: Epistolae Merowingici et Karolini aevi. Munich: Monumenta Germaniae Historica, 1957–.

MGH SRG   Monumenta Germaniae Historica: Scriptores Rerum Germanicarum in usum scholarum separatim editi. Hanover: Hahn, 1871–.

MGH SS   Monumenta Germaniae Historica inde ab anno Christi quingentesimo usque ad annum millesimum et quingentesimum: Scriptores in folio. 32 vols. Hanover: Hahn, 1826–1934.

PG   Patrologia cursus completus: Series graeca. Ed. Jacques-Paul Migne. 161 vols. in 166. Paris: Migne, 1857–1903.

PL   Patrologia cursus completus: Series latina. Ed. Jacques-Paul Migne. Paris: Migne, 1844–91.

RB   Regula Benedicti. Ed. Adalbert de Vogüé, in *La règle de saint Benoît*, 7 vols. SC 181–187. (Paris: Cerf, 1971–72) (cited by chapter and line number)

RM   Regula Magistri. Ed. Adalbert de Vogüé, in *La règle du Maître*. 3 vols. SC 105–107. (Paris: Cerf, 1964–65) (cited by chapter and line number)

SC   Sources chrétiennes. Paris: Cerf, 1941–.

Primary Sources

Alcuin. *Epistolae.* Ed. Ernest Dümmler. MGH Epistolae 4, repr. Munich: Monumenta Germaniae Historica, 1978.

Ambrose. *Enarrationes in XII Psalmos Davidicos.* PL 14, cols. 959–1238.

Apophthegmata patrum. Ed. Jean-Claude Guy, in *Recherches sur la tradition grecque des Apophthegmata patrum.* Brussels: Société des Bollandistes, 1962.

Apophthegmata patrum. PG 25.

Ardo. *Vita Benedicti abbatis Anianensis et Indensis,* ed. G. Waitz, MGH SS 15.1, 200–20. Hanover: Hahn, 1887.

Augustine of Hippo. *In Johannis evangelium tractatus cxxiv,* ed. D. R. Willems. Corpus Christianorum: Series Latina 36. Turnhout: Brepols, 1954.

Augustine of Hippo. *Ordo monasterii.* In *Augustine of Hippo and His Monastic Rule,* ed. George Lawless, 74–79. Oxford: Clarendon, 1987.

Aurelianus. *Regula ad monachos.* PL 68, cols. 385–98.

Basil of Caesarea. *Regula.* Ed. K. Zelzer, Corpus Scriptorum Ecclesiasticorum Latinorum 86. Vienna: Hoelder-Pichler-Tempsky, 1986.

Benedict of Aniane. *Concordia regularum.* PL 103, cols. 393–702.

Bernard of Cluny. *Ordo Cluniacensis sive Consuetudines.* In *Vetus Disciplina Monastica,* ed. M. Herrgott, 136–364. Paris: C. Osmont, 1726.

Caesarius. *Regula virginum.* In *Césaire d'Arles: Oeuvres monastiques,* ed. Joël Courreau and Adalbert de Vogüé. 2 vols. SC 345 and 398. Vol. 1, 170–273. Paris: Cerf, 1988–94.

Columbanus. *Regula monachorum* and *Regula coenobialis fratrum.* In *Sancti Columbani Opera,* ed. G. S. M. Walker. Dublin: Dublin Institute for Advanced Studies, 1957.

Consuetudines Corbeienses. Ed. J. Semmler, CCM 1, 355–422. Siegburg: Respublica Verlag Franz Schmitt, 1963.

Defensor of Ligugé. *Liber scintillarum.* Ed. H. M. Rochais. 2 vols. SC 77 and 86. Paris: Cerf, 1961–62.

Donatus. *Regula ad virgines.* In "La règle de Donat pour l'abbesse Gauthstrude," ed. Adalbert de Vogüé. *Benedictina* 25 (1978): 219–313.

Epistola cum duodecim capitulis quorundam fratrum ad Auvam directa. Ed. H. Frank. CCM 1, 330–36. Siegburg: Respublica Verlag Franz Schmitt, 1963.

Eusebius 'Gallicanus': Collectio Homiliarum. 3 vols., Corpus christianorum: Continuatio medievalis 101. Turnhout: Brepols, 1970–71.

Gregory the Great. *Libri dialogorum.* In *Grégoire le Grand: Dialogues,* ed. Adalbert de Vogüé. 3 vols. SC 251, 260, and 265. Paris: Cerf, 1978–80.

———. *Moralium libri.* PL 75, cols. 509–1162, and PL 76, cols. 9–782.

Hildemar. *Expositio regulae Sancti Benedicti.* In *Vita et Regula SS. P. Benedicti una cum Expositio Regulae a Hildemaro tradita,* ed. Rupert Mittelmüller. Regensburg: Frederick Pustet, 1880.

John Cassian. *De coenobiorum institutis,* In *Jean Cassien: Institutions cénobitiques,* ed. Jean-Claude Guy. SC 91. Paris: Cerf, 1965.

John of Salerno. *Vita Odonis.* PL 133, cols. 43–86.

Memoriale qualiter II. Ed. C. Morgand. CCM 1, 263–82. Siegburg: Respublica Verlag Franz Schmitt, 1963.

Notitia de servitio monasteriorum. Ed. P. Becker. CCM 1, 493–99. Siegburg: Respublica Verlag Franz Schmitt, 1963.

Odo of Cluny. *Sermon de sancto Benedicto abbate.* PL 133, cols. 721–29.

————. *Vita Geraldi.* PL 133, cols. 639–710. Trans. Gerard Sitwell, in *Soldiers of Christ: Saints and Saints' Lives from Late Antiquity and the Early Middle Ages,* ed. Thomas F. X. Noble and Thomas Head, 293–362. University Park: Pennsylvania State University Press, 1995.

Ordo Casinensis I. Ed. T. Leccisotti. CCM 1, 94–104. Siegburg: Respublica Verlag Franz Schmitt, 1963.

Peter Damian. *Epistolae.* PL 144, cols. 205–498.

Regula orientalis. In *Les règles des saints pères,* ed. Adalbert de Vogüé. 2 vols. SC 297–298. Vol. 2, 462–95. Paris: Cerf, 1982.

Regula Pauli et Stephani. In *Regula Pauli et Stephani: Edició crítica I comentari,* ed. J. M. Villanova. Montserrat: Abadia de Montserrat, 1959.

Regula sanctorum patrum. In *Les règles des saints pères,* ed. Adalbert de Vogüé. 2 vols. SC 297–98. Vol. 1, 180–205. Paris: Cerf, 1982.

Smaragdus. *Expositio in regulam S. Benedicti.* Ed. Alfred Spannagel. CCM 8. Siegburg: Respublica Verlag Franz Schmitt, 1974.

Statuta patrum. In *Les règles des saints pères,* ed. Adalbert de Vogüé. 2 vols. SC 297–298. Vol. 1, 274–83. Paris: Cerf, 1982.

Sulpicius Severus. *Vita sancti Martini.* In *Sulpice Sévère: Vie de saint Martin,* ed. Jacques Fontaine. 3 vols. SC 133–35. Paris: Cerf, 1967–69.

Synodi primae decreta authentica. Ed. J. Semmler, CCM 1, 252–68. Siegburg: Respublica Verlag Franz Schmitt, 1963.

Thegan. *Gesta Hludovici imperatoris.* In *Thegan: Täten Kaiser Ludwigs,* ed. E. Tremp. MGH SRG 64. Hanover: Hahnsche Buchhandelung, 1995.

Theodomar. *Epistula ad Theodoricum gloriosum.* Ed. J. Winandy and K. Hallinger. CCM 1, 126–36. Siegburg: Respublica Verlag Franz Schmitt, 1963.

Ulrich of Zell. *Constitutiones Cluniacensis.* PL 149, cols. 643–779.

Valerian of Cimiez. *Homiliae.* PL 52, cols. 691–755. In *Saint Peter Chrysologus, Selected Sermons and Saint Valerian, Homilies,* trans. Georges E. Ganss, The Fathers of the Church 17. Washington, DC: Catholic University of America Press, 1953.

Vitae patrum. PL 73–74. In *The Desert Fathers: Sayings of the Early Christian Monks,* trans. Benedicta Ward. New York: Penguin Books, 2003.

Waldebertus. *Regula ad virgines.* PL 88, cols. 1051–1070.

Secondary Sources

Alexander, Pedro Max. "La prohibición de la risa en la Regula Benedicti: Intento de explicación e interpretación." *Regulae Benedicti Studia* 5 (1976): 225–84.

Anton, Hans Hubert. *Fürstenspiegel und Herrscherethos in der Karolingerzeit.* Bonn: L. Rohrscheid, 1968.

Asad, Talal. *Genealogies of Religion: Discipline and Reasons of Power in Christianity and Islam.* Baltimore: Johns Hopkins University Press, 1993.

Bardsley, Sandy. "Sin, Speech, and Scolding in Late Medieval England." In *"Fama": The Politics of Talk and Reputation in Medieval Europe,* ed. Thelma Fenster and Daniel Lord Smail, 145–64. Ithaca: Cornell University Press, 2003.

Berlière, U. "Le nombre des moines dans les anciens monastères." *Revue bénédictine* 41 (1929): 231–61.

Braga, G. "Problemi di autenticità per Oddone di Cluny: L'Epitome dei *Moralia* di Gregorio Magno." *Studi Medievali* 18.2 (1977): 45–145.

Bredero, Adriaan H. "Cluny et le monachisme carolingien: Continuité et discontinuité." In *Benedictine Culture*, 750–1050, ed. W. Lourdaux and D. Verhelst, 50–75. Leuven: Leuven University Press, 1983.

Brown, Peter. *The Body and Society: Men, Women and Sexual Renunciation in Early Christianity.* New York: Columbia University Press, 1988.

Bruce, Scott G. *Silence and Sign Language in Medieval Monasticism: The Cluniac Tradition (c. 900–1200).* Cambridge Studies in Medieval Life and Thought. Cambridge: Cambridge University Press, 2007.

Burton-Christie, Douglas. *The Word in the Desert: Scripture and the Quest for Holiness in Early Christian Monasticism.* New York: Oxford University Press, 1993.

Carruthers, Mary. *The Book of Memory: A Study of Memory in Medieval Culture.* Cambridge: Cambridge University Press, 1990.

Casagrande, Carla, and Silvana Vecchio. *Les péchés de la langue: Discipline et éthique de la parole dans la culture médiévale.* Trans. Philippe Baillet. Paris: Cerf, 1991.

Chitty, Derwas J. *The Desert a City: An Introduction to the Study of Egyptian and Palestinian Monasticism Under the Christian Empire.* Oxford: Blackwell, 1966.

Constable, Giles. "Cluny in the Monastic World of the Tenth Century." In *Il secolo di ferro: Mito e realtà del secolo X (Spoleto, 19–25 aprile 1990)*, 391–437. Settimane di studio del Centro italiano di studi sull'alto medioevo 38. Spoleto: Presso la sede del Centro, 1991.

Craun, Edwin D. *Lies, Slander, and Obscenity in Medieval English Literature: Pastoral Rhetoric and the Deviant Speaker.* Cambridge: Cambridge University Press, 1997.

De Jong, Mayke. "Power and Humility in Carolingian Society: The Public Penance of Louis the Pious." *Early Medieval Europe* 1 (1992): 29–52.

———. "Carolingian Monasticism: The Power of Prayer." In *The New Cambridge Medieval History*, Volume II, c. 700–c. 900, ed. Rosamond McKitterick, 622–53. Cambridge: Cambridge University Press, 1995.

———. *In Samuel's Image: Child Oblation in the Early Medieval West.* Leiden: Brill, 1996.

De Vogüé, Adalbert. *Les règles monastiques anciennes (400–700).* Turnhout: Brepols, 1985.

———. "The Master and St. Benedict: A Reply to Marilyn Dunn." *English Historical Review* 107 (1992): 95–103.

———. "Obéissance et autorité dans le monachisme ancien jusqu'à Saint Benoît." In *Imaginer la théologie catholique: Permanence et transformations de la foi en attendant Jésus-Christ: Mélanges offerts à Ghislain Lafont*, ed. Jeremy Driscoll, 565–600. Studia Anselmiana 129. Rome: Herder, 2000.

———. *Regards sur le monachisme des premiers siècles: Recueil d'articles.* Studia Anselmiana 130. Rome: Herder, 2000.

———. "Influence de sainte Basile sur le monachisme d'occident." *Revue bénédictine* 113 (2003): 5–17.

Du Cange, Charles. *Glossarium mediae et infimae latinitatis.* 10 vols. Niort: Leopold Favre, 1883–87.

Dunn, Marilyn. "Mastering Benedict: Monastic Rules and Their Authors in the Early Medieval West." *English Historical Review* 105 (1990): 567–94.

———. "The Master and St. Benedict: A Rejoinder." *English Historical Review* 107 (1992): 104–11.

———. *The Emergence of Monasticism: From the Desert Fathers to the Early Middle Ages.* Oxford: Blackwell, 2000.

From Dead of Night to End of Day: The Medieval Cluniac Customs / Du coeur de la nuit à la fin du jour: Les coutumes clunisiennes au Moyen Âge. Ed. Susan Boynton and Isabelle Cochelin. Disciplina monastica 3. Leiden: Brepols, 2005.

Fuchs, Peter. "Die Weltflucht der Mönche: Anmerkungen zur Funktion des monastisch-ascetischen Schweigens." *Zeitschrift für Soziologie* 15 (1986): 393–405. Reprinted in *Reden und Schweigen*, ed. Niklas Luhmann and Peter Fuchs, 21–45. Frankfurt: Suhrkamp, 1989.

Gehl, Paul F. "*Competens Silentium*: Varieties of Monastic Silence in the Medieval West." *Viator* 18 (1987): 125–60.

Gindele, Corbinian. "Bienen-, Waben- und Honigvergleiche in der frühen monastischen Literatur." *Regulae Benedicti Studia* 6 / 7 (1981): 1–26.

Gleason, Maud. "Visiting and News: Gossip and Reputation Management in the Desert." *Journal of Early Christian Studies* 6 (1998): 501–21.

Goehring, James E. *Ascetics, Society, and the Desert: Studies in Early Egyptian Monasticism.* Harrisburg, PA: Trinity Press International, 1999.

———. "The Dark Side of the Landscape: Ideology and Power in the Christian Myth of the Desert." *Journal of Medieval and Early Modern Studies* 33 (2003): 437–51.

Gould, Graham. *The Desert Fathers on Monastic Community.* Oxford: Clarendon, 1993.

Guillaumont, Antoine. "La conception du désert chez les moines d'Egypt." *Revue de l'Histoire des Religions* 188 (1975): 3–21.

Hallinger, Kassius. *Gorze-Kluny: Studien zu den monastischen Lebensformen und Gegensätzen im Hochmittelalter.* Studia Anselmiana 22–25. Rome: Herder, 1950.

———. "Zur geistigen Welt der Anfänge Klunys." *Deutsches Archiv für Erforschung des Mittelalters* 10 (1954): 417–45. English translation: "The Spiritual Life of Cluny in the Early Days." In *Cluniac Monasticism in the Central Middle Ages*, ed. Noreen Hunt, 29–55. Hamden: Archon, 1971.

Hildebrand, Stephen M. "Oboedientia and Oboedire in the Rule of Benedict: A Study of Their Theological and Monastic Meanings." *American Benedictine Review* 52 (2001): 421–36.

Holze, Heinrich. "Schweigen und Gotteserfahrung bei den ägyptischen Mönchsvätern." *Erbe und Auftrag* 69 (1993): 314–21.

Horn, Walter, and Ernest Born. *The Plan of Saint Gall: A Study of the Architecture and Economy of, and Life in a Paradigmatic Carolingian Monastery.* 3 vols. Berkeley: University of California Press, 1979.

Innes, Matthew. "He Never Even Allowed His White Teeth to Be Bared in Laughter: The Politics of Humour in the Carolingian Renaissance." In *Humour,*

History and Politics in Late Antiquity and the Early Middle Ages, ed. Guy Halsall, 131–56. Cambridge: Cambridge University Press, 2002.

Jarecki, Walter. *"Signa Loquendi": Die cluniacensischen Signa-Listen eingeleitet und herausgegeben.* Baden-Baden: Verlag Valentin Koerner, 1981.

Le Goff, Jacques. "Le rire dans les règles monastiques du haut Moyen Age." In *Haut Moyen-Age: Culture, éducation et société. Études offertes à Pierre Riché,* ed. Claude Lepelley et al., 93–103. Nanterre: Editions Publidix, 1990.

Leclercq, Jean. *The Life of Perfection: Points of View on the Essence of the Religious State.* Trans. Leonard J. Doyle. Collegeville, MN: The Liturgical Press, 1961.

————. "Religious Obedience according to the Rule of Benedict." *American Benedictine Review* 16 (1965): 183–93.

Leyser, Conrad. *Authority and Asceticism from Augustine to Gregory the Great.* Oxford: Clarendon, 2000.

Lorenz, R. "Die Anfänge des abendländischen Mönchtums im 4. Jahrhundert." *Zeitschrift für Kirchengeschichte* 77 (1966): 1–61.

McDougall, David, and Ian McDougall. "Evil Tongues: A Previously Unedited Old English Sermon." *Anglo-Saxon England* 26 (1997): 209–29.

McKitterick, Rosamond. *The Frankish Kingdoms under the Carolingians, 751–987.* London: Longman, 1983.

Miller, Patricia Cox. "Jerome's Centaur: A Hyper-Icon of the Desert." *Journal of Early Christian Studies* 4 (1996): 209–33.

Moyse, Gérard. "Monachisme et réglementation monastique en Galue avant Benoît d'Aniane." In *Sous la règle de saint Benoît: Structures monastiques et sociétés en France du moyen âge à l'époque moderne,* 3–19. Geneva: Droz, 1982.

Noble, Thomas F. X. "The Monastic Ideal as a Model for Empire: The Case of Louis the Pious." *Revue bénédictine* 86 (1976): 235–50.

————. "Louis the Pious and His Piety Reconsidered." *Revue Belge de Philologie et d'Histoire* 58 (1980): 297–316.

Oexle, Otto Gerhard. "Les moines d'occident et la vie politique et sociale dans le haut Moyen Âge." *Revue bénédictine* 103 (1993): 255–72.

Prinz, Friedrich. *Frühes Mönchtum in Frankenreich: Kultur und Gesellschaft in Gallien, den Rheinlanden und Bayern am Beispiel der monastischen Entwicklung (4. bis 8. Jahrhundert).* 2nd ed. Darmstadt: Wissenschaftliche Buchgesellschaft, 1988.

Resnick, Irven M. "*Risus monasticus:* Laughter and Medieval Monastic Culture." *Revue bénédictine* 97 (1987): 90–100.

Rosenwein, Barbara H. "St. Odo's St. Martin: The Uses of a Model." *Journal of Medieval History* 4 (1978): 317–31.

Rousseau, Philip. *Ascetics, Authority, and the Church in the Age of Jerome and Cassian.* Oxford: Oxford University Press, 1978.

————. *Pachomius: The Making of a Community in Fourth-Century Egypt.* Berkeley: University of California Press, 1985.

Saenger, Paul. "Silent Reading: Its Impact on Late Medieval Script and Society." *Viator* 13 (1982): 367–414.

Schmitz, G. "*Quod rident homo, plurandum est:* Der Unwert des Lachen im mon-

astische geprägten Vorstellungen der spätantike und des frühen Mittelalters."
In *Stadtverfassung, Verfassungsstaat, Pressepolitik: Festschrift E. Naujoks,* ed. F.
Quarthal and W. Setzler, 3–15. Sigmaringen: Thorbecke, 1980.

Semmler, Joseph. "Karl der Grosse und das fränkische Mönchtum." In *Karl der
Grosse: Lebenswerk und Nachleben,* ed. Helmut Beumann et al. 5 vols. Vol. 2,
255–89. Düsseldorf: L. Schwann, 1965–68.

———. "Pippin III. und die fränkischen Klöster." *Francia* 3 (1975): 88–146.

———. "Mönche und Kanoniker im Frankenreich Pippins III. und Karls des
Grossen." In *Untersuchungen zu Kloster und Stift,* 78–111. Göttingen: Vanden-
hoeck & Ruprecht, 1980.

———. "Benedictus II: *Una regula, una consuetudo.*" In *Benedictine Culture 750–1050,* ed.
W. Lourdaux and D. Verhelst, 1–49. Leuven: Leuven University Press, 1983.

Smith, Julia M. H. "The Problem of Female Sanctity in Carolingian Europe, c.
780–920." *Past and Present* 146 (1995): 3–37.

———. "Gender and Ideology in the Early Middle Ages." *Studies in Church History*
34 (1998): 51–73.

Steidle, Basilius. "Das Lachen im alten Mönchtum." *Benediktinische Monatsschrift* 20
(1938): 271–80.

Sullivan, Richard E. "What Was Carolingian Monasticism? The Plan of St. Gall
and the History of Monasticism." In *After Rome's Fall: Narrators and Sources of
Early Medieval History, Essays Presented to Walter Goffart,* ed. Alexander
Callander Murray, 251–87. Toronto: University of Toronto Press, 1998.

Taylor, Anna. "Just like a Mother Bee: Reading and Writing *Vitae metricae* around
the Year 1000." *Viator* 36 (2005): 119–48.

Wathen, Ambrose G. *Silence: The Meaning of Silence in the Rule of Saint Benedict.*
Washington, DC: Cistercian Publications, 1973.

Weiss, Jean-Pierre. "Le statut du prédicateur et les instruments de la prédication
dans la Provence du Ve siècle." In *La parole du prédicateur, Ve–XVe siècle,* 23–47.
Nice: Z'éditions, 1997.

Wollasch, Joachim. "Zur Verschriftlichung der klösterlichen Lebensgewohnheiten
unter Abt Hugo von Cluny." *Frühmittelalterliche Studien* 27 (1993): 317–49.

———. *Cluny, Licht der Welt: Augstieg und Niedergang der klösterlichen Gemeinschaft.*
Dusseldorf: Artemis & Winkler, 1996.

"Allas, allas! That evere love was synne"
Excuses for Sin and the Wife of Bath's Stars

Edwin D. Craun

For several decades, scholars have been exploring how Geoffrey Chaucer's Wife of Bath presents herself in her prologue by exploiting the commonplaces of authoritative clerical discourse: biblical exegesis, marriage sermons, treatises on virginity, and misogamous satire. In passing, they also have observed that the mode of constructing her life that Chaucer has given her has general affinities with the speech that clerics expected of penitents in auricular confession. Recently, Jerry Root has made two more specific and cogent arguments about confessional speech. First, the Wife appropriates one quality that clerics insisted was necessary for a good or valid confession, its nakedness or literalness, to reject the privileging of the chaste body by figural exegetes. Second, she confesses all her "privetee," as confessors enjoin, but in order to produce "a 'feminist' representation of man" from the words of men—those of her husbands and of clerical writers. In both ways she resists clerical power and control. And she does so by exploiting confessional discourse as "the privileged language of self-presentation and self-knowledge in the period."[1] More than these two general qualities of confessional speech shape the Wife's monologic dialogue with masculine authority, performed for a largely male audience, including several priests who would have directed confessions.[2] Auricular confession is inherently a dialogue between the confessor, who adopts pastoral discourse on sin to question, to instruct, to reprove, and to persuade, and a penitent, who is enjoined to apply that discourse to his or her thoughts, words, and deeds, making sins known in clerically scripted speech. If a penitent resists a clerical reading of herself as sinful, as willingly deviating from divine law, confessional speech itself may become an occasion (in the confessor's optic) for more sin, for Sins of the Tongue, especially for excusing or defending sin.[3]

Excusing sin or defending sin—the terms were interchangeable—became itself a topos in pastoral discourse on sin and confession, coming to the fore as the higher clergy, often university trained, worked to create informed confessors and informed penitents. This pastoral literature flourished especially in England, where diocesan councils and provincial synods tied catechesis to confession. Pastoral catechesis was used both to prepare English Christians for their obligatory annual confession to a priest (or for more frequent confessions, such as those of Margery Kempe) and to address specific sins and areas of ignorance during the confessional dialogue itself.[4] Adopting a rhetorical strategy at least as old as St. Augustine, pastoral authors often developed the topos by creating contained dialogues in which the rebellious penitents speak first, attributing what they are divulging not to their own wills but to supposedly irresistible causes. Then the writer himself at once enters the dialogue and closes it off with counter-reasoning that re-reads what the penitent just has defended as sinful, as evil freely chosen. Such a conflict over how and why someone does something and the kind of person someone desires to be inevitably thrusts human agency to the fore.[5]

Through these pastoral texts, the stock impenitents' reasoning and rhetoric was spread first to clerics and then to laics through preaching, through catechizing, and through directing confession itself. Such a pastoral rhetorical strategy had its obvious perils. It gave potentially subversive sinners a repertoire of causes, with learned terms and an idiom in which to express them. It gave them alternative (nonpenitential) ways of reading their own lives, many of which I have included in a general essay on excuses for sin.[6] Prominent among them was a "cours of kynde [nature]": inclinations produced by the stars, especially by one's natal horoscope or constellation. Every reader of the Wife's prologue knows where this argument is going: to the Wife's approving survey of herself at forty, just after she gave her heart to "oure clerk," twenty-year-old Jankyn. Recalling his legs and feet "so clene and faire" as he followed her fourth husband's bier, she attributes the youthful power of her carnal desires and her often unrestrained sexual behavior to her birth stars:

> [For certes, I am al Venerien
> In feelynge, and myn herte is Marcien.
> Venus me yaf my lust, my likerousnesse,
> And Mars yaf me my sturdy hardynesse;]
> Myn ascendent was Taur, and Mars therinne.

Allas, allas! That evere love was synne!
I folwed ay myn inclinacioun
By vertu of my constellacioun;
That made me I koude noght withdrawe
My chambre of Venus from a good felawe.
[Yet have I Martes mark upon my face,
And also in another privee place.
For God so wys be my savacioun,
I ne loved nevere by no discrecioun,
But evere folwede myn appetit. . . .] (III.609–23)[7]

Before examining the Wife's speech, I will consider how pastoral literature presents confessional dialogue—and, more broadly, any exchange between a sinner and a reprover—as an arena of struggle, an exchange in
which sinners may resist, all too inventively and vigorously, clerical (and
sometimes lay) attempts to interpret and to direct their thinking, speaking,
and acting. I also will trace how clerical texts of various kinds presented
both sinners' claims of astral determinism and clerical counter-arguments
about sin, constructing clashing notions of human agency and the good life.
Then I will argue that the Wife, as one of those agents in the *Tales* "who actively engage and deploy the institutions of their culture both practically
and discursively,"[8] presents herself, at this point in her monologue, by sub-
versively deploying pastoral rhetoric. Finally, I will consider the questions
about her as an agent that Chaucer raises. In telling the story of astral
power about herself, rather than the male clergy's one about sin, what
power does she acquire to shape her self and her future actions? Does her
discursive self-reading become the locus of moral agency, the place where
she takes some (limited) responsibility for governing her own life as she becomes ethically conscious through language?[9] For agency, I believe, is em-
bedded in complex historical languages, and it is the task of the scholar to
re-present, in as much of their complexity as possible, the languages woven
into literary texts.

That Chaucerian pastor and confessor, the Parson, situates defending
or excusing sin firmly in the confessional dialogue when he begins to ex-
pound it as his second sin of the tongue in his discourse on penitence:

Thanne comth of Ire attry [poisonous] angre. Whan a man is sharply
amonested [admonished] in his shrifte to forleten [abandon] his synne, /
thanne wole he be angry, and answeren hokerly [disdainfully] and angrily,
and deffenden or excusen his synne by unstedefastnesse of his flessh; or

elles he dide it for to holde compaignye with his felawes; or elles he seith, the feend enticed hym; / or elles he dide it for his youthe; or elles his compleccioun is so corageous that he may nat forbere; or elles it is his destinee, as he seith, unto a certein age; or elles, he seith, it cometh hym of gentillesse [nobility] of his auncestres; and sembable thynges. (X.583–85)

Of the seventeen "synnes that comen of the tonge" that the Parson treats together in a subtractate on deviant speech,[10] he places only excusing sin and swearing in a definite situation, confessions and conjurations, and he gives voices only to excusers and chiders (although the excusers are distanced somewhat by indirect discourse). These techniques allow him to present specific instances of these types, such as "thou dronkelewe harlot" of uncharitable reproof (X.626). With excusing sin, the general rhetorical effect is to stress confession as its site, where it alone of the seventeen is a response to an authoritative pastoral voice, the confessor's. In the widespread coupling of Bernard of Clairvaux, *defensio peccatorum* is the opposite of *confessio peccatorum*, the eighth of twelve stages or degrees ("gradus") of pride and humility respectively.[11] To engage in one is to deny oneself the other—as the Parson says: "For soothly, no wight that excuseth hym wilfully of his synne may nat been delivered of his synne til that he mekely biknoweth [confesses, makes known] his synne" (X.586).

Pastoral writers trace the voices of those who excuse sin back to the postlapsarian exchange between God and Adam (Gen. 3:11–12). This exchange, as Eric Jager has demonstrated, was seen by patristic and medieval writers as the origin of the rite of confession, with God asking a question to prompt Adam to confess his sin.[12] The early fourteenth-century priest Robert Mannyng uses Adam's response to illustrate excusing sin as he closes *Handlyng Synne,* his handbook on confession for the laity, by warning against several dangers in confession.

> Ʒyt þyr ys an vnþryft [fault]
> Þat doþ moche skaþe [harm] yn shryft,
> Þat þou defendest þe fro plyght [sin]
> And puttest þy synne on god almyght.
> So dede oure fader Adam
> Whan god of heuen to hym cam
> And seyde, "Adam, why art þou yn synne?"
> "Lord," he seyde, "my wyff made me bygynne.
> Þat yche [same] wyff þat þou me wroght,
> She synnede fyrst & y noght."
> Seeþ how Adam bygan to lye

And putte on god hys owne folye,
For god forbede hym þat tre
Þat he ne shuld ete þer of ne she.
Seeþ how he dede þat god forbede
And dede aftyr hys wyues rede [advice].
He wlde [would, willed to] haue excused hys fame
As who seyþ god was to blame.
Þese lewed men seye & erre ful yl,
And seye hyt was al goddes wyl.[13]

While Mannyng's God asks the simple, direct question that emphasizes the sinful nature of the act and the need to examine, and to declare, what caused it, Mannyng's Adam presents a convoluted response, his initial relative clause throwing the weight on God's agency as creator and on Eve's as the initiator of sin.[14] In this genesis of postlapsarian rhetoric, Adam is the eloquent, calculated Artful Dodger, contrasted to Mannyng's plain-style God (like John Milton's in *Paradise Lost*). (Eve, of course, followed suit by deflecting the guilt onto the Creator when she reminded God that he put the serpent in the garden.)[15] The pastoral writers' common Latin verbs for this transferral of guilt—*retorquere, intorquere*, and *refundere*—suggest strenuous effort and voluminousness. Certainly it always involves, for them, rhetorical figures—"excusyng þi-self in colouris," in the words of the compiler of *Jacob's Well*—which are designed to be deceptive, to hide the naked truth expected in penitents' speech.[16]

Adam's artful speech answering God's question authorizes pastoral writers to weave into their texts the voices of sinners as they produce arguments for their confessors or others who have reproved them. Latin texts tend to present many different ways ("modi") of excusing sin, each more sophisticated than the last as sinners cleverly appropriate common clerical moral reasoning: "'Non feci,' aut: 'Feci quidem, sed bene feci,' aut si male: 'Non multum male'; aut si multum male: 'Non mala intentione'" ["I didn't do it" or "Yes, I did it, but it was the right thing to do" or, if wrong, "Not very wrong" or, if very wrong, "Not with an evil intention"].[17] Here, in Bernard's *De gradibus*, the catalogue and the shifting situations expose the sinner's desperate attempts to seize from clerical discourse some argument that will convince: good consequences, the relative gravity of sin, or the doer's intention. In some vernacular texts, these lists collapse into an unrestrained outpouring of excuses that becomes comic in its intensity, its groping for blame, its emphatic repetition, its assonance and alliteration, and its transparency: "'god ȝaf me no myȝt to wyth-stondyn it. oþere folk dyde me don it. It was oþerys defaute & noȝt myn. Myn husbonde dede me don it."[18] Here, in *Jacob's Well,* sin is deflected onto other agents, human and divine, much as Adam's is.

In response, the pastoral writers subvert the sinners' confusing torrent of excuses with blunt restatement followed by sustained argument. Mannyng reduces the excuses of Adam and other "lewed [ignorant, not literate in Latin, wicked] men" to the plain words "And [they] seye hyt was al goddes wyl." Then he proceeds to argue against such heresy, presenting multiple reasons why Adam had the freedom of decision to save himself from doing evil: God would not have forbidden him to eat of the tree in the first place, if God had willed him to do so; Adam could have rejected Eve's offer of the apple; and so on.[19] Therefore, he argues, Adam's descendants cannot claim that necessity forces them to act unchastely. Throughout pastoral literature, excuses for sin thus provide a textual locus for issues of freedom of choice, will, moral agency, and necessity, issues in which Chaucer was interested throughout his writing life. For most excuses constructed by pastoral writers claim that the sinner's will, his or her desire for the good apprehended by reason, was swayed irresistibly by powerful forces: others, especially one's spouse (as in *Jacob's Well*); the devil, youth, destiny, and physiological drives (as in The Parson's Tale). Pastoral writers design these clashing accounts of moral agency to provoke readers and hearers to reflect on causality, responsibility, and the good life. But they distance their audiences from the sinners' voices, which seem irrational, overwrought, and comically deceptive, especially in contrast to the authors' closing sustained theological reasoning.

This strategy of first scripting and then subverting the voices of those who excuse their sin was developed by Augustine of Hippo, often cited by late medieval English pastoral writers on excusing sin, when he commented on several psalms involving confession and excusing sin. And his discredited sinners attribute sins, including sexual ones, to the stars, specifically the Wife of Bath's Mars and Venus. His exegesis of the second penitential psalm, "Beati quorum remissae sunt iniquitates," contrasts guileful excuses for sin to David's confession of sin.[20] "Fatum mihi fecit, stellae meae fecerunt" ["My fate was the cause. My stars were the cause"], his self-exculpators claim when they are reproved for sins. (*Stellae* may refer to the five planets in late antique and medieval Latin, but I render it as *stars* throughout because of its modern astrological sense.) Augustine allows them only this rapidfire outcry before exposing, as Mannyng later was to do with Adam, the "true" claim beneath their guileful words:

et dicunt: Fatum mihi fecit. Quid est fatum? Stellae meae fecerunt. Quid sunt stellae? Certe istae quas in caelo conspicimus. Et quis eas fecit? Deus. Quis eas ordinauit? Deus. Ergo uides quod uoluisti dicere: Deus fecit ut peccarem. Ita ille iniustus, tu iustus; quia nisi ille fecisset, tu non peccasses.[21]

[And they say: "My fate was the cause." What is fate? "My stars did it." What are stars? Surely those we see in the sky. And who made them? God. Who ordered them? God. Therefore you see what you wanted to say: "God caused me to sin." So He is unjust and you are just because you would not have sinned unless He had caused it.]

Augustine focuses on the will that generates sinners' excuses: the will to seem just and the will to attribute their sin to God, the will to utter what is, in Augustine's eyes, false doctrine. It is this will that determines the moral nature of their speech, which makes it sinful in itself, the *excusationes in peccatis* that Augustine promptly labels it.[22] Against this speech Augustine sets the words of David, the model penitent, in what was to become the standard text for late medieval discourse on *excusatio peccati*: "Ne declines cor meum in uerba maligna ad excusandas excusationes in peccatis, cum hominibus operantibus iniquitatem" [Incline not my heart to evil words: to make excuses in sins, with men that work iniquity (Ps. 140:4)]. After authorizing his prohibition of excuses, Augustine turns to those in his culture who authorize such excuses for sin: the "magni viri" whom he often scornfully terms *mathematici* [astrologers]:

At enim magni uiri sunt, qui defendunt peccata sua; magni sunt et qui numerant sidera, et qui computant stellas et tempora, et dicunt quis quando uel peccet uel bene uiuat, et quando Mars faciat homicidam, et Venus adulteram; magni, docti uiri, et electi uidentur in hoc saeculo. Sed quid ait in psalmo? *Ne declines cor meum in uerba mala, cum hominibus operantibus iniquitatem, et non communicabo cum electis eorum.*

[Yes, there are great men who defend their sins; they are also great who number the stars and reckon the stars and times and say when anyone sins or lives a good life, and when Mars causes murder and Venus adultery; they are great men, learned men, and they seem eminent in this world. But what does it say in the psalm? "Incline not my heart to evil words ... with men that work iniquity, and I will not communicate with the choicest of them."]

To David's resolution Augustine adds his own: he rejects the learned and eminent stargazers with the simple theological claim "Cum libero arbitrio me creauit Deus" [God created me with freedom of decision], a claim that leads him to confess sins as his own, not God's as creator of the stars.[23]

Augustine's anti-astrological rhetoric is most fully developed in his exegesis of Psalm 140 ("Domine clamaui ad te"), the psalm most often cited by medieval pastoral writers when they treat excusing sin. The psalms engaged Augustine so intensely because, as he says, he was drawn to David's sins, especially to David's act of adultery with Bathsheba and his plotting of Uriah's death. Hence Augustine's frequent references to Venus and to Mars as the supposed causes of adultery and murder.[24] In his exegesis of Psalm 140:4, he ties excuses for sins to sexual lapses, especially those of women. He recalls the Gospel of Luke's penitent woman, who confessed fornication at Jesus' feet (Luke 7). She did not (in Augustine's paraphrase of the key verse 4) incline her heart to evil words to make excuses for sins. Strengthening the tie between women and sexual sins, he lists social groups of "base" women and then resorts to his usual technique of weaving in the sinners' voices, followed by the contrasting voice of the penitent, here Luke's penitent woman conflated with David:

> Non enim et huic ipsi mulieri, si declinaretur cor eius in uerba maligna, deesset defensio peccatorum. At non quotidie pares eius in turpitudine, sed non pares in confessione, meretrices, adulterae, flagitiosae defendunt peccata sua? Si latuerint, negant; si autem uel deprehensae atque conuictae fuerint, uel publice id egerint, defendunt. . . . O si Deus hoc nollet, non facerem! Hoc uoluit Deus, fortuna hoc uoluit, hoc uoluit fatum. Non dicit: *Ego dixi: Domine, miserere mei*; non quomodo illa peccatrix ad pedes medici ueniens, *Sana animam meam, quoniam peccaui tibi.*

> [For defense of sin would not have been absent in this woman if her heart had been inclined to evil words. But do not her peers in baseness (but not her peers in confession)—whores, adulteresses, disgraceful women—daily defend their sins? If they have hidden them, they deny them; however, if they have been detected and accused, or if they should have done them publicly, they defend them. . . . "Oh, if God did not will it, I would not be doing it! God willed this; fortune willed this; fate willed this." She does not say "I said: O, Lord be thou merciful to me" [Ps. 40:5]; she does not speak as that sinning woman did, coming to the feet of the physician: "Heal my soul, for I have sinned against thee" [Ps. 40:5].]

Then Augustine traces the simplistic reasoning of these "indoci" [un-learned] women to "docti" men, the *mathematici* who sell the women fables that ensnare them ("fabulas laqueorum") and doom them to a spiritual death. These seductive male voices are as simplistic as those of the "base" women:

> Sedent, et computant sidera; interualla, cursus, uolubilitates, status, motus intendunt, describunt, coniciunt. Docti, magni uidentur. Totum hoc doctum et magnum, defensio peccati est. Eris adulter, quia sic habes Venerem; eris homicida, quia sic habes Martem. Mars ergo homicida, non tu; et Venus adultera, non tu.[25]

> [They sit and reckon the stars; they bend their minds to intervals, courses, revolutions, states, motions—and they delineate them and draw inferences from them. They seem to be learned men, great men. This whole learned and great business is defense of sin. "You will be an adulterer because you have Venus as your star; you will be a murderer because you have Mars in this way. Mars therefore is the homicide, not you; and Venus the adulteress, not you."]

The astrologers speak of inevitability, Augustine explains elsewhere, be-cause they believe that the position of the stars at anyone's conception or birth (his or her *constellatio*) dominates the person's will and so determines his or her acts by celestial influence.[26]

Despite its sheer bulk, Augustine's *Enarrationes* was, as Michael Kuczynski has reminded us, one of the most widely disseminated texts in England during the century after the Norman Conquest. Kuczynski also has demonstrated that it was "especially well-used and influential in fifteenth-century Eng-land."[27] But Augustine's rhetorical practices for subverting self-exculpators and his repertoire of their excuses, including the influence of the stars (even that of Venus and Mars), reached medieval England even more fully in the flourishing traditions of psalm exegesis and pastoral literature.

Scholastic exegesis incorporates Augustinian argument wholesale. Peter Lombard's influential commentary includes, in its exposition of Psalm 31, the voices of Augustine's sinners ("Fatum mihi fecit, stellae mihi fecerunt"); then it proceeds, often drawing in Augustine's *enarratio* verbatim, to unmask their accusation against God, to assert freedom of choice ["liberum ar-bitrium"]. On the next "stars psalm," 40, Peter, quoting Augustine, illus-trates such excuses with Venus (for the adulterer) and Mars (for the thief): "non accuso fortunam, non dico: Hoc mihi facit fatum; non dico:

Adulterum me fecit Venus, et latronem Mars, et avarum Saturnus" [I do not accuse fortune. I do not say "My fate causes this"; I do not say "Venus made me an adulterer, Mars a thief, Saturn a miser"].[28] The thirteenth-century exegetes Hugo de Saint Cher and pseudo-Innocent III include Peter's material on Psalm 31, noting that excusers prefer the term *constellatio*, the Wife of Bath's term and the astrological term (as Augustine noted) for the cluster or position of heavenly bodies at one's conception or birth that can serve as the basis for prognostication (*Dictionary of Medieval Latin*, *Middle English Dictionary* 2b).[29] The practice of illustrating astral excuses with Mars and Venus not only survives in the thirteenth-century commentators but also is sometimes revivified by their learning. Early in the century, the English natural philosopher and encyclopedist Alexander Neckam, author of the popular *De naturis rerum*, elaborates the excuse by ranging through all five planets, the sun, and the moon. In his exposition of Psalm 40, those born under Venus claim that it has made them concupiscent and disposed to lust, and, interestingly for readers of the Wife of Bath's prologue, those born under Mars attribute to it their appetite for discord (not homicide, as in Augustine, or theft, as in Lombard). Alexander also firmly locates these excuses in the confessional dialogue.[30]

So pervasive was this topos of the anticonfessional speech of excusers that it flourished in exegesis on one psalm into which Augustine did not introduce it, 74. Flavius Cassiodorus may have begun this tradition when he glossed verse 6a ("Nolite extollere in altum cornu vestrum" [Lift not up your horn on high]) as the sin of making excuses and then glossed 6b ("Nolite loqui adversus Deum iniquitatem" [Speak not iniquity against God]) as the specific excuse of astral determinism ("necessitate stellarum"). Picked up by eleventh- and twelfth-century exegetes, Cassiodorus' passage is incorporated, in a reduced form, into the marginal gloss of the *Glossa ordinaria*, into Lombard's commentary, and into later commentaries such as the late fourteenth-century one of Peter von Herenthals. Cassiodorus also branded excusing sin as the gravest of sins, an attention-getting claim that the *Glossa* links closely to attributing sins to "the necessity of the stars."[31] So widespread was this Latin commentary on Psalm 74 that Richard Rolle renders it into English with an expansiveness unusual for him:

> willes noght heghe [don't desire to lift up] *the* horne of pride. as whasay.
> when ȝe hafe done syn defend it noght. and sett it in namanys [no man's]
> defaute, bot *in* ȝoure aghen [own]. . . . Ill it is to syn. wers it is to dwell *thar*
> in. bot aldi*re* warst [worst of all] it is, defendand his syn. lay *the* wite

[blame] þare of on god, or on any *other*. and *that* is to heghe oure horne. and to speke wickidnes agayns god. for sum says it was my werdis [fate]. sum says *the* sterne of my birth gert [made] me syn. and *this* is wickednes, & defamynge of god. and he says *that* god is vnrightwis.[32]

Here Augustinian rhetoric—the voices of the self-exculpators, their recourse to fate and the stars, the label "defense of sin," the exposure of their "true" claim—finds its way into a vernacular fourteenth-century commentary—and one widely disseminated in England. So, too, does the later exegetes' insistence on the gravity of excusing sin.

These same elements of the topos also appear in pastoral texts written by Englishmen from the early thirteenth century to the early fifteenth. (However, the pastoral writers, like the medieval exegetes, do not transmit Augustine's association of astrological excuses for sexual license with women in his *enarratio* on the key Psalm 140.) When the pastoral handbook *Lucerna conscientie* discusses *accusatoria* as a quality of confession, it contrasts David's prayer for verbal restraint so that he may not maliciously excuse sin (140:3–4) with the voices of, first, Adam and Eve and, then, Bernard of Clairvaux's sinners. Then it adds several specific excuses, culminating in "stellarum inclinacione." *Inclinatio,* the technical astronomical term that the Wife of Bath uses ("I folwed ay myn inclinacioun"), signified (1) the bending of the planets to influence terrestrial life and (2) one's natural disposition due to the position of the planets at one's birth. Finally, the *Lucerna* cites Augustine's arguments that all sin is freely chosen and willed. The anonymous *Distinctiones* in Bodleian Library Oxford MS 4 expounds *propria* [one's own] as a quality of confession by incorporating, like Augustine, the voices of those who believe in astral determinism ("stelle mihi fecerunt").[33] In the more expansive pastoral texts, the excusers' fallacious reasoning is developed and countered more fully with Augustine's authority. Thomas of Chobham's early thirteenth-century *summa* on preaching presents standard excuses for sin so that his clerical readers and their auditors can penetrate the devil's seductive falsehoods ("fallacie"). Thomas gives astral determinism last, casting it, like the two other excuses, in indirect discourse and stressing sinners' fallacious belief that their natal star determines their *complexio,* their temperament as it is constituted by a specific mixture of elements (*Dictionary of Medieval Latin*): "Alii dicunt se habere excusationem in peccatis quia nati sub aliqua constellatione; dicunt se ex conplexione natiuitatis sue non posse abstinere a peccatis" [Others say that they have an excuse for their sins because they were born under a certain constellation; they say that they cannot abstain from sins because of the temperament given them at birth]. While Thomas draws on traditional counter-reasoning and Augustine's authority to dismiss it as invalid ("nullus," "vanus"), Alexander Carpenter's early fifteenth-century encyclopedia on the vices dismisses astral excuses by incorporating extensive Augustinian passages on the human freedom to commit or not to commit sin.[34]

This pervasive topos of excusing sin, especially through the resistant sinner's appeal to astral powers, becomes one discourse with which Chaucer's Wife of Bath constitutes herself:

> [For certes, I am al Venerien
> In feelynge, and myn herte is Marcien.
> Venus me yaf my lust, my likerousnesse,
> And Mars yaf me my sturdy hardynesse;]
> Myn ascendent was Taur, and Mars therinne.
> Allas, allas! That evere love was synne!
> I folwed ay myn inclinacioun
> By vertu of my constellacioun;
> That made me I koude noght withdrawe
> My chambre of Venus from a good felawe. (III.609–18)

First the Wife delivers her natal horoscope to account for having, at forty, "a coltes tooth," having Venus' mark as a birthmark, and having "the beste *quoniam* myghte be" (601–08)—all bodily signs, for her, of lecherousness. Her word "likerousnesse" suggests a carnal greed, a rampant, unrestrained, and frequently indulged appetite like that of Chaucer's Physician's cagey old keeper of game, a former "theef of venysoun, that hath forlaft / His likerousnesse" (VI.83–85). Like the sinners of Augustine and of the medieval exegetes who attribute their acts of adultery to the stars, the Wife gives Venus pride of place: her ascendent is Taurus, a domicile of Venus, a zodiacal place where Venus has "lordship." As the historian of astronomy J. D. North argues, "It is important to stress the attention given to Venus the planet. . . . she gave the Wife her lust, and her lecherousness."[35] Mars, as Chauncey Wood and North have shown elaborately, exaggerates her Venusian character, "turning a loving nature into a lustful one"—and one more boldly so.[36]

If we come to the Wife's reading of her natal horoscope from pastoral discourse on excusing sin, we can grasp the Wife's rhetorical strategy as she accounts for her desire for Jankyn, a man half her age. She reverses the clerical rhetorical embedding of the sinners' speech within theological argument: she embeds the clerical reading of her sexual life as sinful ("Allas, allas! That evere love was synne!") between her horoscope and her claim that her "constellacioun" dictated her powerful desires and thus shaped markedly her sexual conduct. This embedding, like her immediate veering away to the technical astronomical terms used in discourse on excusing sin ("inclinacioun," "constellacioun"), handles the pastoral optic deftly, without direct confrontation. It never is entertained as a possibility. It is dismissed with an overdramatized regret that "love" was ever framed as sin. The power ("vertu") of her constellation is so great that not only does it determine desire but, once its "inclinacioun" is followed, initially accepted as masterful, as providing a track for will and conduct, it also obviates, in individual cases, the freely chosen behavior on which the pastoral concept of sin is grounded: "I koude noght withdrawe [withhold] / My chambre of Venus from a good felawe."[37] Just as the exegetes and pastoral writers subvert the voices of their self-exculpators with technical terms (theological, in their case) and bare assertions of causality (Augustine's "Cum libero arbitrio me creauit Deus"), she subverts their reading with the same rhetorical techniques. Thus, she contains their reading as they contain hers, but she denies them a voice, giving them only their label ("synne"). Thus, while she utters the clerically scripted speech of the sinners who attribute their conduct to lifelong, overwhelmingly powerful astral influences, she draws on the clergy's own exegetical/pastoral rhetoric for controlling opposing voices.

Like the pastoral writers' sinners, the Wife presents her behavior in terms of an inability to withhold herself from sexual activity: "I koude noght withdrawe / My chambre of Venus from a good felawe." Compare the Parson's version of excuses from physiological makeup ("his compleccioun is so corageous he may nat forbere," line X.584), Alexander Carpenter's "dicunt plane se non posse abstinere a libidinibus propter suam complexionem" or Mannyng's "þey mowe nat holde hem fro foly, / And sey þey mowe nat lyue chaste."[38] Despite the similar phrasing, her words are openly and unvarying carnal. For her physical causes—her birth stars—dictate physiological effects, her "Martes mark" on the face and beneath the body's clothing (622–24, lines that may be a scribal addition). Once she has established that principle repeatedly, she sheds even the clerical label "sin" for her unrestrained sexual activity, emphatically rejecting any form of choice, apart from that of sexual desire, as calculating scrupulosity: "I ne loved nevere by no discrecioun / But evere folwede myn appetit, / Al were he short, or long, or blak, or whit" (621–23, also perhaps an addition). That the Wife should disclose and justify undisciplined sexuality in undisciplined speech is not surprising, given the rhetorical tradition that figures rhetoric as "unregulated sexuality."[39] But the Wife also adopts the elaborate, unrestrained rhetoric of those who excuse sin in the psalmodic and pastoral topos: its emphatic repetitions, its assonance and alliteration, its rhetorical figures, its repeated references to Mars and Venus, its learned terms from a domain other than, and often opposed to, the clerical and pastoral—that of the astrologers. And all serves to attribute her conduct largely to astral agents.[40]

That the Wife's unrestrained speech attributes her unrestrained sexual conduct (at least that is how she portrays it at this point)[41] to the stars and to the powerful appetites they bestow on her is of a piece with her self-portrait for her fifth marriage just a few lines later: "I was . . . of my tonge a verray jangleresse" (637–38). "Janglers" such as William Langland's minstrels and the Manciple's mother's imprudent speakers (IX.318–45), were excessive and idle talkers, whose speech veered to the bawdy, the aggressive, and the deceptive. To clerical figures, such as Langland's Dame Study, this loose speech was the fount of all other Sins of the Tongue.[42] This wife's self-labeling at this point in her monologue thus becomes another egregious way to flaunt her defiance of clerical norms for speech. She already has divulged her chiding, lies, false swearing and "grucchyng" (or murmur) during the composite portrait of her first three marriages (lines 224–452), labeling all, defiantly in clerical terms, as Sins of the Tongue, much as she allows that some have labelled "love" as "synne." The Wife's feminine ending to a clerical term ("jangler-esse") gives particular bite to her self-characterization as a speaking wife: it conveys her resistance as a woman to clerical authority over her speech, especially domestic speech, her speech practices as a wife.[43] Lying or false swearing may be sins to clerics, but to her they are tools of the trade, means for obtaining "maisterie" over the very men who taunt her with the stock-in-trade misogyny of husbands. Similarly, she wrests that other sin of the tongue, clerically proscribed excuses for sin, to her own purpose: advertising her uncontrolled following of carnal appetites. That all of this is done "in pleye"—with Rabelaisian verbal excess, ventriloquism, and self-dramatization—only increases her verbal potency, her mastery of her would-be clerical masters. In their terms, her out-of-control confession, with her speech practices properly labelled as sins only to parade her manipulation of them, her lack of interest in penitence, and her lack of verbal restraint, is an instance of confessional speech becoming the locus of more verbal sin, especially excuses for sin.[44]

What the Wife resists with both her habitual speech practices and how she divulges them is, in clerical terms and her own, correction or reproof.

At the beginning of her prologue, the first rhetorical move that she makes to counter those who speak against marrying more than once is to dodge "a sharp word" that Jesus "spak in repreeve of the Samaritan" (lines 14–16). "So nys it no repreve / To wedde me, if that my make dye" (lines 84–85), she later concludes. Thus she displays from the beginning of her self-portrayal an awareness that others are prepared to judge her sexual conduct based on an appeal to authority maintained by clerics. In the first part of the prologue, the authority of reprovers is Christian scripture. In her exchange with the Pardoner, it is *exempla*: "Whoso that nyl be war by othere men, / By hym shul othere men corrected be" (lines 180–81). While any late medieval Christian was licensed—indeed, obliged—to correct sinners, priests and judges and heads of households (always male in this wife's experience) had particular responsibilities for correcting those under their charge.[45] Chaucer criticism routinely has taken account of her husbands' reproofs, but correction was also the work of the confessor, part of his expected speech within the confessional dialogue. (Consider the incident well known to medievalists: that it is by sharply reproving Margery Kempe during her troubled first pregnancy that her confessor reduces her to silence and fear of damnation.)[46] As that master of confessors Raymond of Peñafort asserts, the confessor must reproach sinners in order to uncover blameworthy conduct ("a increpando culpam detegit")[47] of which they may be unaware, thus enabling them to engage in informed self-accusation.[47] Penitents constantly were enjoined not to resist correction verbally, often with the scriptural *sententia* "a man that is prudent and well-instructed will not murmur when he is corrected" ("vir prudens et disciplinatus non murmurabit correctus" [Ecclus. 10:28]).[48] One common means to resist, of course, was to excuse sins, a practice in which sinners could be quite crafty, according to Jacapo da Varazze (Jacob of Voraigne) in a sermon on correction.[49] Thus, the Wife's embrace of astral power functions as one rhetorical strategy among many by which she artfully dodges correction by men and the resulting constraints on her sexual conduct and speech. Like the lady constructed by Amis in the *Roman de la rose*, the Wife hates correction by men and refuses to learn new ways of behaving from any *maistre* (Amis' term).[50]

Does the Wife, then, escape "the prison house of masculine language" (Mann's phrase)?[51] Does Chaucer fashion her as an agent with some autonomy who is able, as she resists the clerical rhetoric of sin, particularly of excusing sin in response to reproof, to set some terms for her own sexual life? Only, I would argue, in a limited sense. Granted, the Wife is able to use clerical rhetoric on excusing sin for purposes quite different from what pastoral writers and exegetes intended. Discourse authored and usually practiced by men has passed into a woman's control. However, to grasp even the outlines of that discourse is to recognize that the Wife's very resistance to clerical norms for divulging sexual conduct involves subjecting herself to two sets of male authorities. This reading of the Wife's reading of her stars works, first, similarly to the general reading of the prologue developed compellingly over the last two decades: the Wife's throw-it-in-your-teeth reaction to masculine misogyny and its authoritative texts makes her dependent on, even subject to and partially constituted by, that textualized culture.[52] Thus, when the Wife comes to reject categorizing "love" as sin, she becomes subject to Christian clerical authority by uttering one of the most conventional of the excuses mockingly presented by clerics from Augustine to the pastoral writers of Chaucer's century: "*the* sterne of my birth gert me syn" (Richard Rolle again). Here, as elsewhere in her monologue, male-authored texts set the terms of her speech, the form of her very opposition to them. Second, I would argue that, in an unusual twist for the Wife's prologue, Chaucer has her adopt another clerisy in resisting the Christian clerisy: that of male astrologers and their texts. In Chaucer's time, astrology, deterministic or modified, seems to have been a province of male learning. It flourished chiefly in two male-dominated domains: among the learned and at courts (although not the English court until Henry IV's reign).[53] And the more deterministic claims were made by "les clercs," according to the speaker of John Gower's *Mirour*.[54] Thus, even in the arena of life where the Wife presents herself as free from clerical control (her indiscriminate following of her astrologically determined desires), she relies on authoritative clerical learning for her self-construction. Moreover, I would argue, Chaucer has her endorse and advocate the branch of learning that could most circumscribe her as an agent. While her account of astral influence eschews the simplistic astral determinism of the self-exculpating sinners of Augustine, the medieval exegetes, and pastoral writers ("Adulterum me fecit Venus"), it subjects her to external powers and limits her freedom of decision to an initial "following" of overwhelmingly powerful, astrally determined inclinations.

What kind of agency, then, does Chaucer endow the Wife with at this point in her monologue? The Wife may be doomed to react forever to learned discourses formulated by men, but she does adopt one discourse over another: she reads—and divulges—her sexual desires and often unrestrained sexual conduct in terms of astral power, of natural forces, not in terms of sin. And that very discursive self-interpretation (here I draw on Charles Taylor in *Human Agency and Language*)[55] further defines herself: by making her reading of sexual desire and her evaluation of it ("love") manifest, it shapes her sense of what she desires to be. She is a child of Venus and Mars, subject to their potent, formative influences. And that is all she aspires to be.[56] What is of value to her as she constructs herself for this audience is pursuing desires understood as overwhelmingly forceful appetites, not resisting them with the will as contrary to divine law ("sin"). Fashioned by a male writer, the Wife of Bath does not stand outside male-authored discourses, and she also becomes more fully constituted by the one she embraces as valid and uses to evaluate sexual desire. And that allows her to see herself as a more limited agent than pastoral discourse in her culture would allow her to be, an agent who believes that, once she has followed her astrally determined "inclinacioun," she is incapable of choice in specific cases.

I would make one further point. The Chaucerian Wife may be "disenchanted" with her male-dominated, textualized culture, including its clerically constructed sin—that is, as Marshall Leicester has argued, she sees it as culturally formed, not naturally or divinely given, and as deployed for personal and institutional interests.[57] But she does not present the power of the stars in a similarly disenchanted way. She does not display an awareness that it, too, may be constructed by men to serve their interests. Instead, she is enchanted with a natural account of "love" that, as Chauncey Wood argued decades ago, validates her desires and her conduct.[58] Just as she flaunts the church's calendar by engaging in "a social intercourse of lusty self-expression" during Lent, she adopts "tabloid astrology and horoscopy" (Friedman's words) as a natural explanation of human behavior that might be seen to rival revealed religion.[59] Counter to the pastoral writers and theologians who insist that planetary influences cannot overwhelm the human will, she asserts that, once followed, they dictate her surrender to any "good felawe." Certainly, the Wife's reading of her horoscope, and of her sexual life in terms of it, involves an easy, uncritical embrace of the planets' mysterious powers that contrasts sharply with her knowing contestation, even manipulation, of male-dominated arenas, such as marriage and confessional speech.[60] Natural causality becomes as much an impersonal, self-justifying authority for her as bookish misogyny does for her fifth husband.

Notes

I am indebted to Kelley Joy, my able research assistant and an R. E. Lee Research Scholar at Washington and Lee University. Questions from my colleagues W. Lad

Sessions and James Perrin Warren helped clarify my thinking on agency, and the essay as a whole has benefitted from questions from faculty and students at Tulane in the fall of 2000. A fellowship from the Washington and Lee Class of 1962 enabled me to do the manuscript research on which the essay is founded.

1. Root, "*Space*," 109–16 and 4.

2. The Wife's awareness of her male audience and her rhetorical responsiveness to it have been treated incisively by Dickson, "Deflection," 76–77; Patterson, *Chaucer,* 286–90 and 307–17; and Cox, *Gender,* 22–23.

3. I have analyzed the clerical semiotic that informs the Sins of the Tongue and the clerical rhetoric that combats them, both in pastoral literature as a whole and in *confessionalia* (*Lies,* 25–72 and 113–56). Casagrande and Vecchio's reliable historical survey of the Sins of the Tongue in moral theology and large-scale pastoral texts (*I peccati*) does not include *excusatio peccati* in its chapters on specific sins.

4. Rusconi, "Prédication," 68–71.

5. In "Displaced Souls," Miller examines how a practical penitential (*Handlyng Synne*) elicits ethical reflection on agency.

6. Craun, "'It is a freletee.'"

7. All quotations from Chaucerian texts are taken from *The Riverside Chaucer,* ed. Benson et al. Of the four passages between lines 575 and 720 that do not appear in the Hengwrt manuscript and may represent revisions, two appear in this passage, 609–12 and 619–26. Following Beidler's practice (*Geoffrey Chaucer: The Wife*), I have marked them with parentheses. While Kennedy has recently argued, on fairly debatable grounds of style, characterization, and erratic appearance in early manuscripts, that the passages were added by a misogynist scribe ("Variant Passages," 86–89; "Rewriting"; "Cambridge MS"), Hanna, working from his extensive knowledge of book production in late medieval England, concludes that these passages are "uniquely extended examples of Chaucer's continued work upon his poem at some time after Hengwrt's exemplars had been prepared" ("Hengwrt," 78). Neither passage is central to the argument of this essay, but it would be foolish to ignore them, given Hanna's weighty arguments for Chaucer's authorship. So, I do not hesitate to consider them below in a subsidiary way, but, as I do that, I recall their uncertain status.

8. Leicester, *Disenchanted,* 23.

9. The cast of these questions and of my thinking about agency has been influenced by Frankfurt's account of second-order desires, desires that humans evaluate and then desire to be their will, what moves them to act (*Importance,* 15–18), and, even more, by Taylor's *Human Agency and Language.*

10. On the Parson's treatment of the Sins of the Tongue, especially its rhetoric, see Craun, *Lies,* 221–26.

11. Bernard, *De gradibus,* ed. Leclercq and Rochais, 13–15 and 51. Bernard's pairing was taken up by thirteenth-century theologians (*Summa fratris Alexandri,* 3.4.2.1.1.2; Thomas Aquinas, *Summa,* 2.2.162,4) and by pastoral writers (Guillelmus Peraldus, *Summa,* reversed C2v).

12. Jager, *Tempter's Voice,* 215.

13. Mannyng, *Handlyng Synne*, ed. Sullens, lines 12347–66.

14. The post-Augustinian exegete Cassiodorus specifically identifies as *metastasis* (the rapid transition from one point to another) the rhetorical practice of transferring guilt to another. Commenting on Psalm 140:4 (which looms large later in this article), he characterizes the speech of those who are reproved and convicted of sin: "alias semper excusationes assumunt, nequando ueritati: acquiescat inuerecunda proteruitas, modo enim tempori, modo necessitati, modo aliis imputando quod peccant. Quae figura dicitur metastasis, id est translatio, dum culpam nostram in alium transferre contendimus" (Flavius Cassiodorus, *Expositio*, ed. Adriaen, 2.1263–64). The CCSL edition of his *Expositio psalmorum* lists, as extant in England, a dozen manuscripts, most of the twelfth century (viii–xiii).

15. Alexander Carpenter, *Destructorium*, fol. fiiiiv; Etienne de Bourbon, *Tractatus*, fol. 114v.

16. *Lucerna*, fol. 111r; *De lingua*, fol. 221v; *Distinctiones*, fol. 16v; Peter of Waltham, *Remediarium*, ed. Gildea, 274; *Jacob's Well*, ed. Brandeis, 180, 184.

17. Bernard, *De gradibus*, ed. Leclercq and Rochais, 51. All translations are mine unless marked otherwise.

18. *Jacob's Well*, ed. Brandeis, 180–81. I quote or refer to nearly twenty such catalogues of excuses, vernacular and Latin, in "'It is a freletee.'"

19. Mannyng, *Handlyng Synne*, ed. Sullens, lines 12367–418.

20. I have used the Old Latin version of the Psalms, which Augustine explicated, but have cited the Vulgate incipits familiar to medievalists. The translation is the Douai, modified by me where the Old Latin text diverges from the Vulgate.

21. Augustine, *Enarrationes*, ed. Dekkers and Fraipont, 31.2.16; compare 91.3 and 58.1.

22. On the primacy of the will in Augustine's conception of deviant speech, see Colish, *Tradition*, 189–98.

23. Augustine's firm dismissal of the *mathematici* stems from his lifelong engagement with issues of freedom of decision and predestination, especially as they relate to the morality of human acts. When he recalls in the *Confessions* how he, as a young teacher of rhetoric, consulted the *mathematici*, he claims that they extinguish the spiritual health that comes through Christian confession because they say "'De caelo tibi est ineuitabilis causa peccandi' et 'Venus hoc fecit aut Saturnus aut Mars'" (76). Augustine's scorn for those who ascribe sin to the planets is part of his refusal to allot any power to the gods and goddesses he dethrones (e.g., in *De civitate dei*, ed. Huffmann, 7.15).

24. Kuczynski discusses the appeal of the psalms for Augustine in *Prophetic Song*, 22. Other passages in the *Enarrationes* (ed. Dekkers and Fraipont) where sinners attribute adultery and murder to Venus and Mars: 31.16, 40.6, 61.23, and 140.9.

25. *Enarrationes*, ed. Dekkers and Fraipont, 140.8; *mathematici* also sell women fables in 61.23. To discredit them further, Augustine depicts one as hypocritical and mercenary when he is confronted by his impudent wife, who tosses his own astrological arguments in his face:

ipse ergo mathematicus si uxorem suam paulo petulantius uiderit conuersari, aut aliquos alienos improbe adtendere, aut fenestram crebro repetere; non ne arripit, uerberat, et dat disciplinam in domo sua? Respondeat illi uxor: Si potes, Venerem caede, non me. Nonne et ille respondebit: Fatua, aliud est quod competit rectori, aliud quod profertur emptori. (140.9)

26. Augustine, *Contra duas epistulas Pelagianorum*, ed. Urba and Zycha, 2.6.12.

27. Kuczynski, *Prophetic Song*, 21.

28. Peter Lombard, *Commentarius*, PL 191, cols. 319 and 410, the latter from Augustine, *Enarrationes*, ed. Dekkers and Fraipont, 40.6. Sixty manuscripts of Peter's commentary, including some written in the fourteenth century, survive in libraries all over England (Stegmüller, *Repertorium*, 4: 322–25).

29. Hugo de Saint Cher, *Postilla*, fol. 82r; Pseudo-Innocent, *Commentarium*, cols. 1016–17.

30. Alexander Neckam, *De horto*, fol. 71v. "Ut confitendo non se excuset sed accuset.Non fatum.non constellationem.non fingat se a luna desidiam contrasisse.a mercurio garulitatem.uel furandi auiditatem.non a uenere concupiscenciam carnis.uel affectum libidinis.non a sole feruorem caloris.aut speciem qua et decepit et deceptus est.non a marte discordiam.non a ioue ambitionem regnandi uel dominandi.non a saturno tristiciam uel auariciam" (fol. 102r). Alexander also refers generally to astral excuses in his explications of psalms 31 (fol. 71v), 74 (fol. 183r), and 140 (fol. 287v). Seven manuscripts of "De horto" are extant in, or recorded by, British libraries (Stegmüller, *Repertorium*, 3: 1163). At the end of the thirteenth century, the widely disseminated French commentator and preacher Nicolas de Gorran adds only the sun to Peter Lombard's list of three planets ("Laudationem," fol. 72r).

31. Flavius Cassiodorus, *Expositio*, ed. Adriaen, 2: 687–88; *Biblia latina*, vol. 3, fol. F3r; Peter Lombard, *Commentarius*, cols. 700–01; Peter von Herenthals, *Expositio*, fol. Dir. Peter von Herenthal's commentary is preserved in eight manuscripts in British libraries (Stegmüller, *Repertorium*, 4: 314–16). Probably from the exegetical tradition on Psalm 74, the excuse "per necessitatem stellarum" entered the widely read thirteenth-century Franciscan theological *summa*, the *Summa fratris Alexandri*, which weighs the relative gravity of blasphemy and *defensio peccatorum / vitium excusationis* (3.3.2.11.5.1).

32. Rolle, *Psalter*, ed. Bramley, 269. Lawrence Muir lists 39 manuscripts containing Rolle's English commentary ("Translations," 538).

33. *Lucerna*, fol. 111r–v; *Distinctiones*, fol. 16r–v. The *Lucerna* survives in three manuscripts in British libraries (Bloomfield, *Incipits*, no. 5952); the *Distinctiones* in two (ibid., no. 1841).

34. Thomas of Chobham, *Summa*, ed. Morenzoni, 209. It survives in one manuscript (lxvi–lxvii). Alexander Carpenter, *Destructorium*, fol. fiiiir. For example, Carpenter buttresses his claim that sin is committed "voluntarie," not by astral coercion, with an Augustinian *sententia* "Omni peccatum est voluntarium" (probably a loose rendering of one of many similar passages in the *Contra Iuliam*), adding "et per consequens talis actus peccandi dependet a voluntate humana:naturali talem docente ratione potest fieri vel non fieri indifferenter.sequitur ergo quod fuit in

potestate eorum non sic si voluissent peccasse." He then rehearses an Augustinian contrast between Nebuchadnezzar and Pharaoh, in which Pharaoh fights the truth of God out of his own free decision ("veritatem libero pugnauit arbitrio"; fol. fiiiir). Carpenter's *Destructorium* survives in two manuscripts in British libraries and one is attested to (Sharpe, *Handlist*, no. 97). *Constellatio* is also listed as an excuse by Robert Holcot in his mid-thirteenth-century commentary on the Book of Wisdom (*Super sapientiam salomonis*), almost certainly known to Chaucer (*lectio* 117, unpaged). Holcot's commentary survives in twenty manuscripts in British libraries (Stegmüller, *Repertorium*, 5: 143–45).

35. North, *Chaucer's Universe*, 65, 292.

36. North, *Chaucer's Universe*, 289–303; Wood, *Country*, 172–80. North even goes so far as to calculate tentatively, from the Wife's astrological references, her natal horoscope, setting it in 1342 and setting her "anniversary horoscope" for 1382, her fortieth year, when she marries Jankyn (302–03). In both years Venus and Mars would have been in "almost perfect opposition" and contrary to Mercury (see the Wife on enmity between the children of Venus and those of Mercury, lines 697–710). Neither North nor Wood considers the textual issue: that lines 609–12 may be a later addition by Chaucer or someone else, perhaps a scribe. However, North does note that simply placing Mars in Taurus and making Mars ascendent is enough to signify that the Wife has a "Venerien" disposition, although that horoscope would not have "coloured it [the Wife's career] as powerfully as the planet Venus could herself have done, given the right circumstances" (292; see Wood, 174–77). Even if we exclude this passage, the Wife remains a child of Venus, with whom she associates herself throughout this section on her fifth marriage, especially lines 697–706 and 603–04, where she claims that she bears "the prente of seinte Venus seel." Therefore, if this is a scribal addition, it simply intensifies what is already in the text. Moreover, the birth-mark of "Venus seel" may be taken, together with her "Martes mark," as a physiog-nomical sign that both planets were in conjunction at her birth"; planets were said to engrave their influence on the body. So, whether line 611, "Venus me yaf my lust, my likerousnesse," was "originally" (whatever that means) part of the passage or not, this section of the prologue signals in multiple ways that Venus gave the Wife her "in-clinacioun" to lechery. And, as North observes, "The suspicion that Venus might have been in her exaltation, and Mercury in his dejection, is strengthened not only by the lines in which the Wife discusses this point of astrology but also by the great appropriateness of their message for a tale that sets pleasure against asceticism, carnality against celibacy, Wife against cleric" (296). Astell argues that the contention between Venusian wives and Mercurial clerks extends throughout fragments III, IV and V of the *Tales* (*Chaucer*, 148).

Alexander Neckam's sinners were not alone in tracing a propensity for discord to Mars as a natal planet (see the influential *Summa fratris Alexandri*, 1.2.5.2.3.2). While the Wife's accounts of her conflict-ridden first four marriages make it pos-sible to read hardiness as aggressive quarreling, as well as audacity, what is germane to this essay is how she overtly uses her natal stars to reject sin as a way of categorizing her sexual conduct.

37. Unlike Tinkle, in her learned *Medieval Venuses and Cupids,* I do not see the Wife "equivocat[ing] over the link between this native inclination and her actions" (in lines 615–26). Whereas Tinkle reads "I folwed" as "assert[ing] self-control over a native predisposition, which passes insensibly into the seeming constraint of 'I koude noght withdraw'" (163), I read "That" as a loose, more open pronoun that takes in the whole of lines 615–16. And while the initial use of the active voice indicates a measure of control, the verb "folwed" suggests that she adopts her "inclinacioun" as masterful, as controlling, as providing a track or path in which she will move thereafter—phrasing quite in accord with the late medieval sense of the power of habit in shaping human action. (Kent has recently argued that later voluntarists, like Thomas Aquinas before them, stressed Aristotle's "definition of moral virtue as a habit involving choice" [*Virtues*], 249.)

38. Alexander Carpenter, *Destructorium,* fol. fiiiir; Mannyng, *Handlyng Synne,* ed. Sullens, lines 12396–97. Other pastoral writers also explicitly tie excuses for sin to lechery: the *Fasciculus morum* (ed. Wenzel), a fourteenth-century handbook for preachers, illustrates blaming God for "sins of the flesh" with the common excuses of pregnant women (476 and 672, 674); defending sin is an advanced stage of the ladder of sinning in the *Rosarium theologie*'s *distinctio* on *luxuria* (fol. 76r).

39. Copeland, "Pardoner's Body," 44–48.

40. Leicester finds lines 613–26 an instance of "retrospective revision," with the Wife shifting from considering the influence of her "constellacioun" Venus, which makes her affectionate, to Mars, which makes her exploitative and aggressive, and from depicting herself as passively inclined ("a deterministic position") to actively following her appetites ("a more active and independent one"). These shifts suggest to Leicester that the Wife is "disenchanted" about astrology as an explanation for her character, that she comes to see it as a "set of alternative explanations of the same behavior" (*Disenchanted,* 107–13, 135–36). What vitiates this reading is its lack of attention to astrological learning. "Constellacioun" refers to the whole natal horoscope, the arrangement of Mars and Venus at her birth, and "inclinacioun" involves having a certain appetite—in this case, given the combined influence of Mars and Venus, aggressively pursued sexual desire. As North has explained, the position of Mars in Taurus as a domicile of Venus involves a conjoined influence on the Wife (*Chaucer's Universe,* 289–303). In addition, Chaucer uses the same verb ("folwed") for the Wife's conduct with respect to both inclination and appetite, suggesting the same measure of fairly passive acceptance and impelling force.

41. Elsewhere in the prologue the Wife presents herself as far from sexually impulsive: for example, when she claims to have withheld her body from an older husband until he "had maad his raunson unto me" (line 411) and when she disclaims using her body to take sexual revenge on her fourth husband (lines 482–88).

42. Langland, *Piers Plowman,* ed. Schmidt, B. Prol. 33–39 and B.10.27–51. On Study's contempt for loose speech, see Craun, *Lies,* 166–73, and on the Manciple's mother's prudential horror of it, 201–12.

43. The *Middle English Dictionary* records no usage of *jangleresse* outside of *The Canterbury Tales* until 1540.

44. Root has argued that the Church sought to stop the movement of confession from the sacramental act to "secular, social space," where people could "produce the confessional self at will," using confessional speech for purposes quite different than confessors intended ("*Space*," 77–78]). The Wife's wresting of confessional speech and the topos of excusing sin from clerical control is similar to her appropriation of biblical exegesis (Knapp, *Chaucer*, 114) and marriage sermons (Galloway, "Marriage Sermons," 13–29).

45. Alexander Carpenter, *Destructorium*, fol. kiv; John Bromyard, *Summa*, C.XVI.iiii; *Corpus*, ed. Friedburg, 1: 173. I am developing the distinction between fraternal correction of sin, the practice of all Christians reproving sin in others, and prelatical correction (by disciplinary authorities, lay as well as clerical) in a book-length study: "Fraternal Correction: Ethics and Power Relations in Medieval English Reformist Writing."

46. *The Book of Margery Kempe*, ed. Meech and Allen, 77.

47. Raymond, *Summa*, 463.

48. For example, in Nicolas Biard, *Distinctiones*, fol. 28v.

49. Jacapo da Varazze, sermon with the *thema* "Si autem peccaverit," fol. 34r; see also James le Palmer, *Omne bonum*, fol. 89v.

50. Guillaume de Lorris and Jean de Meun, *Roman*, ed. Langlois, lines 9679–10014.

51. Mann, *Feminizing Chaucer*, 65.

52. Aers, *Chaucer*, 147; Gottfried, "Conflict," 203–09; Hanning, "Roasting," 16–19; Leicester, *Disenchanted*, 71–75; Mann, *Feminizing Chaucer*, 57–67; Hansen, *Chaucer*, 27–32; Cox, *Gender*, 29–37. These scholars and critics, I should note, differ radically in how they read the textual effects of the Wife's ventriloquistic performance of misogynist stereotypes.

53. For the learned, Tinkle, *Medieval Venuses*, 42–99. For the court, Carey, "Astrology," 41–55; and Patterson, *Chaucer*, 216–17. Carey presents fascinating evidence about the presence and activities of astrologers at the French court in the second half of the fourteenth century and at the English court from Henry IV onward.

54. Gower, *Mirour*, lines 26725–48.

55. Taylor, *Human Agency and Language*, 15–42, 215–41.

56. The Wife's enchantment with Mars and Venus is of a piece with her identification with the astrological and mythographic Venus throughout her account of her marriages to two younger men (for the mythographic Venus here, see Chance, *Mythographic*, 217).

57. Leicester, *Disenchanted*, 65–68; Knapp, *Chaucer*, 115–16; Aers, *Chaucer*, 84–88.

58. Wood, *Country*, 180.

59. Friedman notes the comic juxtaposition of the Wife's "tabloid astrology" with the academic learning she has acquired from Jankyn—and, I would add, from biblical exegesis in various forms ("Astral Destiny," 169). Friedman demonstrates that late medieval treatises on astral fortunes, found in astrological-medical miscellanies, insist that the wise and virtuous people may, by controlling their

passions, shun those things to which their birth stars dispose them. In this, they are akin to pastoral texts. On astrology's rivalry with Christianity, see Brown and Butcher, *Age of Saturn*, 34–35.

60. Tinkle also relates the Wife's use of masculinist astral physiology to her use of masculinist misogamous / misogynous traditions, but she believes that, in both cases, the Wife's simply "translat[ing] from a general scientific principle to individual application—and from masculine institutions of Latin learning to a woman's speech in English poetry" shows that astral physiology is not a "universal truth" (*Medieval Venuses*, 165). But the Wife disputes openly and extensively both Jerome and the book of wicked wives, whereas she adopts uncritically the power of her birth stars.

WORKS CITED

ABBREVIATIONS

CCSL   Corpus Christianorum Series Latina. Turnholt: Brepols, 1953–.
CSEL   Corpus Scriptorum Ecclesiasticorum Latinorum. Vienna: Tempsky, 1866–.
EETS   Early English Text Society. London: Early English Text Society, 1864–.
PL   Patrologia cursus completus: Series latina. Ed. Jacques-Paul Migne. Paris: Migne, 1844–91.

MANUSCRIPT SOURCES

Alexander Neckam. *De horto deliciarum paradisi quattuor emanantur flumina*. Oxford, Bodleian Library, MS Bodl. 284.
De lingua. Oxford, Oriel College, MS 20.
Distinctiones. Oxford, Bodleian Library, MS Bodl. 4.
Etienne de Bourbon. *Tractatus de diversis materiis predicabilibus*. Oxford, Oriel College, MS 68.
Jacapo da Varazze. *Sermones quadragesimales*. Oxford, University College, MS 109.
James le Palmer. *Omne bonum*. London, British Library, MS Royal 6.E.VI.
Lucerna conscientiae. Oxford, Bodleian Library, MS Bodl. 801.
Nicolas Biard. *Distinctiones*. Oxford, Bodleian Library, MS Bodl. 563.
Nicolas de Gorran. "Laudationem Domini loquetur os meum." Oxford, Bodleian Library, MS Bodl. 246.
Rosarium theologie. London, British Library, MS Harl. 3226.

PRIMARY SOURCES

Alexander Carpenter. *Destructorium viciorum*. Paris, 1516.
[Aurelius] Augustine. *Contra duas epistulas Pelagianorum*. Ed. C. Urba and J. Zycha. CSEL 60. Vienna: Tempsky, 1913.

————. *De civitate dei.* Ed. E. Huffmann. CSEL 40. Vienna: Tempsky, 1899–1900.

————. *Enarrationes in Psalmos.* Ed. E. Dekkers and J. Fraipont. CCSL 38, 39, 40. Turnholt: Brepols, 1956.

Bernard of Clairvaux. *De gradibus humilitatis et superbiae.* In *Sancti Bernardi opera,* ed. Jean Leclercq and H. M. Rochais, 3: 13–59. Rome: Editiones Cistercienses, 1963.

Biblia latina. 4 vols. Basel: Johann Froben, 1498.

The Book of Margery Kempe. Ed. Sanford Meech and Hope Emily Allen. EETS o.s. 217. London, Oxford University Press, 1940.

Chaucer, Geoffrey. *Geoffrey Chaucer: The Wife of Bath.* Ed. Peter Beidler. Boston: St. Martins, 1996.

————. *The Riverside Chaucer.* Ed. Larry D. Benson et al. 3rd ed. New York: Houghton Mifflin, 1987.

Fasciculus morum: A Fourteenth-Century Preacher's Handbook. Ed. and trans. Siegfried Wenzel. College Park: Pennsylvania State University Press, 1989.

Flavius Cassiodorus. *Expositio Psalmorum.* Ed. M. Adriaen. 2 vols. CCSL 97, 98. Turnholt: Brepols, 1958.

Friedburg, Emil, ed. *Corpus iuris canonici.* 2 vols. Leipzig: B. Tauchnitz, 1879–81.

Gower, John. *Mirour de l'omme.* Vol. 1 of *The Complete Works of John Gower.* Ed. G. C. MacCaulay. Oxford: Clarendon, 1899.

Guillaume de Lorris and Jean de Meun. *Le roman de la rose.* Ed. E. Langlois. 5 vols. Paris: Firmin-Didot, 1914–24.

Guillelmus Peraldus. *Summa de vitiis.* Cologne: Quentell, 1479.

Hugo de Saint Cher. *Postilla super totum psalterium.* Venice: de Gregoriis, 1496.

Jacob's Well. Ed. Arthur Brandeis. EETS o.s. 115. 1900. Repr. Millwood, NY: Krause Reprint Co., 1975.

John Bromyard. *Summa praedicantium.* Nuremburg: Kroberger, 1518.

Langland, William. *Piers Plowman: A Parallel-Text Edition of the A, B, C, and Z Versions.* Ed. A. V. C. Schmidt. London: Longman, 1995.

Mannyng, Robert. *Handlyng Synne.* Ed. Idelle Sullens. Medieval and Renaissance Studies 14. Binghamton: Center for Medieval and Early Renaissance Studies, 1983.

Peter Lombard. *Commentarius in Psalmos Davidicos.* PL 191. Cols. 55–1296.

Peter of Waltham. *Remediarum conversorum.* Ed. Joseph Gildea. Villanova, PA: Associated University Presses, 1984.

Peter von Herenthals. *Expositio super librorum psalmorum.* Cologne: de Homborch, 1480.

Pseudo-Innocent III. *Commentarium in septem psalmos poenitentiales.* PL 217. Cols. 967–1128.

Raymond of Peñafort. *Summa de poenitentia et matrimonio.* Rome: n.p., 1603.

Rolle, Richard. *The Psalter or Psalms of David.* Ed. Henry Bramley. Oxford: Clarendon, 1884.

Robert Holcot. *Super sapientiam salomonis.* Spier: Drach, 1483.

Summa fratris Alexandri. Ed. Brothers of the College of St. Bonaventura. 4 vols. Florence: Ad Claras Aquas, 1924–48.

Thomas Aquinas. *Summa theologiae.* 60 vols. New York: McGraw-Hill, 1964–75.

Thomas of Chobham. *Summa de arte praedicanitium.* Ed. Franco Morenzoni. Corpus
    Christianorum Continuatio Medieavalis 82. Turnholt: Brepols, 1988.

SECONDARY SOURCES

Aers, David. *Chaucer, Langland, and the Creative Imagination.* London: Routledge
    and Kegan Paul, 1980.
Astell, Anne. *Chaucer and the Universe of Learning.* Ithaca: Cornell University Press,
    1996.
Bloomfield, Morton, et al. *Incipits of Latin Works on the Vices and Virtues, 1150–1500
    A.D.* Cambridge, MA: Medieval Academy of America, 1979.
Brown, Peter, and Andrew Butcher. *The Age of Saturn: Literature and History in "The
    Canterbury Tales."* Oxford: Blackwell, 1991.
Carey, Hilary M. "Astrology at the English Court in the Later Middle Ages." In
    Astrology, Science and Society: Historical Essays, ed. Patrick Curry, 41–56.
    Woodbridge: Boydell, 1987.
Casagrande, Carla, and Silvana Vecchio. *I peccati della lingua: Disciplina ed etica
    della parola nella cultura medievale.* Rome: Istituto della Enciclopedia italiana,
    1987.
Chance, Jane. *The Mythographic Chaucer: The Fabulation of Sexual Politics.*
    Minneapolis: University of Minnesota Press, 1995.
Colish, Marcia. *The Stoic Tradition from Antiquity to the Early Middle Ages.* Leiden:
    Brill, 1985.
Copeland, Rita. "The Pardoner's Body and the Disciplining of Rhetoric." In
    Framing Medieval Bodies, ed. Sarah Kay and Miri Rubin, 138–59. Manchester:
    Manchester University Press, 1994.
Cox, Catherine S. *Gender and Language in Chaucer.* Gainesville: University Presses
    of Florida, 1997.
Craun, Edwin. "'It is a freletee of flessh': Confessional Speech and *Excusatio
    Peccati.*" In *In the Garden of Evil: The Vices and Culture in the Middle Ages,* ed.
    Richard Newhauser, 170–92. Toronto: Pontifical Institute of Mediaeval
    Studies, 2005.
————. *Lies, Slander, and Obscenity in Medieval English Literature: Pastoral Discourse
    and the Deviant Speaker.* Cambridge: Cambridge University Press, 1997.
Dickson, Lynne. "Deflection in the Mirror: Feminine Discourse in the *Wife of Bath's
    Prologue.*" *Studies in the Age of Chaucer* 15 (1993), 61–90.
Friedman, John B. "Alice of Bath's Astral Destiny: A Re-appraisal." *The Chaucer
    Review* 35 (2000), 166–81.
Frankfurt, Harry. *The Importance of What We Care About: Philosophical Essays.*
    Cambridge: Cambridge University Press, 1988.
Galloway, Andrew. "Marriage Sermons, Polemical Sermons, and The Wife of Bath's
    Prologue: A Generic Excursus." *Studies in the Age of Chaucer* 14 (1992), 3–30.
Gottfried, Barbara. "Conflict and Relationship, Sovereignty and Survival: Parables
    of Power in the Wife of Bath's Prologue." *The Chaucer Review* 19 (1985), 202–24.

Hanna, Ralph, III. "The Hengwrt Manuscript and the Canon of *The Canterbury Tales.*" *English Manuscript Studies, 1100–1700* 1 (1989), 64–84.

Hanning, Robert W. "Roasting a Friar, Mis-taking a Wife, and Other Acts of Textual Harassment in Chaucer's *Canterbury Tales.*" *Studies in the Age of Chaucer* 7 (1985), 3–21.

Hansen, Elaine Tuttle. *Chaucer and the Fictions of Gender.* Berkeley: University of California Press, 1992.

Jager, Eric. *The Tempter's Voice: Language and the Fall in Medieval Literature.* Ithaca: Cornell University Press, 1993.

Kennedy, Beverly. "Cambridge MS Dd.4.24: A Misogynous Scribal Revision of the *Wife of Bath's Prologue?*" *Chaucer Review* 30 (1996), 343–58.

———. "The Rewriting of the *Wife of Bath's Prologue* in Cambridge Dd.4.24." In *Rewriting Chaucer: Culture, Authority, and the Idea of the Authentic Text, 1400–1602,* ed. Thomas Prendergast and Barbara Kline, 203–36. Columbus: Ohio State University Press, 1999.

———. "The Variant Passages in the Wife of Bath's Prologue and the Textual Transmission of the *Canterbury Tales:* 'The Great Tradition Revisited.'" In *Women, the Book and the Worldly: Selected Proceedings of the St. Hilda's Conference, 1993,* ed. Lesley Smith and Jane H. M. Taylor, 2: 85–101. Cambridge: Brewer, 1995.

Kent, Bonnie. *Virtues of the Will: The Transformation of Ethics in the Late Thirteenth Century.* Washington, DC: The Catholic University of America Press, 1995.

Knapp, Peggy. *Chaucer and the Social Contest.* New York: Routledge, 1990.

Kuczynski, Michael. *Prophetic Song: The Psalms as Moral Discourse in Late Medieval England.* Philadelphia: University of Pennsylvania Press, 1995.

Leicester, H. Marshall. *The Disenchanted Self: Representing the Subject in The Canterbury Tales.* Berkeley: University of California Press, 1990.

Mann, Jill. *Feminizing Chaucer.* Cambridge: Brewer, 2002. First published as *Geoffrey Chaucer* (London: Harvester, 1991).

Miller, Mark. "Displaced Souls, Idle Talk, Spectacular Scenes: *Handlyng Synne* and the Perspective of Agency." *Speculum* 71 (1996), 606–32.

Muir, Laurence. "Translations and Paraphrases of the Bible, and Commentaries." In *A Manual of the Writings in Middle English, 1050–1500,* 2, ed. J. Burke Severs, 381–410 and 534–52. New Haven: Connecticut Academy of Arts and Sciences, 1970.

North, J. D. *Chaucer's Universe.* Oxford: Clarendon, 1988.

Patterson, Lee. *Chaucer and the Subject of History.* Madison: University of Wisconsin Press, 1991.

Root, Jerry. *"Space to speke": The Confessional Subject in Medieval Literature.* New York: Peter Lang, 1997.

Rusconi, Roberto. "De la prédication à la confession: Transmission et contrôle de modèles de comportement au XIIIe siècle." In *Faire Croire: Modalités de la diffusion de la réception des messages religieux de XIIe au XVe siècle,* 67–85. Collection de l'École Française de Rome 51. Rome: École Française de Rome, 1981.

Sharpe, Richard. *A Handlist of the Latin Writers of Great Britain and Ireland before 1540*. Turnholt: Brepols, 1997.

Stegmüller, Friedrick. *Repertorium Biblicum Medii Aevi*. 12 vols. Madrid: n.p., 1950–77.

Taylor, Charles. *Human Agency and Language*. Cambridge: Cambridge University Press, 1985.

Tinkle, Theresa. *Medieval Venuses and Cupids: Sexuality, Hermeneutics, and English Poetry*. Stanford: Stanford University Press, 1998.

Wood, Chauncey. *Chaucer and the Country of the Stars*. Princeton: Princeton University Press, 1970.

"Janglynge in cherche"
Gossip and the Exemplum

Susan E. Phillips

Barely two weeks into his exhaustive ninety-five day sermon cycle, the preacher of *Jacob's Well* begins to lose control of his chattering congregation.[1] They must choose, he bellows from the pulpit, whether they will listen quietly to his sermon or gossip and be damned, for the devil records every syllable of their "idell woordys, ianglyng [gossip, idle talk], & [their] rownyng [whispering] in cherche."[2] In an attempt to silence them, he employs what is supposed to be the most effective tool of his priestly trade, delivering an *exemplum* on the consequences of idle speech. The narrative he selects is the popular *exemplum* of the angel who counts the hermit's footsteps. Conventionally a cautionary tale about the dangers of convenience to an ascetic life, the narrative usually runs as follows. A weary hermit, whose desert hut lies a fair distance from the nearest water supply, considers easing his burden by moving his house closer to it. He resolves to move his hut five miles further away, however, after meeting an angel who explains that he records the hermit's every step as a good deed.[3] Adapting the narrative to browbeat his loquacious congregation, the preacher of *Jacob's Well* expands the angel's commentary. While the angel records the hermit's footsteps, "feendys noumbre þe steppys of man & womman to synne warde, & alle rownynges & ianglynges in dyvyn seruyse, for to schewe þe noumbre of hem a-for god to mannys dampnacyoun."[4] How far, suggests the preacher of *Jacob's Well*, from the hermit's footsteps in God's service are the sin-ward steps of his gossiping parishioners. Tellingly, of all the steps toward sin that parishioners might take, only gossip's idle words are specifically named.

The addition, unique to *Jacob's Well*, has an awkward feel.[5] The angel's extra remarks to the hermit about the accounting practices of the fiend and the idle talk of lay folk are tagged on, unsolicited by the tale's events. The moral is not so much prompted by the narrative as forced upon, and indeed into, it, as the *exemplum* is contorted to illustrate the dangers of idle talk, when neither speech nor lay men and women have any obvious role in the story.[6] We might, taking a cue from Larry Scanlon and Mark Miller, attempt to plumb the depths of the *exemplum*, taking its superficial disjunction as an invitation to see hidden complexity.[7] In doing so, we might explicate this narrative as a subtle exploration of the small but definite "synne warde" steps parishioners take with each idle word, reading jangling as an act of convenience that makes the labor of attending service less burdensome. However, since the angel teaches the hermit about the consequences of lay verbal transgression within the narrative framework of the story itself, we cannot explain away the addition as pastoral explication. That is, this preacher does not use the angel's words as means to interpret for his audience the figure of the hermit and the concept of convenience he illustrates in terms of their own lives. Rather, he awkwardly seizes upon the opportunity to have the angel condemn his congregation's idle chatter to an innocent (and reclusive) bystander. Jangling, according to this preacher, is a problem with which even angels are preoccupied.

What this tale suggests, then, is not the narrative complexity and power of the sermon *exemplum* but the antagonism between idle talk and the sermon, between the priest and his congregation—a problem not just for the writer of *Jacob's Well* but for a whole host of pastoral writers in late medieval England. Throughout the later Middle Ages, priests and poets clamor in unison about the evils of idle speech—especially when that speech occurs during their sermons.[8] Yet the problem is not simply the essentially practical struggle of an individual preacher trying to drown out the voices of his chattering congregation. Rather, it is a struggle between two competing types of speech—between the unlicensed "ydell tales" of parishioners and the authoritative tales of the preachers' *exempla*, between uncontrolled social voices and the instruments of social control—two categories of speech that have much more in common than their pastoral definitions might suggest.

In this essay, I take as my subject this battle between pastoral discourse and idle talk as it was waged by preachers and pastoral writers in late medieval England. Because I am interested here in the practical means through which priests and penitential writers tried to both instruct and silence their audiences, I restrict my discussion to vernacular pastoral treatises and sermons.[9] Consequently, many of the texts I discuss are Middle English translations and adaptations of Lorens d'Orléans' *Somme le Roi* (1279), the most popular vernacular treatise on the Sins of the Tongue.[10] Attempting to control and curtail the idle talk of their audiences, these texts employed the

standard tools of the pastoral trade designed to combat sin—lists, definitions, *sententiae*, and most important of all, the *exemplum*. Yet, not only does
idle talk prove resistant to such strategies but also the very tools themselves
become contaminated by the speech they seek to condemn. While I survey
the struggle for verbal control as it was waged in a number of late medieval
English texts, the majority of my discussion focuses on two in particular: the
anonymous *Jacob's Well* and Robert Mannyng's *Handlyng Synne* (ca. 1303).[11]
Explicitly calling attention to the competition between gossip and the
exemplum, these two clerics employ quite different tactics for winning that
competition: one relentlessly attacking idle speech, the other appropriating
its strategies.

Before turning to the specific tactics of these two clerics, however, I
want first to examine the logic that numerous English pastoral writers used
to dissuade audiences from idle chatter. Perhaps the primary task for these
writers is explaining what it is that makes idle words idle. The idleness of
jangling in church seems straightforward. Any speech that disrupts the
divine service, thus hindering the common profit by preventing other
parishioners from receiving the word of God,[12] must be unprofitable, must
be an instance of sloth, and must therefore be idle. Parishioners understand,
if they also ignore, the injunction against jangling in church. Idle words in
other contexts, however, are not as easily defined or recognized. According
to pastoral authorities, gossip is an often ignored spiritual threat, which
leads its participants into all manner of venial and deadly sin. To its
speakers' deep mortification and great detriment on Judgment Day, gossip's
idle words "wirken mochel euele werke whiche þat þei beþ not war of."[13]
For, as the oft-quoted passage, Matthew 12:36, explains: "Of every ydel
woord þou spekyst þou schalt ȝyve acountys at þe day of dome."[14] Gossip is
the venial sin with deadly consequences, as one must account for every idle
word.[15] What is understood about idle talk, then, is that it is spiritually
deadly—"Now comth janglynge, that may nat been withoute synne"—but
easily overlooked.[16]

In an effort to make idle talk legible to parishioners, pastoral writers
offer numerous explanations and definitions of jangling's idleness. Geoffrey
Chaucer's Parson, for example, offers this rather theoretical commentary:
"Now comth ydel wordes, that is withouten profit of hym that speketh tho
wordes, and eek of hym that herkneth tho wordes. Or elles ydel wordes been

tho that been nedelees or withouten entente of natureel profit." The Parson's academic approach to "ydel wordes" is due to the fact that Chaucer is following his source, Guillelmus Peraldus' *Summa de vitiis* or a redaction of it, quite closely here.[17] Emphasizing the notion of profit, the Parson expands upon Peraldus' remarks, explaining that idle words are those spoken without the intent of "natureel profit." Yet rather than providing an explication of this profit, he simply expands the category of idle talk to include speech that lacks profitable intention. The Parson's precise meaning is ambiguous. He does not explain whether or how "natureel profit" is distinct from the "profit" mentioned in the previous sentence, nor does he explain what such natural profit might be. The term *natureel profit,* which does not appear anywhere else in Chaucer's work, is rich in interpretative possibilities. It may be synonymous with *common profit,* a term that the Parson uses several times, perhaps suggesting here that, to be profitable, speech must be for the moral and social good of the community. The Parson may be proposing a notion of profit that is instinctive, asserting that men know naturally what speech is profitable. Alternatively, he may be offering a complex term that links the natural, the moral, and the common, maintaining that natural profit necessarily serves both the moral and the common good.[18] In this reading, man would know instinctively (by "kynde") what kind of speech was moral and therefore served the common profit. Or finally, as the *MED* suggests unconvincingly, the Parson may invoke a notion of profit as customary or normal, thereby implying that men expect a particular profit from speech.[19] By invoking this term in his discussion of idle talk, the Parson offers an intriguing glimpse into the late medieval theory of profit and its relationship to speech.[20] However, as numerous pastoral writers—including the Parson himself—acknowledge, one of the central difficulties with idle talk is that parishioners do not naturally recognize their words as unprofitable and therefore idle. The Parson's explanation of idle speech, then, is more effective as an intervention within scholarly debate about the nature of deviant speech than as a tool through which to enable parishioners to recognize the sinful speech they find so elusive. For the Parson, at least, idle talk proves difficult to explain in practical terms.

Texts deriving from the *Somme le Roi* offer a less theoretical, though no less ambiguous, definition of idle talk. Emphasizing its importance and acknowledging it as all-pervasive, these texts give idle talk pride of place, discussing it as the first branch of the tree of wicked tongue.[21] Yet as they describe the details and contours of this branch, their logic is problematic. At times it is circular, as this passage from the *Speculum vitae* reveals: "Furst he þat wille ouer mekille [too often, too much] vse / Idelle spech as jangelers duse / May hynt [suffer] grete harme and lose þerby."[22] Janglers are those who use idle speech, and those who use idle speech are janglers, as readers learn little about what makes idle words idle, even as they are warned about how harmful those words might be. In other moments, the logic of these texts is paradoxical. Idle words are so harmful, argues the *Book of Vices and Virtues*, that idle talk's very name is misleading and inappropriate: "Men clepen [call] hem idele wordes, but þei beþ not ydel, for þei beþ wel dere [costly] and ful of harm and wel perilous, as þilke þat voiden þe herte of al goodnesse and bryngeþ it ful of vanite."[23] Idle words, according to this tradition, are not idle; they are not empty, but full—full of cost, full of harm, full of danger, and full of vanity. The paradox is of course doctrinally sound and is at the heart of the problem with idle speech. Idle talk's triviality is what makes it consequential, as Peraldus and others explain in meticulous detail.[24] Yet, unaccompanied by scholastic explication, the paradoxical definitions of these vernacular treatises do little to teach parishioners how to recognize and thus avoid such speech.

When general statements of gossip's destructive potential fail, pastoral writers take refuge in specificity, meticulously cataloguing the various sub-species of idle talk. Yet the ambiguity and paradox that plagued these earlier summary remarks also contaminates the details of the subspecies. The preacher of *Jacob's Well* inventories the "manners" of idle speech as follows:

> þe first is outrage [excess, intemperance] in here woordys, as a clapp of melle [mill], þat neuere wyll be stylle. þe secunde is veyn woordys, male-apert [impudent], in iangeling, in tellyng of the þynges, & often þei are false & lyerys. þe iij. manere, summe vsyn veyn woordys in sotyll speche to plesyn þe hererys, to makyn hem lawgh. þe iiij. manere, summe vsyn veyne woordys in lesynges [lies] & bourdys [jests, jokes]. þe v. manere, summe vsen veyn speche in scornyng of gode men þat don wel, for þei wolde drawyn hem fro þat vse of goodnes.[25]

Talking too much, telling tales that might not be true, using exaggeration and subtle speech to make people laugh, telling filthy jokes, and scorning one's neighbors for the good that they do—these are the five manners of idle speech. Some of the subspecies have the status of proverb in their own right, as we can tell from the jingle-like quality of "clapp of a melle, that never wyll be stylle."[26] Others appear to blur the boundaries between idle talk and other species of deviant speech—backbiting, derision, lying, and joking. This sense of conflation is due in part to the fact that in the *Somme* tradition, five of Peraldus' verbal transgressions ("multiloquium," "rumor," "scurrilitas," "turpiloquium," and "bonorum derisio"), have become sub-species of a sixth ("ociosa verba").[27] However, even with this explanation, there remains something unstable about the list—a list structured by cate-gories that bleed into one another and are defined by terms that themselves are constantly in flux.[28] "Jangling," for example, is both the whole category of idle speech and one of its specific manners: telling tales. It is both the content of that idle speech (the telling) and the brazen manner in which it is spoken ("male-apert"). Finally, it is both the truth and the lie, as those who jangle often are called liars because of their stories, which may or may not be true.[29] Jangling, like the whole category for which it often stands, thus is defined as a combination of opposites: it is both form and content, both inside and outside. And it is this hybridity that makes jangling so problematic.[30]

However, *jangling* is not the only term creating confusion in the passage. Even the word used to categorize subspecies hints at the amorphous. Rather than the discrete and quantifiable terms used for the other branches: *leves, boughs, partes,* or *graynes*—idle talk has *maners,* a term that refers both to species and the method, to the form and the content.[31] This lack of precision in turn blurs the boundaries between the manners themselves, as the various versions of the passage attest. William Caxton proclaims that there are "vi maners," while listing the same five found in each of the other texts, as if there seem to be more sins involved than actually are listed.[32] Richard Morris, the first editor of the *Ayenbite of Inwyt,* has the opposite problem. While his text explicitly states that there are five manners, in his marginal commentary he numbers only four, as if two of the manners ("multiloquium" and tale-telling) seem so closely related as to constitute a single one.[33] Similarly, scribes who have no trouble calling readers' attention to subdivisions within the other nine sins of the tongue stumble when it comes to idle talk. The scribe of British Library MS Additional 17013, who denotes all other subspecies of deviant speech with individual capitulum marks, distinguishes only three manners of idle talk, allowing entertaining speech and dirty jokes to become aspects of tale-telling.[34] Taking this consolidation one step further, the scribe of the Simeon Manuscript, despite his penchant for detailing subspecies elsewhere, conflates all of idle talk's five manners into a single category.[35]

Confusion and conflation reach their height as these writers discuss tale-telling, the manner explicitly connected to jangling. This subspecies poses the biggest interpretative challenge for translators and adaptors, as none of the Middle English writers who catalogue it can agree on its attributes. While such tale-telling is often condemned as bold—"male-apert"—it is also "curious"—both feigned and well-crafted—and thus its consequences for speaker and audience vary considerably. The scriptural injunction against trafficking in these "curious" tales appears in two of Paul's letters: 2 Thessalonians 3:11, "audimus enim inter vos quosdam ambulare inquiete nihil operantes sed curiose agentes" [For we have heard there are some among you who walk disorderly; working not at all, but curiously meddling], and 1 Timothy 5:13, "simul autem et otiosae discunt circumire domos non solum otiosae sed et verbosae et curiosae loquentes quae non oportet" [And, withal being idle, they learn to go about from house to house; and are not only idle, but tattlers also and busybodies, speaking things which they ought not—Douay]. The speaker may be labelled a fool or a liar because he is a teller of "curious" tales or because those tales leave listeners ill at ease. Moreover, in some versions, it is not the original teller who is condemned but the "efter telleres,"[36] those who re-tell the jangler's tale. In one extreme case, all "bereres of ernedes" [errands, messages] are so slandered due to the "sliʒe" [crafty, sly] words of the jangler.[37] The cause of the listener's distress is in a similar state of flux. He may be ill at ease because the news itself is disturbing, because the news is about him, or because participating in idle talk gives the soul "mesese" [distress]—and each of these possibilities speaks to a different Sin of the Tongue. Becoming ever more elusive the more it is defined, jangling is a shape-shifting speech, involved in countless sins and yet never reducible to any of them.

The blurring of boundaries and terms that pervades these descriptions renders unstable even the notion of idleness that jangling both defines and is defined by. While the author of *Jacob's Well* attempts to reduce confusion, linking all of the categories together through the repetition of the word *veyn*, other writers, in their attempt to distinguish between and emphasize the problematic nature of idle talk's five manners, present their readers with a complicated and unstable notion of idleness. According to these manuals, gossip is idle, not solely because it is unprofitable and worthless but also because it is variously curious, bold, "queynte," "sotil," "schrewed" [wicked, malicious], and "vol of velþ" [full of filth]—competing terms with the potential to make unprofitable speech seem profitable. Increasing this potential exponentially, these manuals combine lists of competing synonyms with a return to paradoxical logic, repeating and expanding upon their earlier remarks about idle talk's misleading name. While men may call them idle words, they are not; they are "wel heuy and wel schrewede," "peryllous &

greuable" [greivous], "wel stinkinde and wel uoule" [foul], "dere," and "muche harme."[38] By cataloguing all that idle speech simultaneously is and is not, these pastoral manuals represent gossip as blurring the boundaries between the light and the heavy, the trifling and the consequential, the worthless and the costly. These paradoxical binaries are, as I have argued, doctrinally consistent. Yet because idle talk consists solely in these oppositions, it becomes, through these pastoral definitions and explanations, speech with the ability to move between the two opposites, changing one into the other. In short, it becomes transforming talk—words that can make the consequential trifling and the worthless costly.

The notion of gossip as transforming talk present in these treatises is not merely the result of a complex or ambiguous passage in the *Somme*.[39] Quite the contrary. Priests and pastoral writers emphasize precisely this trait in discussions of idle talk that bear no relation to this passage. For example, John Mirk, in his *Instructions for Parish Priests,* warns his audience explicitly about idle talk's deadly transformations. Drawing authority from St. Paul—"nolite seduci corrumpunt mores bonos conloquia mala" (1 Cor. 15:33)—he cautions young priests that gossip can destroy their morals:

> Wymmones serues [service, company] thow moste forsake
> Of euele fame lest they the make,
> For wymmenes speche that ben schrewes,
> Turne ofte a-way gode thewes [manners, morals].[40]

Certainly, there are numerous ways to interpret the perversion (the turning away) of good morals here. The speech of shrewish women may contaminate the "gode thewes" of the priest by encouraging him to engage in their idle chatter. Alternatively, their words may transform the priest's morals by giving him evil fame, that is, by presenting his virtue as corrupt in their subsequent jangling. Finally, participating in women's gossip might expose the chaste young priest to the slippage between the idle and the unclean, as his trafficking in jangles leads to far less trifling forms of commerce.[41] Whichever particular perversion the women's speech enacts, what Mirk's warning highlights is the fact that idle talk transforms.

For all their admonitions that gossip's idle words pervert morals, diminish good deeds, and multiply sins, vernacular pastoral writers do more to demonstrate the transformative potential of idle talk than to contain it. Through their explanations and definitions, all verbal transgression seems to be a species of idle talk, and all words seem to run the risk of being idle.

Deadly in its triviality, idle talk is slippery, moving between categories and, in doing so, conflating them. Moreover, by conflating categories, blurring boundaries, and collapsing binaries, idle talk problematizes not just the arguments of individual writers but also the program of lay education enjoined by Fourth Lateran Council and made specific by the Council of Lambeth.[42] The pastoral manuals and aids for priests that result from the decrees of these councils instruct parishioners and their lay clerics in a syllabus that relies upon specific categories, lists, species and subspecies—categories that, as we have seen, contain but are contaminated by idle talk. Thus, the standard tools of the pastoral trade prove wholly ineffective when they tackle idle speech.

More than simply thwarting pastoral logic or complicating the neat categories of penitential treatises, however, idle talk's evil work—the slippages that it both participates in and creates—poses an ideological challenge to ecclesiastic authority. Jangling presents a problem for the *exemplum*, not merely by resisting the particular stories levied against it but also by threatening to undermine the institutional power of the *exemplum* itself. Idle talk thus represents a systemic problem for the Church, not simply one that impacts numerous individual preachers and their chattering congregations but one that, in fact, besieges a fundamental aspect of preaching practice.[43] The indispensability of the *exemplum* to late medieval preachers is due to its powers of persuasion, powers that, as Larry Scanlon argues, derive from its "rhetorical specificity as narrative."[44]

As ecclesiastical authorities repeatedly assert, stories are more persuasive than straightforward reasoning. Moreover the *exemplum*'s powers of persuasion continue to act long after the sermon has ended. These narratives, as Edwin Craun explains, act on conduct through memory, creating in audiences a revulsion for sin ("detestatio") that is reinforced as details of the story are replayed in the minds of parishioners.[45] However, the *exemplum*'s "rhetorical specificity as narrative"—its ability to be remembered and retold—is precisely what leaves it susceptible to gossip's transforming talk, rendering it unsuccessful in the battle against idle speech and ultimately weakening it as a pastoral tool. This is particularly clear when we examine the exemplary practices of Robert Mannyng and the preacher of *Jacob's Well*—clerics whose pastoral projects are constructed around the battle between pastoral speech and idle talk. While *Jacob's Well* demonstrates the abject failure of the *exemplum*'s powers of persuasion, Mannyng's *Handlyng Synne* reveals just how close to idle talk this pastoral practice might be.

In late medieval England, there is no priest or penitential writer more obsessed with idle talk than the preacher of *Jacob's Well*. The ambition of his project is the likely cause of this preoccupation: he will deliver one sermon a day for ninety-five days, instructing his parishioners—his "freendys"—in how to turn the shallow pit that is their body into a pure well of virtue by purging the ooze of deadly sin. Undoubtedly, the sermons, which promise to sustain this metaphor through the three-and-a-half-month cycle, run the risk from the outset of being too lengthy and monotonous to hold the congregation's attention. In fact, as early as day two, the preacher is already admonishing his parishioners for entertaining any notion of leaving the church before his sermon has finished. It is hardly surprising, then, that this preacher delivers weekly diatribes against idle talk.[46] The condemnations become so frequent that his parishioners must have wondered whether there was any topic that did not have a connection to idle talk. When he talks about Sloth, he talks about jangling;[47] when he talks about Gluttony, he talks about jangling. When he talks about Pride, humility, temperance, prayer, confession, and the Fourth Commandment, he talks about jangling. And judging from these repetitions and their increasing virulence, his congregation does not seem to be listening at all.

When repeated lists and condemnations fail to silence his parishioners,[48] the preacher deploys an astonishing number of *exempla*, devoting more than ten percent of his narratives to the subject of idle talk.[49] Often these tales, like the narrative of the Angel and the Hermit, are not conventionally employed to illustrate idle speech and its consequences. For example, when the crucifix stops its ears in other pastoral writings, it does so against usurers, those who could not bear to hear God mentioned, and those who would not listen to any sermon, rather than against mere janglers.[50] Similarly, the young man who is told that penitential medicine cannot work while he continues to consume unwholesome food is given to lechery, not idle words, in all the pastoral texts in which he appears.[51] Yet for the preacher of *Jacob's Well*, each of these narratives provides the opportunity to address his congregation's jangling, however ill-fitting and disjunctive the moral. He even uses a version of the "Dancers of Colbek"—that complex and critically acclaimed narrative about cursing and sacrilege told by Robert Mannyng—to berate parishioners who chatter in church and "wille noȝt cese for þe preestys byddyng."[52] By turning countless narratives to the purpose of condemning gossip, he illustrates both how persistent a problem idle speech presents and how ineffective the sermon *exemplum* is in solving it.

By far his favorite *exemplum* for the vilification of idle speech, however, is the story of Tutivillus, that famous recording demon whose specific task it is to take written account of jangling in church. Here, the spirit of Matthew 12:36, that *sententia* so popular in vernacular treatises on idle speech, is made incarnate in the demon who sits on the shoulders of chattering parishioners.[53] Moreover, this is likely to be the fiend that the author of *Jacob's Well* introduced into his adaptation of the Angel-Hermit *exemplum*. As Margaret Jennings's exhaustive study shows, by the late fourteenth century, Tutivillus had become a commonplace, appearing on church walls and misericords as well as in a vast number of penitential, sermonizing, and literary texts.[54] It is hardly surprising, then, that Tutivillus would find his way into *Jacob's Well*.[55] What is striking is not that story occurs, but that it recurs. Given this preacher's penchant for manipulating the exemplary corpus to suit his silencing needs, it is quite telling that he chooses to repeat this particular *exemplum*.[56] Repetition in fact becomes a characteristic of the narrative. There are two strains to the Tutivillus story: one features the sack carrier who collects words skipped by clerics; the second depicts the recording demon who keeps track of lay verbal transgression. Depending on his audience, "the preacher could concentrate on the inattention expressed through idle talking or through careless recitation of the prayers of the Office."[57] The author of *Jacob's Well* strangely, though perhaps predictably, chooses to use both. While Jennings catalogues several texts that mention both the sack carrier and the recording demon, *Jacob's Well* is the only text that tells both at the same time. Claiming Jacques de Vitry as his authority, the author of *Jacob's Well* begins with a short narrative about a demon who bears a heavy sack filled with the over-skipped verses of clerks. He quickly turns to the problems of the congregation at hand, however, explicating this first portion of the *exemplum* with a moral not about priestly sloth but about gossiping: "fforsothe, þanne I trow [believe] þe feend hath a gret sacche full of ȝoure ydell woordys, that ȝe iangelyn in cherche in slowthe." Thus, the author of *Jacob's Well* does not tell both strains of story in order to address separately the two halves of his potentially hybrid lay-clerical audience, but rather uses both strains to address the same transgression.[58]

Yet, the image of the devil's sack filled with his congregation's idle words only serves as prologue to the more relevant strain of the *exemplum*. Tutivillus has been recording on a scroll all the gossiping in church. Running out of room on his parchment, he attempts to stretch it with his teeth.

The parchment breaks, however, and he hits his head on the church wall. When a holy man witnesses this spectacle, he asks the devil to explain himself, and Tutivillus responds as follows:

> I wryte þise talys of þe peple in þis cherche, to recordyn hem a-fore god at þe doom for here dampnacyoun, and my book is to narwe to wryten on alle here talys; þei say so manye. þerfore I drawe it out braddere, þat none of here talys schulde be vnwretyn.[59]

According to this priest, just as angels are preoccupied with idle speech, so devils are oppressed by it. In explaining his task—I write down what you say in church—Tutivillus in effect repeats the *exemplum*, just in case the congregation missed it the first (or indeed second) time. In other versions of the *exemplum*, writers draw explicit attention to the tale's humor: in some, the thud of the devil's head against the wall is so loud that the whole congregation hears; in others, the holy man who sees the devil hit his head laughs and is reprimanded by his superior.[60] But for the author of *Jacob's Well*, jangling in church is no laughing matter.[61] Neither the holy man nor the preacher cracks a smile. Even the demon is deadly serious about his task. This preacher's lack of humor is matched by his pessimism. Whereas John Mirk suggests that janglers can be rehabilitated, by having the priest confront the women with their idle talk, reading to them from the devil's scroll, and shaming them into repentance,[62] the author of *Jacob's Well* offers no such possibility. The devil's scrolls will be read against his parishioners on Judgment Day.[63] This preacher's attitude towards gossip is so black and white that he does not cut the men in his audience the usual slack when it comes to idle talk: the janglers in his *exemplum* are not explicitly women. Where wall paintings and stained glass windows, most medieval poets, and many modern dictionaries all gender gossip as women's work, the author of *Jacob's Well* recognizes it as an all-too-universal occupation.[64]

The futility of this preacher's efforts, however, is evident even in the moral that he adds to this tale. Other texts conclude their *exemplum* with generic statements of moral instruction, such as the Vernon Manuscript's exhortation to think on God's wrath and *Handlyng Synne*'s straightforward explanation, "For ianglers þys tale y tolde, / þat þey yn cherche here tunges holde." In contrast, the preacher of *Jacob's Well* speaks with all-too-vivid specificity as he imagines the response of his wayward congregation: "I drede me þanne, þe feend hath a gret book aȝens [against] ȝou, wretyn of ȝoure ianglynges in cherch, & ȝit ȝe excusyn ȝow þere-in and seyn: 'me must speke to hym þat spekyth to me ."[65] Proposing the idea or, quite probably, attesting to the fact that his parishioners disputed him on this topic, this preacher's response is both comic and strange. Staging this contentious dialogue with his audience, the author of *Jacob's Well* demonstrates not just the continual temptation to idle talk or the difficulty a habitual sinner has in recognizing and renouncing his sin but also the explicit defiance of an audience that considers conversation an essential and unavoidable part of daily life. The chapters of *Jacob's Well*, then, are a far cry from Larry Scanlon's description of the penitential manual as a "closed, stable text" whose authority is "total and unassailable within the text" itself.[66] The depiction of jangling here is far more immediate, more persistent, and more threatening than the conventional pastoral depiction of sin as ever-present and all-pervasive. This priest is not winning the battle against sin; he is being overwhelmed by it.

The preacher's sense of the hopelessness of his cause is more pronounced three weeks later, when he retells the Tutivillus story during a sermon on idleness. After first quickly repeating the tale, he gives a more in-depth commentary on how this *exemplum* relates to his church in particular:

> I trowe þe feend hath nede to drawe lengere & braddere his rolle here; for it is ellys to lytel to wryten on alle þe talys tolde in þis cherch, for it is neuere left, but it be at sacre [communion; the consecrating of the bread], for prechyng, ne schryfte [confession], ne schame, ne dreed of god ne of þe world.[67]

The tone is desperate and exasperated. Nothing, it seems, will stop the jangling in "þis cherche": not praying, not confession, not shame, not dread of God, not dread of the world, not his litany of *exempla*. His hostility is unmistakable; his failure palpable.

Even more belligerent than this commentary, though, is the second *exemplum* that he attaches to this story. In one final attempt to silence his jangling parishioners, he recounts the gruesome tale of the talkative nun:

> A nunne, chast of body but ydel in woordys, in iapys, & in foly speche, & dely3ted þerin, sche deyid, & was beryid in þe cherch. þe next ny3t after, þe kepere of þe cherch sey3 [saw] here be led wyth feendys a-forn an awtere [alter]. þe feendys, wyth a brennyng sawe, kutten here in þe myddys, & þe ouer part of here þei brentyn [burned] fro þe wast vpward for here ydell woordys. þe nethir [lower] parte fro þe wast dounward was hole, for sche was chast in body.[68]

The story is remarkable enough in its own right, and precisely what it signifies about the sins of the tongue and their consequences for the soul is far from clear, as the different versions of the story reveal. Pope Gregory the Great tells it as an example of why church burial does not guarantee one's bodily safety.[69] In Caesarius of Heisterbach, though prompted by women's chattering in church, it is told about a shrewish and quarrelsome noblewoman rather than a talkative nun.[70] *Handlyng Synne* first attaches it to the fifth commandment and speech that slays, and then later to lechery, intimating that the nun's speech was less than chaste, and thereby making sense of the punishment.[71] Not surprisingly, the author of *Jacob's Well* explicates this *exemplum* in terms of idle speech. Here there is no hint of lecherous talk or wrathful scolding; rather, the nun's transgressions are her "ydell woordys."[72] In the moral he delivers as the tale's conclusion, his virulence is at its height: 'I drede me, þanne, ȝe that arn ydell in woord, thouȝt, & dede, schal be brent & sawyd wel werse þan sche was but ȝe leuyn it."[73] Petty and aggressive in its tone—what, for example, would it mean to be burnt and sawed worse than this half-charred nun?—this sermon on day thirty-six is a far cry from the first one in which he addressed his audience with "Rygyt so, frendys." In the battle for verbal control, these friends have become the preacher's foes. The futility of his efforts is unmistakable: he has lost control of his sermon and his congregation. And for all the gruesome detail and unchecked vehemence with which he conveys the image of the half-charred nun, attempting to burn the consequences of idle speech into the memories of his parishioners, he is unsuccessful. For the remaining seven weeks of the sermon cycle, he must continue to chastise his congregation for their jangling in church. The sermon *exemplum*, the most powerful weapon in his pastoral arsenal, completely fails to silence his chattering congregation.

Idle talk, then—at least for the author of *Jacob's Well*—is immune to the *exemplum*'s powers of persuasion. Despite turning numerous narratives to the purpose of condemning idle speech, layering them with gruesome details about the consequences of such speech, and sealing them with scathing morals designed to shame his audience into submission, the author of *Jacob's Well* is unable to silence his congregation. Placing the *exemplum* in direct competition with idle talk, he is unable to defeat it.

Robert Mannyng adopts a quite different strategy, suggesting a perhaps more effective means for controlling idle talk. His method is one of substitution rather than direct competition, as he trades on the ability of tale-telling to hold an audience's attention, turning his *exemplum* into a kind of officially sanctioned jangling. In explaining his purpose for writing *Handlyng Synne*, Mannyng outlines this practice explicitly:

> For many beyn of swyche manere,
> Þat talys & rymes wyle bleþly [happily] here;
> Yn gamys, yn festys, & at þe ale,
> Loue men to lestene trotouale.

Given that men love "to lestene trotouale"—that is, to listen to idle tales and vain talk—the only way to teach them morals is to tell moral stories.[74] If parishioners listen to tales constantly, in games, feasts, and taverns, the only way to get them into church is to entice them with a good story. Mannyng substitutes for idle, sinful occupation the more spiritually productive work of religious devotion, recognizing all the while that he can achieve this only by catering to the sinful tastes of his audience. While this practice does not distinguish Mannyng from numerous other priests and pastoral writers, his explicit admission of his strategy does.

Announcing his strategy of narrative substitution, Mannyng acknowledges and asserts not the persuasive power of the *exemplum* but its ability to entertain. That master storyteller and money-maker, Chaucer's Pardoner, understands the principle well:

> Thanne telle I hem ensamples many oon
> Of olde stories longe tyme agoon.
> For lewed [unlearned] peple loven tales olde;
> Swiche thynges kan they wel reporte and holde.[75]

The Pardoner ensures his audience and, by extension, his profit, by recounting numerous *exempla*—these ever-popular, old stories. His motive in employing this practice, however, is far from simple. He tells tales not merely because his audience delights in them and therefore will pay him, nor purely because his audience can "holde" them, learning and continuing to gain spiritual benefit from them after the sermon is over—the *exempla* continuing to act on the conduct through memory—but also because his audience can "wel reporte" them. The curious addition is ambiguous. Either the Pardoner wants his audience to report the tales they hear to their neighbors, encouraging them to gossip about his *exempla*, for their own entertainment or as a means of ensuring and enlarging his next audience; or he is encouraging his audience to repeat the *exempla* in order to educate those neighbors.

In this second reading, we can see a dangerous side-effect to the practice of authorized tale-telling. What the Pardoner imagines here is a kind of alternative religious / moral community telling its own *exempla,* with their own morals—morals that may or may not be those of the Church. In either interpretation, this alternative community is problematic, taking away the authority of priests, providing a space for heresy, or making the Church complicit in its idle talk. The tale-telling of this imagined community gives rise to a worrying question: what precisely is the difference between the stories the preacher tells and those of his gossiping congregation? The distinction seems to be primarily one of context rather than content: parishioners are involved in intimate, privy, and therefore suspect exchange; the priest is at the pulpit delivering a public address. Yet, given that idle talk resides in both form and content, drawing its power from its ability to transform through its "manere," the distinction is tenuous at best. While the Pardoner imagines parishioners appropriating the narratives of their priests, far more worrying for ecclesiastic authority is the notion that the borrowing might operate in the opposite direction, that *exempla* are based on gossip.

Even as clerics championed the *exemplum*'s persuasive powers, concern over the questionable use of non-biblical *exempla* in sermons was widespread, as authorities attempted to determine which sources were acceptable for exemplary narratives.[76] Chaucer's Parson articulates the orthodox critique of exemplary practice, proclaiming his complete distrust of these unruly stories:

> Thou getest fable noon ytoold for me,
> For Paul, that writeth unto Thymothee,
> Repreveth hem that weyven [turn aside from] soothfastnesse
> And tellen fables and swich wrecchednesse.

The words of the Gospel and not gossipy stories—those "ineptas autem aniles fabulas" [foolish and old wives' tales] prohibited by St. Paul's letter and pedaled by Chaucer's Pardoner—are the proper vehicles for pastoral instruction.[77] As Edwin Craun has argued, the Parson is using Paul's words to Timothy to set up the "binary opposition between salvific teaching and loquacity," constructed by Alain de Lille's *Summa de arte praedicatoria* and the tracts on deviant speech by Peraldus and his followers.[78] In doing so, the Parson does more than condemn those stories that distract from the truth;

he equates exemplary practice with idle talk.[79] Indeed, he excludes all *exempla* from his "myrie [merry] tale," with one curious exception. The Parson includes a single *exemplum* about an angry schoolmaster who is taught a lesson in patience by the words of his wayward student. It is perhaps not coincidental that this single "tale" follows quickly on the heels of his catalogue of the Sins of the Tongue, which concludes with idle talk, jangling, and japes. It is as if the Parson, having completing his critique of idle and deviant speech, is compelled to offer a tale that illustrates the proper use of speech—a tale about speaking "sothe" and counselling virtue.[80] While the narrative seems far from the "wrecchednesse" the Parson denounces in others' fables, the source of the narrative is unknown.[81] Thus, without scriptural foundation—or perhaps authority of any kind—it is a tale that, for all its preoccupation with the idea of speaking "sooth," might in itself be one of the those false "fables" the Parson so abhors.

The Parson is not alone in his rigid attitude toward such narratives. Wycliffite writings are adamant in their condemnation of those "nouelries," "fablis & newe soteltes," which become incontrovertible evidence of the orthodoxy's failed preaching: "þei techen opynly fablys, cronyklis and lesyngis [lies] and leuen cristis gospel and þe maundementis of god."[82] With its emphasis on the novel, the new, and the subtle, the deviant speech of orthodox preachers more closely resembles news than sermon. A priest under the pope's authority is far more likely to sin in his sermon than to teach his congregation about sin: "þis prechoure may synne on many maners bi þat þat he sowiþ not good seed, but iapis [jokes] & gabbingis or oþere tryuolis [trifles], & leeueþ to preche þe word of god."[83] According to John Wycliffe's followers, orthodox sermons become the idle chatter that they have been trying to suppress.

Nowhere is Wycliffite criticism of orthodox priests' idle speech more applicable, however, than in Mannyng's *Handlyng Synne*. Like many of his contemporaries, Mannyng worries about the authority of his tales. However, the concern he reveals and repeats is not about delivering classical *exempla* or new verse chronicles but about committing a more illicit kind of tale-telling. That is, the worry is not that the source of the tale is inappropriate for sermons but that the practice of reading *exempla* might itself be a kind of backbiting—that the sermon might become a species of gossip. As he catalogues the contents of his text, Mannyng adds a protective disclaimer:

> Talys shalt þou fynde þer ynne,
> And chauncys þat haue happyd for synne;

> Meruelys, some as y fond wretyn,
> And ouþyr þat haue be seye & wyten [witnessed; known];
> None be þer ynne, more ne lesse,
> But þat y fond wrete, or hadde wytnesse.
> Þarfore may hyt & gode skyle why [for good reason],
> 'Handlyng synne' be clepyd oponly;
> For hyt touchyþ no pryuyte,
> But opon synne þat callyd may be.[84]

He will tell many marvellous stories but will reveal "no pryuyte." Unlike the transgressive details of other people's private and backbiting gossip, his stories are in the realm of the public, tales that are already open or at least speak of sins already made public. Not surprisingly, this distinction is quite tenuous. While Mannyng insists that all of his *exempla* have proper authority, the nature of that authority is suspect. He relies not only on traditional *auctoritas*, what has already been written, but also on his own experience and on the experience of his acquaintances. Moreover, Mannyng's assertion of authority through stories that have "be seye or wyten" or that he "hadde wytnesse" is dangerously close to gossip's own verifying rhetoric.[85]

Throughout his text, Mannyng acknowledges the potential slippage between the two discourses, as he reminds both himself and his congregation that his tale-telling sermons are always in danger of spilling over into the realm of idle talk's "ydel tales." At the conclusion to one *exemplum*, appropriately about a backbiting monk, Mannyng quickly catches himself before committing the sin that he expounds:

> Þis tale y wote [know] and vndyrstande
> Where hyt fyl, yn ynglande,
> At a ful namecouth [famous] abbeye
> Þat y ne wyle telle, ne bewreye [betray; reveal].
> Swych peyne ys for hem dyght [prepared]
> Þat kun nat kepe here tung ryght.[86]

Mannyng's concluding warning here is a provocative variation on Larry Scanlon's argument about the relationship between the *exemplum* and its moral. Here, not only is the moral "apprehended narratively,"[87] growing organically out of, and confirming, the narrative, but also it runs the risk of being too successful a confirmation, coming dangerously close to being another instance of that narrative.[88]

It is precisely these moments on the verge of transgression and the tenuous disclaimers that accompany them that make Mannyng's *exempla* so engaging and persuasive—so like the "queynte," "sotil," and "curiouse" words of idle talk. Even though the majority of Mannyng's stories are derived from the *Manuel de pechiez* or borrowed from collections of *exempla*, he manages to make them seem new and exciting—the kind of story that his parishioners want to hear. By claiming that a tale took place in a famous abbey in England that shall remain nameless, Mannyng renders his *exempla* more immediate, more transgressive, more like the tales of his chattering congregation. The problem with this sensationalizing rhetoric, however, is that it renders the *exemplum* an instance of that which it seeks to control. Even while this posturing gives the *exemplum* its power to bridle the congregation's chatter, it makes the *exemplum* complicit in that tale-telling.

Yet if Mannyng commits verbal transgression here, what, as a cleric licensed to teach through *exempla*, is the nature of that transgression? What he performs is not an instance of backbiting, not least because this monk's transgression has been repeated in numerous sermons and collections of *exempla*. Nonetheless, Mannyng asserts his need to be vigilant about that particular sin. In fact, this is one of the few instances in which he calls for a general, communal shriving: "Of þys synne, y rede [advise, counsel] we vs shryue / And take oure penaunce by oure lyue."[89] Whereas Mannyng's morals usually address the congregation in the second person plural, here he includes himself in the company that needs to atone for this popular sin. But he clearly stays within the letter of the law on backbiting, not revealing the Monk's "privitee," by not disclosing either the abbey's identity or the Monk's name. While the Monk reveals his identity to his former colleague—"and tolde hys name"[90]—Mannyng does not convey this private information to his audience. Nor does Mannying attempt to slander surreptitiously this anonymous English monk. This is not, for example, the Pardoner's barely concealed slander, through which the audience knows the subject of his story though the Pardoner never reveals proper names. Mannyng's *exemplum* is not malicious nor is it unprofitable, for its content is morally useful to its audience, or at least has the intent of being so. Yet, with its emphasis on the "curiouse" and the sensational, it is a manner of deviant speech—it is the jangling of idle talk. The notion of jangling I raise here is not the fear of ineffectual or unproductive speech that Mark Miller suggests haunts Mannyng throughout his text—the perhaps common concern of a priest that his words, for all his good intentions, are unprofitable.[91] Nor is this the jangling that preoccupies William Langland—the idle speech that inappropriately debates matters of religion.[92] It is instead a transgression both more and less obvious than these two.

By hiding behind his avoidance of backbiting, Mannyng masks his sin of jangling. Yet, throughout this text, he plays blatantly and deliberately with the line between idle talk and productive salvific speech, repeatedly reminding his readers that his tales are no "tryfyls" even as he draws on the attention-grabbing power of the "trotouale" [idle tales, vain words]. Not simply a favorite term or even a constant preoccupation, "trotouale" is Mannyng's narrative mode.[93] While he begins his text with "a tale of auctoryte" "wretyn, al and sum, / Yn a boke of vitas patrum," his citation of patristic authority quickly gives way to the advertising rhetoric of the "trotouale": "Y shal ȝow telle what me was tolde / Of a prest þat sagh and fond / Þys chaunce yn þe holy lond."[94] Of course, the narrative preceded by this claim comes not from the first-hand account of a priest who traveled to the Holy Land but directly from Mannyng's source, the *Manuel de pechiez*. Mannyng uses the convention of citing "auctoryte" as a means to entice his audience with the new and exciting. Similarly, when he adds narratives of his own to the collection, he emphasizes the novel and immediate, rather than the distant and the authoritative. Of the seven *exempla* that he contributes to his text, four are set explicitly in England, with one occurring quite close to home in Lincolnshire.[95] These are tales drawn not from appropriate "auctoritee" but from Mannyng's own experience: "Yn cambrygshere, yn a toune / Y herd telle of a persoune."[96] Even tales that he borrows from appropriate authorities, he alters to make more immediate both in time and place. The tale of the wicked executors becomes the tale of the wicked Kesteven executors, as the *exemplum* takes place not far away but here in the audience's very midst: "Y shal ȝow telle of a kas / Þat fyl now late yn kesteuene; / But þe name y wyl nat neuene [name]."[97] Mannyng moves his *exempla* from the timeless past of gospel and patristic history into the here and now of Lincolnshire. Thus the danger of backbiting he voices here becomes quite real. Yet read against a similar remark made in the all-too-familiar tale of the backbiting monk, this disclaimer must be understood as something more than an avoidance of sin. Through it, Mannyng—like those "male-apert" janglers from pastoral writing on idle talk—creates curiosity in his audience. He offers the temptation to privy details, but withholds those details, as a way of both denying the idleness of his tales and trading on it. Whereas the Pardoner traffics in old tales, Mannyng traffics in new ones, or at least old stories masquerading as new.

Mannyng's exemplary practice thus trades on—and inspires—his audience's desire for illicit specificity. While he never completely capitulates to that desire, in the "Dancers of Colbek" he all but does so. Drawn from "kronykeles," among the least reputable of pastoral sources, it is a narrative consumed with idle talk. Yet Mannyng's preoccupation with idle speech here is not, as Mark Miller suggests, a worry about his own potentially inefficacious teaching or his sentimentalizing rhetoric; rather, it is a further extension of the curious tale-telling in which that teaching often engages. A narrative obsessed with naming, this *exemplum* provides more specific and identifying details than any other in Mannyng's collection, a fact he makes clear as he introduces the tale. Even as he tells his audience that this marvel is as "soth [true] as þe gospel," he promises to let them in on what he suggests is his secret knowledge: "Here names of alle þus fond y wrete, / And as y wote [know], now shul ȝe wete [learn]."[98] Throughout his work, Mannyng reveals names only when they belong to holy men and church fathers who witness, but do not commit, sin. Here, however, he tells a tale of a priest named Robert, resident of the town of Colbek during the reign of King Edward, preacher at the church of Saint Magnus, and father of two children, Aȝone and Aue, who was menaced one Christmas by carollers named Gerlew, Merswynde, and Wybesyne. The tale, as Miller has shown, is as much about Robert's failings—his unprofitable admonitions, his idle and ill-advised swearing, his inability to control both his children and his temper—as it is about the carollers' sacrilege. Thus the narrative traffics in the distressing and private details of Robert's life, instead of the transgressions of an anonymous sinner. While the tale is not backbiting, since it speaks of sins already made open by other writers, it is nonetheless reliant on the illicit specificity of gossip's idle talk. Nor does there ever have to have been such a Robert, for Mannyng to trade on his secrets. Rather, it is the illusion of such disclosed "pryvytee" that Mannyng uses to engage his audience. What he displays in the "Dancers of Colbek" is not a concern over idle talk but an exploitation of it.

The consequences of Mannyng's exemplary strategies, however, become clear in the *exemplum* that immediately follows the "Dancers of Colbek": the story of Tutivillus. In telling this tale, Mannyng does not follow the *Manuel de pechiez* but, rather, continues to develop both his theme and his method, inserting a narrative that resonates with the previous one. Yet, although it is loosely connected to his discussion of sacrilege—"Ianglyng longeþ to sacrylage"—this *exemplum* seems to have more to do with the kind of speech in which Mannyng has been engaging than with this larger topic. Quite unlike the preacher of *Jacob's Well*, he highlights the narrative's humor, introducing it not as a didactic tale, but as a joke, "And y shal telle as y kan, / A bourd [joke, amusing story] of an holy man."[99] And it is this humor that undoes the tale. In Mannyng's hands, the *exemplum* becomes a story about the fiend's embarrassment and frustration, both at being thwarted by inflexible parchment and at suffering the indignity of having his failure observed by a cleric. Mannyng repeatedly draws his audience's attention, not to the jangling of a congregation, but to the antics—the feet stomping and grimacing—of a buffooning devil. The story is far more entertaining than it is persuasive, teaching his audience more about the temperament of the devil than about the dangers of idle speech, especially as his scroll is completely obliterated in his attempt to stretch it. Thus while Mannyng's exemplary strategies—his "bourdes," marvels, and curious tales—may succeed in holding the attention of his audience, they undermine the persuasive potential and pastoral efficacy of the *exemplum*.

What Mannyng, in his officially sanctioned jangling, and the author of *Jacob's Well*, with his relentless yet futile attempts to control idle speech, demonstrate is not the power of pastoral discourse but the evil work of idle talk—its ability to transform and appropriate. Gossip's idle words infect the comic, the subtle, and even the pastoral, co-opting those modes for their own purposes—shifting one kind of speech into another. Idle talk is thus a favorite topic of priests and pastoral writers, not just because it is the venial sin in the face of which all parishioners much be vigilant but also because it competes with and contaminates pastoral discourse itself, undermining the very means used to control it. Attempts to define and contain it merely reinforce its slipperiness. And *exempla* that seek to persuade against it either demonstrate idle talk's resistance to such tools or show the utility of idle talk as a mode of narration, for priests as well as their audiences.

The strategies of these two priests, however, teach us more than the immunity of gossip to the tools of the pastoral trade. They ask us to reconsider our understanding of exemplarity. For all the assertions to the contrary, by late medieval writers and contemporary medievalists alike, the *exemplum* seems to lack the persuasive power so often associated with it. Its "rhetorical specificity as narrative," while giving the *exemplum* its persuasive potential, also limits and makes problematic that potential. As narratives, *exempla* can be manipulated and transformed to suit the needs of individual priests and particular occasions. But as the preacher of *Jacob's Well* reveals, the more a priest enacts such manipulation, the more transparent, and thus ineffective, this pastoral tool becomes. Moreover, these narratives, celebrated for their ability to act on the memory, are retold and reinvented not just by poets and priests but also in the minds and conversations of parishioners. The *exemplum*'s spectacular scenes, so useful in grabbing an audience's attention, run the risk of obscuring and even erasing the moral. The nun's half-charred body borne aloft by cackling fiends is far more memorable than the constantly shifting transgression for which she was punished. And the slapstick physical comedy or disgruntled remarks of the overworked fiend inspire more laughter than fear. Finally, that illicit specificity, which Mannyng exploits in the extreme but which finds its way into *exempla* of all kinds, while capturing an audience's attention, draws that attention toward the specific and the personal rather than the general and the ethical. That is, when it comes to idle talk, pastoral exemplarity runs the risk of setting quite a bad example.

In the last decade, several scholars have argued persuasively for the need to reassess the power and potential of the *exemplum*. Yet these re-evaluations have overlooked the limitations and problematic appropriations that are endemic to late medieval exemplarity. Most recently, Mark Miller has offered a brilliant reading of the "Dancers of Colbek," arguing for the complexity of Mannyng's exemplary practice—his modeling of what it means to handle sin—as abjuring any straightforward connection between sin and its remedy, an *exemplum* and its moral, one species of transgression and another. While I do not disagree with Miller's reading—quite the contrary, he makes an insightful intervention into the theory of medieval agency—I would suggest that his interpretation requires and assumes a medieval reader wholly sympathetic to the theoretical intentions of the priest. That is, in his theory of exemplarity, Miller ignores, as does Larry Scanlon, those resistant and recalcitrant readers to whose tastes Mannyng continually caters and against whom the preacher of *Jacob's Well* perpetually rails. Yet it is precisely these readers who have much to tell us about exemplarity, not in theory, but as it was practiced—resistant readers who tell tales, reinterpret narratives, and jangle in church.

Notes

1. I follow Carruthers and Atchley, here, in taking the author at his word that these sermons were in fact delivered (Carruthers, "The Liturgical Setting," 11–23, and "Allegory and Bible Interpretation," 1–14; Atchley, "Wose," 40–66). For a more cautious account, see Spencer, *English Preaching*, 214–15. According to Carruthers

and Atchley, these ninety-five daily sermons were in all likelihood delivered during the liturgical period from Ash Wednesday to Pentecost. Though the date is uncertain, scholarly consensus places the manuscript in the first quarter of the fifteenth century. Brandeis edited the first fifty sermons; Atchley recently has edited the remaining forty-five.

2. *Jacob's Well*, ed. Brandeis, 111/21. While "gossip" itself does not acquire the signification of idle and trifling talk until the 19th century (*OED*, *gossip* 4), its medieval godparent is "jangling," the idle speech that scorns neighbors, tells new and distressing tales, and never ceases (*OED*, *MED*, *jangling*).

3. The *exemplum* is #2143 in Tubach's *Index exemplorum*. Originating in the *Vitae patrum* (PL 73, col. 900), the tale appears in Jacques de Vitry, Odo de Cheriton, the *Speculum laicorum*, and the *Alphabet of Tales*, to name a few.

4. *Jacob's Well*, ed. Brandeis, 111/14–17.

5. According to Gregg, the changes are original to *Jacob's Well* (*Narrative Exempla*, 179–80 and 267–68). I have not found the variation in any of the texts or manuscripts I have examined.

6. This *exemplum* from *Jacob's Well* is a striking counter-example to Scanlon's argument that an *exemplum*'s moral must be "apprehended narratively," growing organically out of the narrative that precedes it (*Narrative*, 30).

7. Scanlon, *Narrative*; Miller, "Displaced Souls." Both Scanlon and Miller have called for a redefinition and reconsideration of the *exemplum*, arguing that we must read these tales not as straightforward and passive vehicles of moral teaching, as repositories of authority, but as complicated, appropriating, and ideologically powerful narratives. By declaring the lack of complexity and subtlety in the exemplary practice of *Jacob's Well*, I am not refuting Scanlon and Miller's clever and insightful readings; rather, I am drawing attention an author who really is using *exemplum* as a straightforward vehicle for doctrine, and is failing miserably in his efforts as a consequence.

8. See Owst's humorous description of the various ways in which preachers were besieged (*Preaching*, 169–86).

9. Thus, I must for the most part relegate to the margins medieval academic theories of gossip's deviant speech, such as those proposed by Guillelmus Peraldus, Etienne de Bourbon, and the author of *De lingua*. For a detailed and insightful discussion of these writers and their theories of the Sins of the Tongue, see Craun, *Lies*, esp. 1–72. As will be evident throughout this essay, I am deeply indebted to Craun's work.

10. As Craun explains, there are at least eleven Middle English versions of the *Somme*, which survive in at least sixty-five manuscripts and two printed editions. The most popular of these is the *Speculum vitae*, which itself boasts at least forty extant manuscripts. For a complete list of the eleven versions, see Craun, *Lies*, 18n. The texts I consider here are the *Speculum vitae* (ca. 1375), *A Myrour to Lewede Men and Wymmen* (ca. 1400), the *Book of Vices and Virtues* (ca. 1375), *Ayenbite of Inwit* (ca. 1340), Caxton's *Ryal Book* (1486), and *Jacob's Well* (ca. 1425).

11. A translation of the Anglo-French poem, *Manuel des pechiez*, which Mannyng began in 1303.

12. *The Myroure of Oure Lady* refers to those who gossip as "vayne or comberous people . . . the fendes chyldren" who "ar bad felowes for they let the comon profyt of all theyre felyshyp" (ed. Blunt, ed., 45).

13. *The Book of Vices and Virtues*, ed. Francis, 55/11–14.

14. *Jacob's Well*, ed. Brandeis, 228/26–27. The Vulgate reads, "Dico autem vobis quoniam omne verbum otiosum quod locuti fuerint homines reddent rationem de eo in die iudicii." Numerous medieval sermons and penitential manuals, from the *Ayenbite of Inwyt* and *The Book of Vices and Virtues* to Mirk's *Festial,* echo this warning, repeatedly proclaiming that their readers and congregations will be made accountable for every syllable of their idle speech (*Ayenbite*, ed. Morris, 58/5–7; *Book*, ed. Francis, 55/24–25; Caxton's 1491 edition of Mirk's *Festial*, fol. R2v).

15. For Guillelmus Peraldus, idle talk is the quintessential venial sin. In fact, he uses idle speech as a means to introduce the topic of the venial, suggesting that the two concepts are inextricably linked. In the 1474 edition, the section on idle speech reflects this linkage in its title: "De verbo ocioso & peccatis venialib(us)" (*Summa*, fol. NN₃v).

16. Chaucer, The Parson's Tale, X. 649, in *The Riverside Chaucer*, ed. Benson et al. All subsequent references to Chaucer's Tales refer to this edition. The author of *Jacob's Well*, however, offers no such concession.

17. Chaucer, The Parson's Tale, X.647. According to Wenzel, this section on the sins of the tongue is one of the moments in which Chaucer seems to depart from *Quoniam* to follow Peraldus more closely ("The Source," 364). See also the parallel that Peterson cites, "Sequitur de verbo ocioso et quid sit. Notandum ergo quod verbum ociosum, secundum Hiero., est quod sine utilitate loquentis dicitur, aut audientis" (*Source*, 60).

18. White's argument that the medieval notion of "kynde" has a moral component offers a useful perspective here (*Nature*, 48–67).

19. In both the *MED* and in Benson, *Glossorial Concordance to the Riverside Chaucer*, the "natural" in the Parson's phrase is categorized as that which is "normal, customary, expected." This reading of *natural* seems to me the least likely, as the "customary" profit—that is the usual profitlessness—of speech is exactly what the Parson and his clerical brethren are attempting to remedy.

20. On the late medieval concept of profit more generally, see Kaye, *Economy and Nature*, especially 116–22.

21. In the *Somme* tradition, the tree of wicked tongue has ten branches. Guillelmus Peraldus, by contrast, places *ociosa verba* seventeeth in his list of twenty-four. However, the two Middle English translations of Peraldus (BL MS Add. 30944 and BL MS Harley 6571), while following his order, place greater emphasis on idle talk by adding as preface to the whole treatise on the Sins of the Tongue several *Somme*-inflected lines about idle speech. The scribe of BL MS Add. 30944 calls attention to this shift of emphasis by initiating the tractate on deviant speech, with the header "Of ydelle speche" (fol. 129r) instead of the running header "Of kepyng

of þ(e) tunge in comyn(n)" that appears on each of the successive pages (fols. 129v–133r). The text of these two translations has been edited by Diekstra, *Book for a Simple and Devout Woman*. The tractate on the Sins of the Tongue with its opening remarks about idle talk begins on 262; the chapter on idle talk occurs on 293–95.

22. *Speculum vitae*, ed. Smeltz, lines 13891–93. Defining idle talk through the janglers who engage in it is a strategy that also appears in *A Myrour*, ed. Nelson (211/30–32); and *Jacob's Well*, ed. Brandeis (148/20–21).

23. *Book*, ed. Francis, 55/20–23. This passage appears with some minor variations in all of the texts that derive from the *Somme*.

24. Chief among Guillelmus Peraldus' arguments about the gravity of idle speech are the notion that mouth as the gate of heaven should not be opened without momentous circumstances and the claim that the tongue, the pen of the Holy Ghost, becomes the pen of the devil when abused in idle speech (*Summa*, fols. NN3v–5r).

25. *Jacob's Well*, ed. Brandeis, 148/24–32.

26. Cf. Chaucer, The Clerk's Tale (IV.1200), The Parson's Tale (X.406) and Whiting, *Proverbs*, C276 and M557.

27. For a complete listing of Peraldus' twenty-four Sins of the Tongue, see Craun, *Lies*, 15–16.

28. While blurring certainly occurs in the cataloguing of sin more generally, idle talk seems to have been particularly prone to such conflation, to the point that it becomes not an occasional trait but a defining feature of this transgressive speech.

29. Jangling here exhibits gossip's talent for blending truth with falsehood. Part of the problem with gossip, for medieval and contemporary critics alike, is that one never can be sure whether it is true or false. Cf. the sworn brotherhood between a "lesyng and a sad soth sawe" that "tydynges" produce in Chaucer's *House of Fame* (line 2089).

30. The instability that accompanies "jangling" here appears in texts outside the *Somme* tradition. For example, in The Parson's Tale, "jangling" is at one moment synonymous with idle chatter—"Janglynge is whan a man speketh to muche biforn folk, and clappeth as a mille, and taketh no keep what he seith" (X. 406)—and at other moments separate from it (X. 647–50). Moreover, the confusion extends beyond pastoral discourse. As the *MED* explains, "jangling" can involve idle talk generally, as well as the specific infractions of too much talking, gossip, slander, and dispute.

31. *MED* 1a, 1b, 3a.

32. Caxton, *Ryal Book*, fol. F3v.

33. *Ayenbite*, ed. Morris, 58. Here the first and second manners are combined.

34. BL MS Add. 17013, fols. 17v–18r. While I have not consulted the manuscript in person, according to Francis's edition of the *Book of Vices and Virtues*, the scribe of Hun. MS HM 147 appears to follow the same pattern.

35. BL MS Add. 22283, fol. 97v.

36. *Ayenbite*, ed. Morris, 58.

37. *Book*, ed. Francis, 55/33–36.

38. *Book,* ed. Francis, 56/6; Caxton, *Ryal Book,* fol. F3v; *Ayenbite,* ed. Morris, 58; *Speculum,* ed. Smeltz, line 13940; *Myrour,* ed. Nelson, 212/17.

39. While I have not been able to examine all extant manuscripts of the *Somme,* those I have consulted do not exhibit the level of confusion and conflation, either in text or decoration, that appears in the Middle English adaptations and translations.

40. Mirk, *Instructions,* lines 57–60.

41. Numerous penitential manuals highlight the slippage between jangling and intimate exchange in their discussions of chastity and the worldly practices that threaten it. See the warning to virgins in *A Myrour,* ed. Nelson, 169, and to young widows in *Book,* ed. Francis, 256.

42. In the introduction to his edition of the *Book of Vices and Virtues,* Francis argues that the Constitutions of the Lambeth Council, while not the earliest formulation of the pastoral syllabus, is certainly the most important (ix). See also Boyle's discussion of Fourth Lateran Council's pervasive influence on manuals of popular theology ("Fourth Lateran Council," 30–43).

43. As Heffernan has argued, "the use of the exemplum was the single most important development in the success of the *ad populum* sermon of late medieval England" ("Sermon Literature," 183).

44. Scanlon, *Narrative,* 31.

45. Craun, *Lies,* 63. Following Aquinas, Craun argues that producing *detestatio,* "the reason's adverse reaction against sin during the process of contrition," is a primary goal for pastoral writers handling the Sins of the Tongue, who seek to convert the will of deviant speakers (58).

46. Discussions of jangling in church occur in chapters 2 (excommunication), 16 (sloth), 17 (sloth), 24 (lechery), 27 (confession), 28 (confession), 29 (satisfaction), 36 (idleness), 37 (humility), 42 (the "grauel of mysgouernaunce"), 46 (righteousness and steadfastness), 59 (chastity), 61 (temperance), 82 (the third commandment), and 83 (the fourth commandment). By week three, the author has more than compensated for the early hiatus. After Easter—chapter 45, if we accept Atchley's argument about liturgical setting—condemnation for jangling occurs less frequently, though with no less vehemence. For a discussion of liturgical setting, see Atchley, "Wose," 49–58.

47. In fact, during his two-day sermon on Sloth (110–17), all four of his *exempla* and most of his commentary are concerned with idle talk: "ffor ȝif þou be slawȝ and sluggy, þou art lyche an hungry dogge . . . þin erys hungryn gredyly newe tydynges, slaundrys, & lesynges, & iapys, & ribaldrye" (113/24–29).

48. Where other pastoral texts contain one or two lists of verbal transgression, *Jacob's Well* has three: the ten branches of the tree of "wicked tongue" (148–56); the twenty-two misconducts of the tongue, a list quite close to Guillelmus Peraldus' twenty-four (260–63); and the "sins of the mouth," a seemingly endless list containing everything from bearing false witness to foolish laughter and making faces and including more than sixty verbal transgressions (294–95). Moreover, this preacher does not employ this level of thoroughness and compulsion for all manner of sins but, rather, reserves it exclusively for verbal transgression. For example, in his discussion of the misconduct of the heart, tongue, and deed, the priest devotes six lines to the

misconduct of the heart, nine to misconduct in deed, and over one hundred to the tongue's transgressions.

49. A statistic made all the more remarkable by the fact that in its ninety-five chapters, *Jacob's Well* exhaustively addresses each aspect of the pastoral syllabus, including the seven deadly sins, the cardinal and theological virtues, the ten commandments, and the parts of confession.

50. Tubach #1844; *Jacob's Well*, ed. Brandeis, 110.

51. Tubach #3253; *Jacob's Well*, ed. Brandeis, 230–32.

52. Atchley, "Wose," 185. See Miller, "Displaced Souls," throughout, but esp. 625–32.

53. The narrative also resonates with Guillelmus Peraldus' assertion that while the virtuous man's tongue is the pen of the Holy Ghost, the deviant speaker's tongue is the pen of the devil (*Summa*, fol. NN4r).

54. Jennings, "Tutivillus," esp. appendix I, 86–87. See also Tubach #1630 a & b. The misericord in Ely Cathedral is particularly vivid in its detailed representation of the Tutivillus *exemplum*. On the right-hand side, the devil is shown tugging at the scroll with his teeth. In addition to the Ely misericord, Tutivillus appears in wall paintings at Peakirk, Seething and Little Melton, Melbourne, and Colton, and in misericords at Gayton and Enville (Anderson, *Drama and Imagery*, 173–77). See also Alexander and Binski, *Age of Chivalry*, esp. 444–46; Rouse, *Medieval Wall Paintings*, esp. 68–69.

55. In *Jacob's Well*, as in many other texts that Jennings cites, the recording demon is not named.

56. *Exemplum* repetition is rare in this collection of sermons. In all other instances, the repeated *exemplum* is used for two different purposes, as in the *exemplum* of the half-burned woman, who first appears as a quarrelsome noble-woman (95) and later as a talkative nun (*Jacob's Well*, ed. Brandeis, 231).

57. Jennings, "Tutivillus," 8.

58. *Jacob's Well*, ed. Brandeis, 115/6–7. Atchley argues from internal evidence that the *Jacob's Well* congregation is both lay and clerical, suggesting Bury St. Edmunds as a likely setting ("Wose," 28–31).

59. *Jacob's Well*, ed. Brandeis, 115/13–17.

60. "How to hear mass," in *The Minor Poems of the Vernon Manuscript*, ed. Horstmann, p. 501/313–18; Jennings, "Tutivillus," 26–27. In some versions, Mary intervenes on the holy man's behalf, and the *exemplum* becomes more about the power of Mary's intercession than about gossip.

61. Gregg takes note of the preacher's austere tendencies more generally: "By rigidly excluding any tale that could even remotely be suspected of levity, the English sermon composer evinces an unwillingness to compromise his homiletic material that was not wholly typical of his age" ("The Exempla," 374).

62. Mirk, *Festial*, 279–80. Similarly, in Jacques de Vitry, when the priest in the narrative tells his audience what he has seen, their fear-inspired penitence erases the devil's scroll (Crane, *Exempla*, 6, #19).

63. While the narrative, in its many versions, stages a competition between the oral and the written, between the words of parishioners and a scribal culture that can record and condemn it, the contest emphasized by the author of *Jacob's Well* is not primarily that of an oral culture vs. a scribal one, but rather that of two competing kinds of speech.

64. Mirk, for example, in addition to having Tutivillus sit on women's shoulders, offers an extended discussion of women's loquacity in his sermon on the Visitation, observing that since Mary spoke only four times in the gospels, contemporary women should curtail their speech (*Festial*, fols. R₁r–R₃v). Departing from Peraldus, the *Book for a Simple and Devout Woman* offers a similar argument (196). See also Jennings's discussion of the "female presence" strain of the *exemplum* ("Tutivillus, 11–27).

65. "How to hear mass," in *Vernon Manuscript*, ed. Hortsmann, 503 / 395–400; Mannyng, *Handlyng Synne*, ed. Sullens, lines 9312–18; *Jacob's Well*, ed. Brandeis, 115 / 18–20.

66. Scanlon, *Narrative*, 13.

67. *Jacob's Well*, ed. Brandeis, 232 / 15–19. Here, again he has the demon explain his task to the audience, thereby repeating the tale.

68. *Jacob's Well*, ed. Brandeis, 232 / 22–9.

69. Gregory the Great, *Dialogues*, II. 23. His is a story of two nuns who are threatened with excommunication for their chattering (Tubach #723).

70. A monk, disturbed in his prayers by the chattering of two women, tells this tale to their husbands in order to shame and silence them (Caesarius of Heisterbach, *The Dialogue on Miracles*, IV. 22. Cf. *An Alphabet of Tales*, 277, #405).

71. Mannyng, *Handlyng Synne*, ed. Sullens, lines 1547–1600 and 8291–96.

72. Far more concerned with "jangling" than with lechery, the author of *Jacob's Well* has removed almost all of the foulness of "foly speech."

73. *Jacob's Well*, ed. Brandeis, 233 / 1–2.

74. Mannyng, *Handlyng Synne*, ed. Sullens, lines 45–48. As Miller observes, *trotouale* appears to be a "favorite word" of Mannyng's ("Displaced Souls," 626). What is more, Mannyng appears to be one of the few English writers to use the word. And while the other two texts in which the word appears offer only a unique instance, Mannyng uses the word four times in this text. *OED, MED* "trotëvale" [*sic*].

75. Chaucer, *Tales*, VI. 435–38.

76. While most orthodox commentators accept patristic writers as exemplary sources, they cast suspicion on chronicles, romances, and classical texts. See Spencer, *English Preaching*, 78–91.

77. Chaucer, *Tales*, X. 31–34; 1 Tim. 4:7. Just as Chaucer surveys clerical ranks and the spectrum of abuses associated with them, so he covers the range of clerical opinion on exemplarity.

78. Craun, *Lies*, 216.

79. Chaucerians long have debated the intent behind the Parson's rejection of "fables," interpreting it variously as a condemnation of the Host's less-than-virtuous tastes and as rejection of all narratives, including those that comprise the *Canterbury Tales*. For Strohm, the Parson rejects "fabulation itself," radically

altering the conditions of the tale-telling competition and leading pilgrims away from the "rampant narrativity" that has characterized their collective endeavor (*Social Chaucer*, 176). For Craun, the Parson's injunction against tales is not absolute, but rather speaks only of those tales which are morally unprofitable (*Lies*, 217–21). I restrict my discussion here to the *exempla* that the Parson so studiously avoids in his penitential "tale."

80. Chaucer, *Tales*, X. 670–73. In the four lines of the *exemplum*, *sothe* is repeated three times.

81. Wenzel, in his notes to *The Riverside Chaucer*, suggests a possible parallel with Guillelmus Peraldus.

82. Wycliffe, *Comment on the Testament of St. Francis* (*English Works*, ed. Matthew, 50); *The Order of Priesthood* (*English Works*, ed. Matthew, 175); *Of the Leaven of Pharisees* (*English Works*, ed. Matthew, 16).

83. Wycliffe, *De Officio Pastorali*, in *English Works*, ed. Matthew, 442. Along with numerous other instances of this critique in Wycliffite writings (59, 73, 153, 195, and 438), see the *Lantern of Li3t*, which lists the faults of preachers in the devil's church, "þei prechen cronyclis; wiþ poyses & dremyngis / & manye oþir helples talis; þat ri3t nou3t availen" (ed. Swinburn, 55/26–28).

84. Mannyng, *Handlyng Synne*, ed. Sullens, lines 131–40. Mannyng's preoccupation with committing this verbal sin is evidenced by the fact that he makes a similar disclaimer even earlier in the text, as he outlines his project: "Of pryuytees speke y nou3t; / Þe pryuytees wyle nat name / For noun þarefore shuld me blame" (lines 30–32). It is almost as if the very premise of *Handlyng Synne* requires such a disavowal.

85. "I heard it from so-so who was there," "I saw it with my own eyes," etc. Cf. the speech tags that accompany tidings in Geoffrey Chaucer's *House of Fame*, lines 2051–54.

86. Mannyng, *Handlyng Synne*, ed. Sullens, lines 3617–22.

87. Scanlon, *Narrative*, 30: "the moral can only be apprehended narratively. Indeed, it can only be apprehended narratively because it is produced narratively."

88. Chaucer's The Manciple's Tale provides a humorous echo of Mannyng's concern. To his *exemplum* about the dangers of not holding one's tongue, the Manciple adds a fifty-line *moralitas*, in which he ventriloquizes his mother's voice. What she provides in the form of advice from parent to child is a monotonous list of proverbs and parables about idle speech. The tale, it seems, is actually about jangling, as many of the species of idle speech find their way into her discussion. But in its seemingly endless repetition of injunctions against too much speaking, the Manciple's *moralitas* (or at least his mother's) commits the sin against which it speaks, with jangling triumphing over its condemnation.

89. Mannyng, *Handlyng Synne*, ed. Sullens, lines 3631–32.

90. Mannyng, *Handlyng Synne*, ed. Sullens, line 3604.

91. Miller, "Displaced Souls," 626–32.

92. See Clifton, "Struggling with Will," 29–52; and Blythe, "Sins of the Tongue," 119–42.

93. In "Displaced Souls," Miller argues that "the topic of 'trotëvale' is a considerably more troubling one for Mannyng than a simple contrast between idle talk and the good work of pastoral literature might suggest" (609). While I agree with Miller's assertion, my argument differs from his in that I take Mannyng's preoccupation with this topic not as the concern of a priest over his potentially ineffectual speech but as the implementation of a tool he exploits to maintain the attention of his audience.

94. Mannyng, *Handlyng Synne*, ed. Sullens, lines 168–70 and 1252–54.

95. Kemmler lists five original *exempla*: the tale of Witch and the Cow-sucking bag (line 499), the tale of Bishop Grosteste (line 4743), the tale of the Norfolk Bondman and the cattle that defile the churchyard (line 8669), the tale of the derelict midwife (line 9627), and the tale of the Bishop's corpse (line 11083); *Exempla*, Appendix IV, 202–04. To these, following Sullens, I add the tale of the Suffolk man (line 10403) and the tale of the Cambridgeshire Parson (line 6175); *Handlyng Synne*, ed. Sullens, Appendix II, 381–87. These two *exempla* do not appear in the *Manuel de pechiez* and are listed by Tubach (#3213c and #1487, respectively) as unique occurrences.

96. Mannyng, *Handlyng Synne*, ed. Sullens, lines 6175–76.

97. Mannyng, *Handlyng Synne*, ed. Sullens, lines 6378–80. Tubach #1933. In his Prologue, Mannyng identifies Kesteven as the part of Lincolnshire that includes the priory of Sempringham, his home while composing *Handlyng Synne* (lines 57–86).

98. Mannyng, *Handlyng Synne*, ed. Sullens, lines 9014 and 9027–28.

99. Mannyng, *Handlyng Synne*, ed. Sullens, lines 9258 and 9264–65.

Works Cited

Abbreviations

EETS   Early English Text Society. London: Early English Text Society, 1864–.
PL   Patrologia cursus completus: Series latina. Ed. Jacques-Paul Migne. Paris: Migne, 1844–91.

Manuscript Sources

The Book of Vices and Virtues. London, British Library, MS Add. 17013 and MS Add. 22283, fols. 92r–116r.
"Frende ne sybbe who so byholdeth hys lothely lokys And his outward countenaunce." London, British Library, MS Add. 30944, fols. 3r–154v.
Lorens D'Orléans. *Somme le Roi*. London, British Library, MS Royal 19.C.ii.
"Mi dere lord seynt Johan in þe book of reuelaciones þat is cleped þe apocalips." London, British Library, MS Royal 18.A.x, fols. 16r–55v.
"Sent Ion þe Ewangelist in a boke þat he made þat men clepyn þe Apocalips." London, British Library, MS. Add. 37677, fols. 61v–83v.

"Seynt Johon þe evangelist in his boke of pryuytes." London, British Library, MS Harley 6571, fols. 1r–78v.

PRIMARY SOURCES

An Alphabet of Tales. Ed. Mary Macleod Banks. EETS o.s. 126, 127. London: EETS, 1904.

Atchley, Clinton Parham Edwin. "The 'Wose' of *Jacob's Well:* Text and Context." Ph.D. diss., University of Washington, 1998.

Ayenbite of Inwit, Part II. Ed. Pamela Gradon. EETS o.s. 278. London: EETS, 1979.

Biblia sacra juxta vulgatam versionem. Ed. Robert Weber. 3rd ed. Stuttgart: Deutsche Bibelgesellschaft, 1983.

The Book of Vices and Virtues. Ed. W. Nelson Francis. EETS o.s. 217. London: EETS, 1942.

Caxton, William. *The ryal book, or A book for a kyng.* Westminster: William Caxton, 1486.

Chaucer, Geoffrey. *The Riverside Chaucer.* Ed. Larry D. Benson et al. 3rd ed. New York: Houghton Mifflin, 1987.

Dan Michel's Ayenbite of Inwyt, or, Remorse of Conscience: In the Kentish Dialect, 1340. Ed. Richard Morris. EETS o.s. 23. London: Trübner, 1866.

The Exempla or Illustrative Stories from the "Sermones Vulgares" of Jacques de Vitry. Ed. Thomas Frederick Crane. London, 1890.

Guillelmus Peraldus. *Summa de vitiis.* Basel: Rodt, 1474.

Jacob's Well. Ed. Arthur Brandeis. EETS o.s. 115. London: EETS, 1900.

Langland, William. *The Vision of Piers Plowman, A Complete Edition of the B-Text.* Ed. A. V. C. Schmidt. London: J. M. Dent & Sons, 1978.

Mannyng, Robert. *Handlyng Synne.* Ed. Idelle Sullens. Binghamton: Medieval & Renaissance Texts & Studies, 1983.

Manual des pechiez in Robert Mannyng's *Handlynge Synne.* Ed. Frederick J. Furnivall. EETS o.s. 119, 123. London: EETS, 1901.

The Minor Poems of the Vernon Manuscript. Ed. Carl Horstmann. EETS o.s. 98, 117. London: EETS, 1892–1901.

Mirk, John. *Festial.* London: William Caxton, 1491.

———. *Mirk's Festial.* Part I. Ed. Theodor Erbe. EETS e.s. 96. London: EETS, 1905.

———. *Instructions for Parish Priests.* Ed. Gillis Kristensson. Lund Studies in English 49. Lund: Carl Bloms, 1974.

A Myrour to Lewede Men and Wymmen: A Prose Version of the "Speculum Vitae." Ed. Venetia Nelson. Middle English Texts 14. Heidelberg: Carl Winter, 1981.

The Myroure of Oure Ladye. Ed. John Henry Blunt. EETS e.s. 19. London: EETS, 1873.

"*Speculum vitae:* An Edition of British Museum Manuscript Royal 17.C.viii." Ed. John W. Smeltz. Ph.D. Diss., Duquesne University,1977.

Wycliffe, John. *The English Works of Wycliffe.* Ed. F. D. Matthew. EETS o.s. 74. London: EETS, 1880.

———. *The Lanterne of Liȝt.* Ed. Lilian Swinburn. EETS o.s.151. London: EETS, 1917.

Secondary Sources

Alexander, John, and Paul Binski. *Age of Chivalry: Art in Plantagenet England.* London: Royal Academy of Arts, 1987.

Anderson, M. D. *Drama and Imagery in English Medieval Churches.* Cambridge: Cambridge University Press, 1963.

Benson, Larry D. *Glossorial Concordance to the Riverside Chaucer.* New York: Garland, 1993.

Blythe, Joan Heiges. "Sins of the Tongue and Rhetorical Prudence in 'Piers Plowman.'" In *Literature and Religion in the Later Middle Ages,* ed. Richard G. Newhauser and John A. Alford, 119–42. Binghamton: Medieval and Renaissance Texts and Studies, 1995.

Boyle, Leonard E. "The Fourth Lateran Council and Manuals of Popular Theology." In *The Popular Literature of Medieval England,* ed. Thomas J. Heffernan, 30–43. Tennessee Studies in Literature 28. Knoxville: University of Tennessee Press, 1985.

Carruthers, Leo. "Allegory and Bible Interpretation: The Narrative Structure of a Middle English Sermon Cycle." *Literature and Theology* 4:1 (1991), 1–14.

———. "The Liturgical Setting of *Jacob's Well.*" *English Language Notes* 24:4 (1987), 11–23.

Clifton, Linda J. "Struggling with Will: Jangling, Sloth, and Thinking in *Piers Plowman B.*" In *Suche Werkis to Werche: Essays on "Piers Plowman" in Honor of David C. Fowler,* ed. Míċeál F. Vaughan, 29–52. East Lansing: Colleagues Press, 1993.

Craun, Edwin. *Lies, Slander and Obscenity in Medieval English Literature.* Cambridge: Cambridge University Press, 1997.

Gregg, Joan Young. "The Exempla of *Jacob's Well*: A Study in the Transmission of Medieval Sermon Stories." *Traditio* 33 (1977), 359–80.

———. "The Narrative Exempla of *Jacob's Well*: A Source Study with an Index for *Jacob's Well* to *Index Exemplorum.*" Ph.D. diss., New York University, 1973.

Heffernan, Thomas J. "Sermon Literature." In *Middle English Prose: A Critical Guide to Major Authors and Genres,* ed. A. S. G. Edwards, 177–208. New Brunswick: Rutgers University Press, 1984.

Jennings, Margaret. "Tutivillus: The Literary Career of the Recording Demon." *Studies in Philology* 74 (1977), 1–95.

Kaye, Joel. *Economy and Nature in the Fourteenth Century: Money, Market Exchange, and the Emergence of Scientific Thought.* Cambridge: Cambridge University Press, 1998.

Kemmler, Fritz. *"Exempla" in Context: A Historical and Critical Study of Robert Mannyng of Brunne's "Handlyng Synne."* Tübingen: Gunter Narr Verlag, 1984.

Miller, Mark. "Displaced Souls, Idle Talk, Spectacular Scenes: *Handlyng Synne* and the Perspective of Agency." *Speculum* 71 (1996), 606–32.

Owst, G. R. *Preaching in Medieval England: An Introduction to Sermon Manuscripts of the Period, c. 1350–1450.* Cambridge: Cambridge University Press, 1926.

Petersen, K. O. *The Source of the Parson's Tale.* Radcliffe College Monographs 12. Boston: Athenæum Press, 1901.

Rouse, Edward Clive. *Medieval Wall Paintings.* Princes Risborough: Shire Publications, 1991.

Scanlon, Larry. *Narrative, Authority and Power: The Medieval Exemplum and the Chaucerian Tradition.* Cambridge: Cambridge University Press, 1994.

Spencer, H. Leith. *English Preaching in the Late Middle Ages.* Oxford: Clarendon, 1993.

Strohm, Paul. *Social Chaucer.* Cambridge, Mass.: Harvard University Press, 1989.

Tubach, Frederic C. *Index Exemplorum: A Handbook of Medieval Religious Tales.* Helsinki: Suomalainen Tiedeakatemia, 1969.

Wenzel, Siegfried. "The Source of Chaucer's Seven Deadly Sins." *Traditio* 30 (1974), 351–78.

White, Hugh. *Nature, Sex and Goodness.* Oxford: Oxford University Press, 2000.

Whiting, Bartlett Jere. *Proverbs, Sentences, and Proverbial Phrases; From English Writings Mainly before 1500.* Cambridge, Mass.: Belknap, 1968.

LANCELOT AS CASUIST

Peter R. Schroeder

As Sir Thomas Malory's *Le Morte Darthur* moves toward its dolorous conclusion, Lancelot, on the verge of returning Queen Guinevere to King Arthur, makes two long and problematic speeches. By this point, of course, Lancelot has been ambushed in Queen Guinevere's chambers by a malevolent gang of knights led by Gawain's brothers Mordred and Agravaine; has succeeded in escaping, killing Agravaine in the process; has rescued Guinevere from burning, in the process killing Gawain's favorite brother, Gareth; and has fled with the queen to his castle of Joyous Garde, pursued by Arthur and Gawain. Arthur, finally convinced that Lancelot and Guinevere long have been maintaining an adulterous affair, accuses Lancelot of treason; Gawain accuses Lancelot of having deliberately and maliciously slain Gareth.

Malory has made it clear that the first of these charges is true and the second false. The affair between Lancelot and Guinevere is a central and undeniable component of the story, however much Malory himself may want to gloss over it, while the killing of Gareth is an unfortunate accident, which Lancelot regrets more than anyone. But in his speeches, which charitable critics have characterized as a mix of lies, equivocations, sophistry, and blasphemy,[1] Lancelot denies, or seems to deny, both charges. This poses a fairly substantial problem for admirers of Lancelot, of whom the chief is Malory himself. How, that is, can we reconcile what Lancelot says with the admiration that Malory obviously feels, and wants us to feel, for his noble knight?

The usual solution is to claim that we modern readers see a problem where Malory would not. "For the author as for the character the *fact* of the lie does not exist," says Mark Lambert.[2] To Lambert and Terence McCarthy, that is because we are operating according to the standards of a "guilt culture," while Malory is presupposing a "shame culture"—a system with very different standards. Thus, according to McCarthy, "if we see Lancelot as a liar . . . , Malory, it is clear, does not"; Lancelot's defense "is both logical and truthful viewed from within the system. If *we* find it less than convincing, it is simply because we are outside that system."[3] In the same vein, D. S. Brewer claims that "distinction between right and wrong must go when honour's at the stake. Thus an honourable man must sometimes tell lies. Lancelot is justified by honour in his various quibbles, prevarications, and downright lies to preserve the Queen's good name."[4] Larry Benson, more guardedly, suggests that an alternative system of "perfect chivalry" serves to justify Lancelot's apparent transgressions.[5] In any case, the basic claim is that truth in those days was not the same as truth nowadays, and that neither Malory nor Malory's Lancelot would have been disturbed by what we, anachronistically, see as a misleading farrago of lies and equivocations.

This solution strikes me as implausible. A distinction between truth and falsehood is not entirely a modern invention, and I think that Malory is quite aware that Lancelot in this scene faces a number of conflicting ethical imperatives, none of which has any clear and absolute primacy. According to the chivalric code of *amour courtois*, his first obligation is to protect his lady and her reputation. According to the religious values that still linger from the Grail quest, his first obligation is to God. According to some high-medieval comitatus principle, his first obligation is to his king and (by extension) to the well-being of the kingdom. Yes, Lancelot and Malory subscribe to the values of a "shame culture." But they also—and simultaneously—subscribe to the values of a "guilt culture," and to a few other values as well. In earlier stories, and in earlier parts of Malory's own narrative, it was indeed possible to segregate these different value systems. But at this point in the story they are all competing with each other. How, then, can Lancelot be true, simultaneously, to God, Guinevere, Arthur, the kingdom, the truth, and his own heroic sense of self?

My central argument will be that Malory recognizes this problem and tries to solve it by making Lancelot a kind of casuist. In essence, that is, while Malory knows the difference between truth and falsehood, he makes a moral distinction between an outright lie and a misleading equivocation, and he carefully frames Lancelot's speeches to avoid any outright lies. But before we construct that argument, it would be well to try weakening the two central props of the "usual solution": that Malory's notion of truth would have differed substantially from our own, and that, in any case, what we would regard as a lie would be morally justified in the kind of shame culture that Malory presupposes.

In his recent study of truth in fourteenth-century England, Richard Firth Green provides interesting evidence from many cultures that *truth* (or its equivalent word) can indeed mean a good many things besides "factuality."[6] But—whatever we may think of Green's linkage between the changing conception of truth and an increasing dependence on literacy—his own detailed discussion seems to make clear that in England, by the fifteenth century, the primary sense of *truth* was very much what it is today. In this respect, as in others, Malory may feel a kind of nostalgia for an earlier day. But he (and his readers) surely was aware that, for better or for worse, truth had come to mean primarily conformity to fact. And it seems unlikely that he would be capable of the kind of exercise in cultural relativism—imagining an Arthurian world not yet familiar with the "modern" conception of falsehood—that, as Green notes, is difficult even for scholars today.[7]

Richard Firth Green, then, while making a strong case for what some might call the socially constructed nature of truth and falsehood, ends up lending support to the idea that by Malory's time the construction would have been very like our own. That is, it seems reasonable, on a good many grounds, to believe that Malory would have shared our view of what a lie is. But would he have regarded a lie, in this case, as wrong? Or is Lancelot's mendacity justified by the code of the shame culture?

In fact, of course, whatever our code, we all tend to make distinctions: there are lies and there are lies. We may well find ourselves sharing Athena's view that the incessant lies of Homer's Odysseus are a sign of cleverness rather than moral depravity, and few of us are likely to condemn Lancelot for his analogous tendency to disguise himself at tournaments. But his speeches to King Arthur are different. Here, Lancelot is making an eloquent and misleading public denial of a serious accusation. "An honourable man," says D. S. Brewer, "must sometimes tell lies." But is this one of those times?

D. S. Brewer's discussion of honor and shame—which in turn serves as the basis for Mark Lambert's claims[8]—draws heavily on a study in which Julian Pitt-Rivers, after summing up a number of general principles governing the code of honor, supports and refines them from his research among Andalusian villagers.[9] That there is some fundamental similarity between these general principles and the principles embodied in Malory's world seems to me beyond dispute. But I am by no means convinced that these principles exonerate Lancelot. True, in the code of honor the appearance of sincerity seems to count more than truth: "the way things are said is more important than the substance of what is said. . . . The apology that does not sound sincere aggravates the offence."[10] Moreover, someone who intends to deceive is not necessarily dishonored if he is discovered to have lied. As Pitt-Rivers goes on:

> We can explain now something which appears anomalous in the literature of honour: on the one hand honour demands keeping faith and to break one's word or to lie is the most dishonourable conduct, yet in fact a man is permitted to lie and to deceive without forfeiting his honour.[11]

Yet again, though, there are lies and there are lies. "To lie is to deny the truth to someone who has the right to be told it and this right exists only where respect is due."[12] The intentional lie, that is, shows a lack of respect for the person to whom the lie is told; the liar is not dishonored as long as his lie can be interpreted as an insult to the recipient. But surely, in Lancelot's case, "respect is due" to King Arthur, and there is no evidence that Lancelot ever intends to withhold such respect.

Moreover, Julian Pitt-Rivers is summing up the principles of a "code of honor" uncontaminated by any alternative ethical system. But he himself acknowledges that, in Andalusian practice and elsewhere, this code "has conflicted with the law of the Church and the law of the land."[13] And there is evidence that Lancelot, for all his concern with honor and shame, is nothing like a pure embodiment of this code. Even if we set aside his self-flagellating responses to the rebukes he keeps receiving from assorted holy hermits during the Grail quest, what do we make, for example, of the values presupposed in his interchange with the lady whom Meleagaunt has ill-advisedly set to guard him in his "cave full of straw"? The lady, of course, wants Lancelot to lie with her; when Lancelot refuses, she points out that without her help Lancelot will languish in prison and Guinevere will be burned. Lancelot continues to resist.

> "Than ar ye shamed," seyde the lady, "and destroyed for ever."
> "As for the worldis shame, now Jesu deffende me! And as for my distresse, hit ys welcom, whatsomever hit be that God sendys me."
> So she cam to hym agayne the same day that the batayle shulde be and seyde,
> "Sir Launcelot, bethynke you, for ye ar to hard-harted. And therefore, and ye wolde but onys kysse me, I shulde delyver you and your armoure, and the best horse that was within sir Mellyagaunce stable."
> "As for to kysse you," seyde sir Launcelot, "I may do that and lese no worshyp. And wyte you well, and I undirstood there were ony diswor-shyp for to kysse you, I wold nat do hit."[14]

While "worship," in Malory, is normally a public virtue aligned with fame and honor, the "disworshyp" that Lancelot fears in this passage seems to have little to do with the "worldis shame" that he earlier shrugs off. We assume that no hidden video cameras lurk in Meleagaunt's cave, nor that the lady will be invited to Camelot to risk an awkward encounter with Guinevere. What restrains Lancelot here, one gathers, is something akin to an inner moral sense, the sort of thing one associates with a culture of guilt rather than of shame. And this is not a unique instance.

My hope so far is to have tossed at least a few grains of reasonable doubt on the claim that Malory's "system" would have kept him from recognizing the moral complexity of Lancelot's situation. But if Malory shared our sense that a lie, in this case, would not be to Lancelot's credit, and if Malory does not want us to think ill of Lancelot (an assumption to be scrutinized more closely later), then we need to reconsider how Malory sets about trying to resolve this dilemma. How, that is, can he make Lancelot deny the charges of treason, assert the unsullied honor of the Queen, and yet avoid lying?

In its general form, Lancelot's problem is by no means unique. Ethical theorists since antiquity have tried to figure out what to do when one ethical imperative seems to collide with another. We know that the road to hell is paved with good intentions, and we may feel uneasy at the notion that justice should be done even if the heavens fall, but how exactly do we weigh such things as intention and effect in evaluating the morality of a particular act? St. Thomas Aquinas himself, no mush-headed moral relativist, acknowledges that one should allow some flexibility in applying moral rules: "a thing taken in its primary sense, and absolutely considered, may be good or evil, and yet, when some additional circumstances are taken into account, by a consequent consideration may be changed into the contrary."[15] And in the "great flurry of pastoral manuals"[16] that, after the Fourth Lateran Council in 1215, aimed to help confessors sort out the sins of their flocks, we find that a central concern is how "circumstances" should contribute to the ethical evaluation of any specific act. Thus the Diocese of Exeter in 1287 provides a mnemonic for remembering the circumstances that a confessor would need to take into account in evaluating the severity of a sin: "who, what, where, by whose aid, why, how, and when."[17]

Now, Malory was no philosopher, but I do not think he was a fool. If he indeed recognized that Lancelot was in a bind, it seems at least plausible that, instead of invoking some hypothetical all-embracing ethical system that would turn the Problem of the Lying Knight into a non-problem, he might try to draw from the practical ethics of his time a way to negotiate a solution. Such a negotiation almost certainly would involve some version of what we know as casuistry.

Casuistry takes its name from *casus conscientiae*, a "case" of conscience. Malory lived a century before the efflorescence of "high casuistry," with its seemingly magical ability to transmute vice into virtue, false oaths into true. But he almost certainly was familiar with the more practical proto-casuistry of the fifteenth century, when (according to the *OED*) we begin to find examples in popular literature of "to put" or "set the case"—the formula used in canon law to begin the examination of a hypothetical example.[18] The focus of this earlier development—usefully sketched in Albert Jonsen and Stephen Toulmin's *The Abuse of Casuistry*, one of whose goals is to rehabilitate the rather tarnished concept of casuistry itself—was to consider how precisely those "additional circumstances" could modify general principles in a particular ethical case, and how competing ethical claims could be reconciled. Even the early casuists could come up with some fairly strange arguments, and I am not confident that viewing Lancelot's speeches as casuistical will make *me* any happier with what he actually says. But the question is whether Malory might have viewed this as a tenable way of getting Lancelot out of his messy predicament.

Let us turn now to the actual speeches. In the first, Lancelot, besieged in Joyous Garde, is responding to Arthur's accusation that he has "slayne my good knyghtes and full noble men of my blood" and that he has "layne by my quene and holdyn her many wynters, and syththyn, lyke a traytoure, taken her away fro me by fors" (3:1187). Lancelot says that the King:

> "may sey what ye woll, for ye wote well wyth youreselff I woll nat stryve. But thereas ye say that I have slayne youre good knyghtes, I wote woll that I have done so, and that me sore repentith; but I was forced to do batayle with hem in savyng of my lyff, othir ellis I muste have suffirde hem to have slayne me. And as for my lady quene Gwenyver, excepte youre person of your hyghnes and my lorde sir Gawayne, there nys no knyght undir hevyn that dare make hit good uppon me that ever I was traytour unto youre person. And where hit please you to say that I have holdyn my lady, youre quene, yerys and wynters, unto that I shall ever make a large answere, and prove hit uppon any knyght that beryth the lyff, excepte your person and sir Gawayne, that my lady, quene Gwenyver, ys as trew a lady unto youre person as ys ony lady lyvynge unto her lorde, and that woll I make good with my hondis. Howbehyt hit hath lyked her good grace to have me in favoure and cherysh me more than ony other knyght;

and unto my power agayne I have deserved her love, for oftyntymes, my lorde, ye have concented that she sholde have be brente and destroyed in your herte, and than hit fortuned me to do batayle for her, and or I departed from her adversary they confessed there untrouthe, and she full worsshypfully excused. And at suche tymes, my lorde Arthur," seyde sir Launcelot, "ye loved me and thanked me whan I saved your quene frome the fyre, and than ye promysed me for ever to be my good lorde. And now methynkith ye rewarde me evyll for my good servyse. And, my lorde, mesemyth I had loste a grete parte of my worshyp in my knyghthod and I had suffird my lady, your quene, to have ben brente, and insomuche as she shulde have bene brente for my sake; for sytthyn I have done batayles for your quene in other quarels than in myne owne quarell, mesemyth now I had more ryght to do batayle for her in her ryght quarell. And therefore, my good and gracious lorde," seyde sir Launcelot, "take your quene unto youre good grace, for she ys both tru and good." (3:1188)

Some pages later, after the intervention of the papal emissary, Lancelot delivers Guinevere to Arthur "as ryght requyryth":

"And if there be ony knyght, of what degre that ever he be off, except your person, that woll sey or dare sey but that she ys trew and clene to you, I here myselff, sire Launcelot du Lake, woll make hit good uppon hys body that she is a trew lady unto you.

"But, sir, lyars ye have lystened, and that hath caused grete debate betwyxte you and me. For tyme hath bene, my lorde Arthur, that ye were gretly pleased with me whan I ded batayle for my lady, youre quene; and full well ye know, my moste noble kynge, that she hathe be put to grete wronge or thys tyme. And sytthyn hyt pleased you at many tymys that I shulde feyght for her, therefore mesemyth, my good lorde, I had more cause to rescow her from the fyer whan she sholde have ben brente for my sake.

"For they that tolde you tho talys were lyars, and so hit felle uppon them: for by lyklyhode, had nat the myght of God bene with me, I myght never have endured with fourtene knyghtes, and they armed and afore purposed, and I unarmed and nat purposed; for I was sente unto my lady, youre quyne, I wote nat for what cause, but I was nat so sone within the chambir dore but anone sir Aggravayne and sir Mordred called me traytoure and false recrayed knyght." (3:1197)

Gawain at this point interrupts ("Be my fayth, they called the ryght!") and, in spite of Lancelot's review of the many services he has rendered Gawain and his kinsmen, continues to insist that "two of hem thou slew traytourly and piteously" (3:1199). Finally, Lancelot kisses the queen and announces "Now lat se whatsomever he be in thys place that dare sey the quene ys nat trew unto my lorde Arthur, lat se who woll speke and he dare speke" (3:1202). No one takes up the challenge.

What exactly has Lancelot said? He admits that he has killed the knights but—against Gawain's continuing accusations—denies that he has done so intentionally. It seems likely that a jury of readers would accept as straightforwardly true Lancelot's account of his actions in rescuing the queen and of his deep regret at Gareth's death.[19] Gawain's misguided and hysterical insistence that Lancelot has acted "in the despite of" Gawain (3:1189) thus serves as a kind of red herring, deflecting our attention from Lancelot's reply to the other charge, that he has been lying with the queen "many wynters." There seems little doubt that this charge is true. What we now need to consider is whether Lancelot's (seeming) denial of the charge is in fact a lie, and whether, even if it is a lie, it is in some sense morally justified.

To begin with the second of these, Albert Jonsen and Stephen Toulmin note that theologians of the thirteenth century made some interesting revisions to St. Augustine's blanket prohibition against lying ("One must not do evil, even to prevent greater evil"). Aquinas grants that in certain circumstances "it is licit to hide the truth prudently by some sort of dissimulation," and Raymond of Peñafort divides lies into three types: the "pernicious," which does harm to another; the "jocose," which harms no one; and the "officious," or dutiful, which benefits someone other than the liar.[20] If Lancelot is lying, then, is his lie intended to benefit himself or to harm another? The answer to both questions would seem to be no. The immediate result of his denial is that he loses the queen. As he points out, "For and the quene had be so dere unto me as ye noyse her, I durste have kepte her frome the felyshyp of the beste knyghtes undir hevyn" (3:1202). Guinevere only can be returned—with her reputation intact and some hope of restoring both private and public domestic tranquility—if the affair goes unacknowledged. And in addition, of course, to acknowledge the affair would be a hideous violation of the codes of courtly love.

Lancelot's denial, then, gains nothing for himself but benefits everyone else. Is this his intent? It seems likely. Elsewhere, as with the Fair Maid of Astolat and (as we have seen) Sir Meliagaunt's rather forward prison warden, he is scrupulously attentive to the competing demands of deed, motive, and effect. Malory's Lancelot is far from Tennyson's debauched and debauching relativist. But he seems equally far from the critics' Lancelot who thinks "that a liar is a man who cannot prove the truth of his words with his sword."[21] After all, his defenses of the queen against Sir Mador and

Sir Meliagaunt succeed at least in part because in those cases he *is* in the right. Guinevere is not guilty of the specific allegation made against her by the slimy Meliagaunt, and she is certainly innocent of poisoning Sir Patryse at a dinner that, as she truthfully says, "I made for a good entente and never for none evyll" (3:1050).

So if Lancelot does lie, the lie would seem to be of the venial, "officious" variety. But *does* Lancelot in fact lie at all? In the first of his self-exculpatory speeches Lancelot explicitly denies nothing. Rather he claims that "there nys no knyght undir hevyn that dare make hit good uppon me that ever I was traytour unto your person," and that, in response to the accusations:

> "I shall ever make a large answere, and prove hit uppon ony knyght that beryth the lyff, excepte your person and sir Gawayne, that my lady, quene Gwenyver, ys as trewe a lady unto youre lord as ys ony lady lyvynge unto her lorde, and that woll I make good with my hondis."

The nature of the speech act here is somewhat elusive: Is "I shall ever make a large answer" the same as actually making a "large answer," whatever that might be, or is it simply a hypothetical? And what about the comparative claim? If Lancelot's sampling of other "ladies" consists, as it does for us, of Morgan le Fay, Morgawse, La Beall Isode, and possibly the wives of Sir Marrok and Sir Segwarydes, he might plausibly believe that Guinevere was indeed their equal in fidelity. Finally, after pointing out—quite truly—the many public services that he has done the queen and the falseness of earlier accusations made against her, he reaches his only real affirmation: "take your quene unto youre good grace, for she ys both tru and good." And here, I think, we find an equivocation for which Malory carefully has prepared the way. The well-known passage in which he compares the "olde love" of King Arthur's days, free of "lycoures lustis," with the instability of love "nowadayes" concludes with the assertion "that whyle [Guinevere] lyved she was a trew lover, and therefor she had a good ende" (3:1120). We have been given reason to believe, that is, that Guinevere is indeed "true," although not specifically true to Arthur.

When he delivers the queen to Arthur, Lancelot follows the same pattern, beginning with a hypothetical: "if there be ony knyght, of what degre that ever he be off, except your person, that woll sey or dare say but that she ys trew and clene to you, I here myselff, sir Launcelot du Lake, woll make hit good uppon hys body that she ys a trew lady unto you." Again, his only real assertion is that he will fight. He then calls his accusers liars, which they self-confessedly are—among other things, for not telling Arthur about the affair earlier.[22] His account of the many services he has done the king and Gawain is not only true but also relevant in reaffirming the kind of person he is—a noble knight, not a traitor. We need not make an imaginative leap into the past to accept that the "who" circumstance, emphasized here by his formal self-identification—"I here myselff, sir Launcelot du Lake"—makes a difference. Jurors today, confronted by witnesses who give contradictory versions of an event, are instructed to take into account the characters of the witnesses: Are they the sort of people whose testimony is credible? And we are likely to agree with Bors's somewhat earlier distinction between King Arthur and King Mark, when Lancelot is questioning the wisdom of trusting the king: "ye knowe well that kynge Arthur and kynge Marke were never lyke of condycions, for there was never yet man that ever coude preve kynge Arthure untrew of hys promyse" (3:1173). In its extreme form, in the Inquest of Fame, according to Henry Charles Lea, "the general character of the accused, as found by a jury, was accepted as an indication of the guilt or innocence of the prisoner."[23]

Having established his character, Lancelot gives his account of the fatal ambush: "for I was sente unto my lady, youre quyne, I wote nat for what cause, but I was nat so sone within the chambir dore." This is, of course, evasive. Charged with holding the queen years and winters, he is denying that *on this particular occasion* they were doing anything wrong. Whereas the French Book's Lancelot, entering the queen's chamber, immediately takes off his clothes and jumps into bed, Malory has prepared the way for a plausible denial by introducing another weird contrast between love then and now: "and whether they were abed other at other maner of disportis, me lyste nat thereof make no mencion, for love that tyme was nat as love ys nowadayes" (3:1165). As a result, we have no reason to disbelieve Lancelot's particular claim, though the claim in fact fails to respond to the more general charge that Arthur has made against him.[24] Lancelot's final words, as he delivers the queen, seem to take the form of a vague threat rather than a straightforward truth-claim: "now lat se whatsomever he be in thys place that dare sey the quene ys nat trew unto my lorde Arthur, lat se who woll speke and he dare speke." No one, of course, dares speak.

The poet "nothing affirmeth, and therefore never lieth," writes Sir Philip Sidney, "for, as I take it, to lie is to affirm that to be true which is false."[25] Lancelot affirms very little, and what he does affirm is in some sense true: his accusers are liars (though the accusations may not be lies); the queen is true (as a lover, to Lancelot); on this particular night he may indeed have been innocent of lying with the queen. But he certainly equivocates, and the effect—as, almost certainly, the intent—of his words is to mislead. Do we have reason to believe that Malory might have forgiven a misleading equivocation yet condemned an outright lie?

Evidence that he indeed might have done so comes from two parallel yet largely independent casuistical strands. Albert Jonsen and Stephen Toulmin focus on the first of these, the theologico-philosophical strand that, beginning in the thirteenth century, developed increasingly elaborate theoretical justifications for using misleading words in a good cause. Thus Raymond of Peñafort , last seen distinguishing species of lies, considered that someone harboring an innocent fugitive (in a hypothetical dilemma posed by Augustine) might—if silence and distraction fail—"respond 'in equivocal words.' An ingenious Latin equivocation is suggested: '*non est hic*,' which can mean either 'he is not here' or 'he does not eat here.'"[26] And in the sixteenth century, say Jonsen and Toulmin, "the casuists refined and elaborated the concepts relevant to judgments about telling or concealing the truth; sorting out interpretations they morally could tolerate from those they found unacceptable. They finally formulated a distinction that drew a sharp line between equivocation and mental restriction. The former takes advantage of the fact that linguistic usage permits a phrase to have several legitimate meanings: the speaker merely avoids making it clear which meaning he intends his utterance to have, hoping that his questioner will interpret it in some sense other than he intends."[27] What is crucial here, of course, is the legitimation of misleading words ("for she ys both tru and good," for example) if *in some sense* they can be construed as true.

Although Malory may not strike us as someone likely to while away his time in prison reading Raymond of Peñafort or the *Summa theologica*, these theoretical ideas, as we have noted, were diffused through pastoral manuals dealing with confession. But Malory almost certainly was familiar with the analogous casuistical strand, legal and popular, that Richard Firth Green discusses in a section devoted to "equivocal oaths."[28] Here, among Green's examples, is Lancelot's defense of the queen against the accusations of Meliagaunt, where Meliagaunt's:

> mistaken belief that the man who had left the bloodstains on Guinevere's bedsheets must have been one of the ten wounded knights in her chamber offers her champion Lancelot a chance to plead what customary law would have called a *thwertutnay* and to offer battle on this specific charge: "but as to that I saye nay playnly, that this nyghte there lay none of these

ten wounded knyghtes wyth my lady Quene Gueneuer, and that wil I
preue with my handes, that ye say vntruly in that now."[29]

In general, says Green, "casuistry plainly offered the only possible alternative to perjury for those who, knowing themselves to be guilty, were faced
with having to swear to their innocence"; though the practice made some
(in both law and literature) uneasy, "straightforward verbal equivocation
seems generally to have been regarded as a perfectly legitimate tactic."[30] We
certainly sense that, in Lancelot's battle against Meliagaunt, we are not
meant to hold the misleading intent of the oath against him.

My emphasis so far has been on what might, in a legal prosecution, be regarded as "opportunity": trying to establish that Malory might well have regarded casuistical equivocation as "a perfectly legitimate tactic" to get Lancelot
off the hook. Let us now circle back to the question of motive. What evidence
is there—beyond a more or less unanimous chorus of critics—that Malory
thought that Lancelot needed getting off the hook at all?

Here it might be well to examine yet again, in dutiful medievalist
fashion, some of the changes that Malory made in his sources. In the *Stanzaic Morte Arthur*, as in the French Book, Lancelot's tryst with the queen, before he is ambushed, is clearly not innocent: "To bed he goeth with the
queen, / And there he thought to dwell all night."[31] In both, Lancelot dis-
patches a damsel to deliver his initial disclaimer:

> Et s'il dit que ce est por madame la reine dont l'en li a fet entendant que ge
> li ai fet honte, si li dites que ge sui prez de deffendre encontre un des
> meilleurs chevaliers de la cort que de ceste chose ne sui veraiement encorpez.

> [And if he says that it is for my lady the queen for whom he has heard that
> I have done him shame, then tell him that I am ready to defend against one
> of the best knights of the court that I am not truly guilty of this thing.][32]

The effect of proforma (and secondhand) evasiveness is even stronger in the
English poem, where Lancelot sends the richly clad damsel:

> Hastely in message for to fare
> To the king of mikel might,
> To prove it false—what might he more?—
> But proffers him therefore to fight.[33]

Finally, when the French Lancelot returns the queen to Arthur, he focuses on the disloyalty of those who had wanted to kill her and points out
that, if he were indeed guilty of the mad love of which he has been accused,
he would not be returning her at all, since she could not have been taken by
force: "se ge amasse la reine de fole amour, si com l'en le vos fesoit entendant,
ge ne la vos rendisse des mois et par force n'eussiez vos pas" [If I loved the
queen with mad love, as you have been made to understand, I would not give
her back to you on my own, and you would not be able to get her by force].[34]
The Lancelot of the English poem edges closer to Malory in his assurances:

> Sir, I have thee brought thy queen,
> And saved her life with the right,
> As lady that is fair and sheen,
> And trew is both day and night;
> If any man sayes she is not clene,
> I proffer me therefore to fight.[35]

Here, certainly, we find the kernel of Malory's more full-fledged evasions,
yet the effect is surely different. Neither the French nor the stanzaic
Lancelot is likely to trouble us in the way that Malory's Lancelot does.

Part of the difference, in the English poem, may arise from the way the
formulaic quality of the verse itself ("what might he more," "fair and sheen,"
"day and night") lends a formulaic air to the substance of Lancelot's words:
we sense that he is simply going through the motions. A deeper difference is
that neither of Malory's sources invites us to admire Lancelot as unequivocal-
ly as Malory does. The Lancelot of the *Stanzaic Morte Arthur, pace* Larry Benson, is likely to strike us as little more than a plot function,[36] whose various
self-contradictions result from the various roles he must play in the story.
And the effect of the French Lancelot is nicely summed up by E. Jane Burns:

> Lancelot, on the other hand, does not conform to the single-minded
> purposefulness of this text and his actions remain, as a result, both
> illogical and problematic. Although he is depicted as an adulterer, a
> criminal, and an outlaw, Lancelot is honored throughout the romance by
> the title that later appears on his tombstone: 'LI MIEUDRES CHEVALIERS QUI
> ONQUES ENTRAST EL ROIAUME DE LOGRES.' . . . Within the realistic framework
> of *LA MORT* . . . the paradoxical behavior of Arthur's favorite knight
> appears unpalatable, even absurd.[37]

In neither case, then, would we feel terribly disconcerted at an outright lie, let alone the rather mild evasions that these two Lancelots go in for.

Malory, sensing the same unpalatable absurdity in the French Lancelot that E. Jane Burns does, would seek some way to mitigate it. He admires Lancelot and wants us to admire Lancelot. The healing of Sir Urry serves as a public validation of what we already know: Lancelot is "the beste knyght of the worlde" (3:1146), not simply because he can defeat all other knights at battle or joust but also because, within the constraints of the story, he embodies the central virtues of knighthood. He is a good person. He always tries to do the right thing. Stuck with the basic outline of the story, Malory must figure out some way to make the best of a hopeless situation.

How? He could, of course, have Lancelot take the uncompromising Augustine as his guide and tell the truth, letting the chips fall where they may. We can imagine some such speech as:

> And wyte you well, my lorde, I have holdyn my lady, youre quene, yerys and wynters, and lovede her unmesurably and oute of mesure longe, and oure synne and wyckednes hath brought us unto grete dishonoure. And she and I togydirs have ben false to you and to God, and thys forthynketh me muche.

But the effect of any such speech would clearly be disastrous. If the queen is to be restored, in full honor, to her husband, everyone must agree on the public fiction that the queen is, in fact, innocent of the charges against her, so that Arthur can "take hys quene agayne" (3:1194) and Gawain (for example) can continue to claim, "As for my lady the quene, wyte thou well, I woll never say her shame" (3:1189). The circumstances, then, make straightforward truth an unpalatable option.

But, since Malory could scarcely be unaware that it is a sin to tell a lie, an outright lie—along the lines of "the queen and I are completely innocent of these charges"—would further besmirch the character of Lancelot; and Malory, as we have noted, does not want to besmirch the character of Lancelot. The germ of his solution lay at hand, in the weasely and half-hearted evasions of his sources: first sending the damsel to deliver a kind of proxy denial; then, in effect, saying "Here's the queen, and I'll fight anyone who has bad things to say about her." The fact that he has chosen to expand these evasions into full-fledged speeches—set pieces that, as Ann Dobyns notes, are quite unlike Lancelot's normal discourse[38]—suggests to me that Malory sees in these speeches nothing to taint the nobility of his favorite knight. And this, in turn, as I hope to have indicated, is best explained if we suppose that Malory accepted the casuistical distinction be-tween a lie and an equivocation.

Ladies and gentlemen of the jury, Malory's motive was strong: to ex-onerate his favorite knight. His opportunity was at hand, in the various strands of casuistry that justified misleading equivocation in a good cause. And his means lie before us, in Lancelot's speeches and in the shrewd alterations Malory has made in his sources to prepare the way for those equivocations. No other explanation holds water. I rest my case.

NOTES

1. Thus Lambert, *Malory*, 177: "One's first impulse is to take this as Malory's condemnation of Lancelot through his own words: here is the noblest knight of the world reduced to lying, sophistry, blasphemy."

2. Lambert, *Malory*, 179. There are, of course, dissenters from this usual view. Thus Dobyns ("'Shameful Noyse'") claims, in her close stylistic analysis of the speeches, that Lancelot "clearly lies to those closest to him" and that "the pattern of Lancelot's speeches suggest a condemnation of the chivalric society he represents" (99). This conclusion, it should become clear, likewise strikes me as implausible.

3. McCarthy, *Reading the "Morte Darthur,"* 103.

4. Thomas Malory, *The Morte Darthur: Parts Seven and Eight*, ed. Brewer, 28–29.

5. Benson, *Malory's "Morte Darthur,"* 231.

6. Green, *A Crisis of Truth*, especially 31–40.

7. See Green, *A Crisis of Truth*, 36: "When even the great Frederic Maitland could show himself insensitive to the possibility that for medieval people truth might have 'other referents' ('our ancestors perjured themselves with impunity' [P&M 2:543]), I can hardly expect that this attempt to characterize our distance from the cultural norms of the Middle Ages in terms of the gulf that separated the Turtons and Burtons of British colonialism from their unfortunate subjects will meet with universal acceptance."

8. Lambert, *Malory*, 178–79: "The usefulness of the shame-guilt distinction for an understanding of how Lancelot and other characters behave in *Le Morte Darthur* was first pointed out by Brewer in his edition of Malory's final tales, and his insight is of fundamental importance. It seems to me, in fact, that the distinction is even more basic than Professor Brewer considers it to be. It is Malory himself, not just his characters, for whom honor and shame are more real than innocence and guilt. *Le Morte Darthur* is *of* rather than *about* a shame ethos."

9. Pitt-Rivers, "Honour and Social Status," 19–77. The other essays in his *Honour and Shame* are likewise relevant.

10. Pitt-Rivers, "Honour," 27.

11. Pitt-Rivers, "Honour," 32.

12. Pitt-Rivers, "Honour," 33.

13. Pitt-Rivers, "Honour," 47.

14. Malory, *Works*, ed. Vinaver, 3:1136. All parenthetical in-text Malory citations are to this edition.

15. Thomas Aquinas, *Summa theologica* 1.19, 6, in *Introduction*, ed. Pegis, 204.

16. *Pastors*, ed. Shinners and Dohar, 122.

17. *Pastors*, ed. Shinners and Dohar, 178.

18. Jonsen and Toulmin, *The Abuse of Casuistry*, 116. Malory himself uses this formulation a number of times, as when Lancelot seeks advice on what to do if in fact the queen is condemned to death: "'Then I put thys case unto you,' seyde sir Launcelot, 'that my lorde, kyng Arthure, by evyll conceyle woll tomorne in hys hete put my lady the quene unto the fyre and there to be brente, than, I pray you, counceile me what ys beste for me to do'" (3:1172).

19. It is interesting that Lancelot's intentions should become a central issue here. According to Green, English law traditionally had regarded only the deed itself—in this case, the killing of Gareth—as important: an accidental killing was still a killing. Only in 1470 does Green find "intent" being taken into account (*A Crisis of Truth*, 300–01).

20. Jonsen and Toulmin, *The Abuse of Casuistry*, 197. The authors go on to note that "Each of these kinds of lies, regardless of harm done, remained sinful because the malice of a lie depended not on its consequences but on the very discrepancy between what is in the mind and what is uttered. However, because by the thirteenth century theologians had come to distinguish more clearly between mortal and venial sin, Raymond noted that even if the pernicious lie would always be mortal, dutiful and jocose lies might be venial, depending on the circumstances."

21. McCarthy, *Reading the "Morte Darthur,"* 103.

22. This point is even more explicitly made in one of Malory's sources, the *Stanzaic Morte Arthur*, when Agravain tells Arthur "And we have false and traitours been / That we ne wolde never to you diskere" (*King Arthur's Death*, ed. Benson, lines 1734–35).

23. Lea, *The Duel*, 71, quoting Pike's *History of Crime in England*.

24. Lancelot's sleight-of-hand transmutation of one allegation into another apparently can mislead even an astute modern critic. Thus Harris, "Lancelot's Vocation," claims that "the insistence of these allegations [the allegations that Lancelot has been lying with the queen "many wynters"] has little to do with what is true or false, since Malory has made sure that no one knows with certainty if Lancelot and the queen were 'abed'" (229).

25. Sidney, "The Defence of Poesy," in *Selected Prose and Poetry*, 136.

26. Jonsen and Toulmin, *The Abuse of Casuistry*, 197.

27. Jonsen and Toulmin, *The Abuse of Casuistry*, 201. A modern American reader might recall the quibble over the meaning of the richly ambiguous "is" in the dispute over whether President Clinton was guilty of perjury in testifying about his relationship with Monica Lewinsky.

28. Green, *A Crisis of Truth*, 112–19.

29. Green, *A Crisis of Truth*, 114. The OED defines a "thwertutnay" as "a complete or absolute 'Nay,' a downright 'No'; a flat denial by the defendant of the plaintiff's charge."

30. Green, *A Crisis of Truth*, 113. A kind of analogous equivocation could be invoked to explain why the guilty party sometimes was, in fact, victorious in the "wager of battle." In such cases, according to Lea, "legal casuists assumed a condition of being, guilty in the sight of God, but not in that of man," or "that the unfortunate victim, though not guilty of the special offense charged, suffered in consequence of other sins" (*The Duel*, 136–37).

31. *King Arthur's Death*, ed. Benson, lines 1806–07.

32. *La mort le roi Artu*, ed. Frappier, 140.

33. *King Arthur's Death*, ed. Benson, lines 2050–53.

34. *La mort le roi Artu*, ed. Frappier, 158.

35. *King Arthur's Death*, ed. Benson, lines 2382–87.

36. "The poet's interest in the feelings of his characters humanizes them ... and we feel that Lancelot, Guenevere, and Arthur are real people caught in a real web of tragic circumstance" (*King Arthur's Death*, ed. Benson, xvi).

37. Burns, *Arthurian Fictions*, 160–61.

38. Dobyns, "'Shameful Noyse,'" 92. As was noted earlier, Dobyns takes these deceitful speeches as a sign that Malory is condemning Lancelot and the chivalric society that he represents. This is certainly possible, but (to me) it goes against the assorted ways by which Malory tries to increase our admiration for Lancelot.

WORKS CITED

Benson, Larry. *Malory's "Morte Darthur."* Cambridge, Mass.: Harvard University Press, 1976.

Burns, E. Jane. *Arthurian Fictions: Rereading the Vulgate Cycle.* Columbus: Ohio State University Press, 1985.

Dobyns, Ann. "'Shameful Noyse': Lancelot and the Language of Deceit." *Style* 24 (1990), 89–102.

Green, Richard Firth. *A Crisis of Truth: Literature and Law in Ricardian England.* Philadelphia: University of Pennsylvania Press, 1999.

Harris, E. Kay. "Lancelot's Vocation: Traitor Saint." In *The Lancelot-Grail Cycle: Texts and Transformations*, ed. William W. Kibler, 219–37. Austin: University of Texas Press, 1994.

Introduction to Saint Thomas Aquinas. Ed. Anton C. Pegis. New York: Random House, 1948.

Jonsen, Albert R., and Stephen Toulmin. *The Abuse of Casuistry: A History of Moral Reasoning.* Berkeley: University of California Press, 1988.

King Arthur's Death: The Middle English "Stanzaic Morte Arthur" and "Alliterative Morte Arthure." Ed. Larry Benson. Exeter: Exeter University Press, 1986.

Lambert, Mark. *Malory: Style and Vision in "Le Morte Darthur."* New Haven: Yale University Press, 1975.

La mort le roi Artu. Ed. Jean Frappier. Geneva: Droz, 1964.

Lea, Henry Charles. *The Duel and the Oath.* Ed. Edward Peters. Philadelphia: University of Pennsylvania Press, 1974.

Malory, Thomas. *The Morte Darthur: Parts Seven and Eight.* Ed. D. S. Brewer. Evanston: Northwestern University Press, 1974.

———. *The Works of Sir Thomas Malory.* Ed. Eugene Vinaver, rev. P. J. C. Field. 3 vols. 3rd ed. Oxford: Clarendon; New York: Oxford University Press, 1990.

McCarthy, Terence. *Reading the "Morte Darthur."* Cambridge: D. S. Brewer, 1988.

Piers, Gerhart, and Milton B. Singer. *Shame and Guilt: A Psychoanalytic and a Cultural Study.* Springfield, IL, 1953.

Pitt-Rivers, Julian. "Honour and Social Status." In *Honour and Shame: The Values of Mediterranean Society,* ed. J. G. Peristiany, 19–77. Chicago: University of Chicago Press, 1966.

Shinners, John, and William J. Dohar, eds. *Pastors and the Care of Souls in Medieval England.* Notre Dame: University of Notre Dame Press, 1998.

Sidney, Philip. *Sir Philip Sidney: Selected Prose and Poetry.* Ed. Robert Kimbrough. New York: Holt, Rinehart and Winston, 1969.

Punishing Deviant Speech

"Tongue, you lied"
The Role of the Tongue in Rituals of Public Penance in Late Medieval Scotland

Elizabeth Ewan

In "The Flyting of Dunbar and Kennedy," written around 1500, two Scottish poets, Walter Kennedy and William Dunbar, take turns "flyting" or hurling insults at each other. Kennedy orders his rival Dunbar to come to the market cross of Edinburgh on his knees and confess his crime:

> Cum to the croce on kneis and mak a crya,
> Confesse thy crime, hald Kenydy the king,
> And wyth ane hauthorne scurge thy self and dyng [hit]
> Thus dree [suffer] thy penaunce wyth *deliquisti quia*.

But this is not the end of the poet's punishment—Dunbar's tongue has been at fault, and therefore Kennedy, ironically using his own tongue, insults him:

> Cursit, croapand [croaking] craw, I sall ger crop [have the tip cut off] thy
>   tong
> And thou sall cry *cor mundum* on thy kneis.
> Duerch [dwarf], I sall dyng the quhill thou dryte and dong [hit you until
>   you defecate and drop dung],
> And thou sal lik thy lippis and suere thou leis [swear you lie].[1]

Deliquisti quia was the opening phrase of the priest to a penitent; *Cor mundum*, from Psalm 51:10, was the prayer of the penitent to the priest.[2]

There was, however, more than the sacrament of penance involved here. Priscilla Bawcutt has pointed out that these lines of "The Flyting" have parallels to ritual punishments for slander imposed by the secular courts of Scottish towns in the late Middle Ages.[3] The sixteenth-century poet Richard Maitland makes specific reference to one part of this punishment in his criticism of libelous poets, "Of the Malyce of Poyetis," when he orders them to "Cry toung I leid [lied] throw all yis natioun."[4]

In Dundee on 6 July 1521, the town clerk recorded that Besse Pilgus, wife of David Burn, came to the market cross in the presence of the town magistrates and admitted that she had called James Wichthand a thief, granting her fault openly. Besse then admitted that what she had said was false, "sayd tong, scho leit [she lied]," and asked him forgiveness, agreeing that if she were ever convicted of slandering him in the future, she would be banished from the town.[5] In Aberdeen on 13 November 1528, Wat Saneray, who had said "impertinent language" to Duncan Mar, one of the town magistrates, by accusing him of corruption, was expelled from his office of sergeand. Furthermore, he was ordered to come to the parish church the following Sunday before Mass with a wax candle in his hand and, before the council and good men of the town sitting in the choir, to offer the candle to the high altar and say "Twng, ye leid of the forsaid wordis." Then he was to beseech them to ask Duncan to forgive him for his fault. If he did such a thing again, he would be banished from the town forever.[6]

The formula "tongue, you lied" appeared in ritual punishments for slanderers in at least six pre-Reformation Scottish towns, including Aberdeen, Dundee, Inverness, Linlithgow, Perth, and Stirling. It may have been used elsewhere as well, although the extremely patchy survival of late medieval records for many Scottish towns, unfortunately, makes this impossible to ascertain. In those towns where it was used, it generally was reserved for those cases that were seen as particularly grievous, involving the slander of high-ranking local officials or offences by persistent offenders. While the formula may have been used sparingly by the medieval authorities, however, it appealed to the new Protestant church magistrates. After the Reformation of 1559–60, the medieval formula was adopted by many kirk sessions, the local Church courts, to punish those guilty of defamation.[7] A Church court formulary of 1722 from Aberdeen shows it still being used there in the eighteenth century.[8] In this case, as in many others, a ritual used by the Scottish Reformation Church had its roots in medieval practice.

The use of the formula "tongue, you lied" (or sometimes "false tongue, you lied") appears to have been unique to Scotland. John Webster Spargo, in his short discussion of it, cited two comparable examples, one a town statute from twelfth-century Preston in England and one from sixteenth-century Germany.[9] However, they are not exactly the same. The English example requires those who defame women's sexual reputation to take themselves by the nose and say they lied—this seems to be related to the symbolism of the nose as a sign of sexual activity, rather than to the erring tongue.[10] In Germany, the ritual involved actual physical punishment. The person guilty of defamation was required to publicly hit himself on the mouth, saying "Mouth, since you said those words, you lied." If he refused to do this, the hangman was to stand beside him, condemn him on behalf of the person who had been insulted, and give him a hard blow on the mouth. Hitting oneself on the mouth was also a custom in Sweden.[11]

This essay examines the influences that may have contributed to the shaping of the "tongue, you lied" formula in Scotland. The ritual appears to have been shaped by at least three different sources: the rituals of public penance imposed by the medieval Church; the statutes passed by Scottish towns to preserve public peace, especially by prohibiting disobedience to officials; and the literature of the sins of the tongue that flourished in the later Middle Ages. Language referring to the tongue (or its receptacle, the mouth) suffused all three.

A number of elements of the ritual are familiar to medievalists from aspects of public penance imposed by the western Church throughout Christendom. The Fourth Lateran Council in 1215 made yearly confession to a priest mandatory for all Christians and hence gave a new importance to private penance, but it did not altogether displace earlier customs of public penance.[12] Indeed, public penance continued to be used by Church courts, especially for sins that were seen as an offence to the community as a whole. Defamation, which not only hurt an individual but also fomented discord in the community, was one of these. From 1225, the Scottish Church statutes, which were modeled closely on those of the English and continental churches and, so, reflected similar influences from canon law, included defamation as one of the sins that could incur excommunication. By the fifteenth century, they included "al common sclanderaris" as liable to excommunication.[13]

The punishments imposed by ecclesiastical courts also were adopted by some secular courts. The use of penitential rituals to punish defamation cases can be found in surviving Scottish town court records from the later fifteenth century onwards, although the earliest example yet discovered that specifically uses the "tongue, you lied" formula dates from 1509.[14] Such use of penitential ritual is not surprising when one considers that the town authorities saw the spiritual health of the community to be their responsibility, as well as that of the Church.[15] Defamation endangered the soul of the sinner, but by fomenting tension and anger among the neighbors of a town, it endangered the godliness of the whole community as well. The earliest record of a Scottish town court, a fragment from Aberdeen in 1317, includes a defamation case.[16]

Penance might have been designed initially to secure the salvation of the sinner's soul by bringing him to the necessary contrition required for God's forgiveness, but the publicity of the ritual and the way in which the entire community shared in it, both as audience and as those who forgave the sinner, were beneficial for the rest of the town as well.[17] The sacrament of penance gave people experience confessing their sins on an individual level to their local priest; the public ritual thus spoke to an experience that all should recognize. Confession originally had been mandated by the Church to be made once a year, but by the later Middle Ages more frequent confession had become common. The Scottish writer John Ireland in his "Treatise on Penance and Confession" (ca. 1490) commented that, while people were obliged to confess once a year at Easter, it was better to confess every month and indeed whenever one knew one had committed a deadly sin.[18] This is reflected in the timing of the "tongue, you lied" rituals, which were not confined to Easter but occurred throughout the year.

The public nature of both the sin and the restitution was important. Private sins could be amended by private confession, but public sins, such as publicly destroying someone's reputation, needed to be atoned for before the whole community. Peter of Poitiers in the 1170s wrote that if one sinned against a neighbor, one sinned against God, the Church, and the neighbors, and must do penance to all three, doing penance for the sin against God and the Church and doing satisfaction to the neighbor by asking his forgiveness.[19] The thirteenth-century *Summa Confessorum* of Raymond of Peñafort discussed sins against one's neighbors in its second book, following this with a long section on the Sacrament of Penance in Book Three. Antoninus of Florence (1389–1459) wrote in his *Confessionale (Defecerunt)* that penitents who were unwilling to make full restitution to their victims for loss of reputation or property should not be absolved by priests.[20] Moreover, on a less strictly spiritual side, the sight of the humiliation that the sinner had to undergo acted as a deterrent for others tempted to commit similar sins. The Perth Hammermen guild stated after imposing a public penance on a guild brother who had insulted its deacon in 1547, "This we do for observing and keeping of gud rewle."[21]

Although works of pastoral theology were written primarily for churchmen, the ideas contained in them were disseminated to those responsible for keeping order in the secular world through preaching and devotional literature. Unfortunately, little sermon material survives from medieval Scotland, but there are fragmentary fifteenth-century remains of works of spiritual guidance such as Frere Laurent, *Somme des Vices et de Vertus* (1279) and the mid-fourteenth-century English derivative work *Speculum Vitae*, suggesting that much more once existed.[22] Many Scottish poets also addressed these issues. The "Contemplacioun of Synnaris," a long devotional work written in the later fifteenth century by the Observant Franciscan William of Touris, probably for the Scottish king James IV (1488–1513), became one of the most copied of Middle Scots poems, spreading its influence far beyond the court.[23] Penance and confession were important parts of the work. Dunbar wrote two poems on the practice of confession, "The Maner of Passyng to Confessioun" and "The Tabill of Confession," while penitential formulas such as *Cor mundum* were used not only in "The Flyting of Dunbar and Kennedy" but also in several other flyting poems, including the mid-sixteenth-century "Answer to the King's Flyting" by David Lindsay and the later sixteenth-century "Flyting of Montgomerie and Polwart."[24] The connection between flyting or slander and its punishment by public penance was well established in contemporary literature. Moreover, many of the works of devotional literature were preserved in manuscripts written by Scottish notaries of the fifteenth and sixteenth centuries.[25] Notaries, many of whom served both Church and civil courts, religious and lay clients, acted as a bridge between the sacred and secular worlds.

Public penance usually included certain ritual gestures such as kneeling before one's victim. In her study of thirteenth-century French towns, Mary Mansfield stated that "The imposition of public penance in the cities depended on a well-established common language of gestures of humiliation." Kneeling, however, was also the sign of a penitent at confession before the priest.[26] Most uses of the "tongue, you lied" ritual involved the offender kneeling before the victim. Gestures like this were important because "they gave legal actions a living image." Gestures expressed the movements of the soul (in this case genuine contrition) through the use of the body. "Gestures were considered expressions of the inner movements of the soul, of feelings, of the moral values of individuals."[27] The use of the body to express humility was echoed in the use of the tongue to carry out the three elements required for proper penance: to express contrition, to confess the sin, and to make restitution.

Public penance, as imposed by the Church courts, and some lay courts as well, involved the sinner coming in procession to the local church at the time of high mass, often holding a candle (or sometimes a white wand). There, on his or her knees before the congregation, the penitent confessed the sin and asked forgiveness of God, the Church, the people, and the offended party. The Aberdeen town court form of the rituals, which usually took place in the church at the time of high mass and included offering a candle to the high altar or the altar of the Holy Blood (the altar most associated with the town magistrates), most closely met these requirements. To heighten the humiliation, but also to stress the religious nature of the ritual, the offender was often bare-headed, bare-footed, and dressed in penitential garb. In Scotland, such garb might consist of "sark alane [shift alone]" or of "linen clothes," probably a gown of repentance.[28] In Inverness in 1560 John Abram and his wife Margaret Ogilbe were found guilty of defaming Henry Kar the elder and his wife, calling them "commond theyfis" and the wife "ane rank veche [witch]." They were ordered to pass in "linen clothes" to the four ports of the town, and then to come to the market cross and say "false tung, tha leyd." The humiliation involved is suggested by the fact that they were to choose between this punishment and banishment from the town.[29]

This case was unusual in requiring the offenders to wear penitential clothes outside the church; the only other surviving cases involving both the "tongue, you lied" formula and penitential garb were carried out in the church. Janet Bell of Stirling, who accused Janet Scharp in 1545 of bearing a child to a man other than her husband, was ordered to go in penitent's garb to the church and ask both Janet and her husband forgiveness, saying "Toung, you leid on hir." Agnes Henderson was sentenced to a similar punishment—going to the church, dressed in a sark, with a wax candle in her hand—for defaming Annabell Graham and her mother. She had called Annabell a "friar's get [brat]" and a "friar's yawd [jade]," and insinuated that her mother was a heretic. She was ordered to say to her tongue "You leid that said Annapill Graheme [was a friar's get, etc.]" and to ask both Annabell and her mother forgiveness.[30]

Rituals of public penance were carried out in the church, at the market cross, or sometimes at the place where the offence occurred. To some extent the practice depended on local custom. In Aberdeen, for example, it was common for the town to use the parish church as the site of rituals of forgiveness. The penitent was required to ask the town authorities to intercede with the victim, rather than to ask forgiveness directly; the church seemed the most appropriate place for such intercession to take place. In Inverness, the ritual took place in secular spaces: the market cross, the tolbooth (town hall), or the gates of the town. In Stirling, the site of the ritual apparently depended on the nature of the offending words, reflecting the division of responsibility for "crime" between the secular and religious authorities.

Those accusing others of theft usually were punished at the market cross, while those making accusations of sexual immorality, such as bearing illegitimate children or fornication with priests, were punished in the church.

In many ways, the cross was an especially appropriate place for the ceremony. It symbolized the king's peace, a peace that had been broken by the evil words of the defamer. It was also the heart of secular burgh life and, thus, represented in physical form the community that had been injured. For these reasons, the market cross was a common site of punishment for many crimes, not just defamation. It was also the site at which public proclamations, including announcements of local statutes and acts of parliament, were made, a place where constructive use of the tongue was made to teach citizens the laws under which they should govern their conduct and behavior. The cross was the place where open proclamation of the banishment of those who did not obey these laws was announced. On 22 Oct. 1532, a man and two women were banished from Aberdeen for their demerits, and the assise "ordanit opin proclamatioun to be maid hereof at ye merkat croce."[31] On a more practical level, it represented the one place besides the local church where maximum publicity could be given to the humiliation of the sinner. This was important because "publicity of offence brought both public humiliation and future public accountability."[32]

The use of the tongue to confess the sin and to make restitution was crucial in such rituals. In the poem "The Maner of Pasyng to Confessioun," which, Bawcutt points out, makes use of characteristic late medieval penitential language and imagery, Dunbar instructs the penitent "With thine awin mouth thi synnes thou suld tell."[33] Essentially what was sought was "open penance by the offender and restoration of the plaintiff's reputation."[34] As one Scottish court put it, an offender "for reformation [of his action] was to ask forgiveness [of his victim] and to restore her to her fame."[35] Richard Maitland asked libelous poets to do the same for their victims: "repent ze ralaris [raillers] and restoir / To yame yair fame quhome [whom] ze sklandrit befoir."[36]

The very open nature of the ritual meant that part of the restitution made by the offender for the sin involved public humiliation. The use of public humiliation in Scottish towns can be traced to the collection of statutes known as the *Leges Burgorum* [Laws of the Burghs], which were drawn up between the mid-twelfth and late thirteenth centuries. They were intended as a guide for Scottish towns and seem to have been adopted in whole or in part throughout Scotland.[37] Early public humiliation included being placed on the cuckstool. Burgh laws imposed this punishment on those guilty of brewing offences, who would not pay their fines, and on petty thieves.[38] In 1405 the Aberdeen cuckstool was assigned a new use: someone who had cursed ("maledixerit") the provost, bailies, or other officials of the burgh was sentenced to be placed on the cuckstool and there befouled with mud, dung, eggs, and suchlike.[39] Such punishment perhaps was referred to by Kennedy, who threatened Dunbar: "I sall degrade the, graceles [villain], of thy greis [grace], / Soile the for scorn." The language of soiling recalls the comment of Guillelmus Peraldus in his thirteenth-century *Summa de vitiis* that lying "befouls that part of the body which should be clean, that it makes the liar false,"[40] while the pun on grace and graceless recalls the sacramental nature of penance.

Indeed the connection between contempt for authorities and public humiliation was made in the early burgh laws themselves, and it is here that one of the sources of the later ritual may be found. One law states that if any person "dispersons" or "missays" ("dispersonaverit") the provost in full court, he must, with his friends, deny it "with open mouth ("aperto ore") saying that he lied" in what he said and ask his mercy. He was then to swear on the holy sacrament that he never knew ill of him. If he insulted him again, he would be at the mercy of the alderman and his neighbors, and must make amends to his victim.[41]

Sandy Bardsley recently has drawn attention to the overlap between offenses of disrespect to community officials and the growth of presentments for scolding in England in the later fourteenth and fifteenth centuries,[42] while Anthony Fletcher has shown for the sixteenth century how crucial reputation was to those charged with governing the community. As he points out, men could gain credit if they were seen as concerned for justice, but lose it if gossip criticizing their conduct circulated.[43] Unfortunately, no fourteenth-century town records and too few fifteenth-century ones survive for Scotland to demonstrate that there was a similar development there. However, from other sources it does appear that there was some connection between attempts to control such disobedience and attempts to deal with other cases of ungoverned speech.

As seen above, the earliest statute that resembles the "tongue, you lied" ritual was concerned with verbal disobedience to the alderman, the head of the town government, in a specific place (the town court), where the leading members of the community would be gathered together. This concern with disrespect to those in authority was later broadened beyond the court. From the early fourteenth century, the king's chamberlain, who conducted a yearly ayre in each royal burgh, was to enquire if any one had dispersoned [abused] the bailie in court or outside it. By the later fourteenth century, he was to enquire if anyone had dispersoned the bailie or sergeands in doing their office or impeded them in their carrying out the law. It may not be coincidental that the chamberlain was also to enquire if there were any common slanderers ("scandalizatores communes") in the burgh; by the later fourteenth century, they were grouped together as slanderers, rebellers, or walkers on the night ("defamatores vel rebelles siue noctiuagi") and placed in the same chapter as those dispersoning the bailies.[44]

The connection of slander and disobedience to officials is found in several of the cases where the "tongue, you lied" formula or a variation was used. In 1552, David Stewart of Dundee, who had insulted the town magistrates, was ordered to ask the provost's, bailies', and council's forgiveness and to "refrane his twng fra sic [such] sayingis in tyme cumming."[45] Ewan Talyeour, who insulted the town officers of Inverness, was ordered first to stand in the govis [pillory] on Palm Sunday, where he would be seen by the congregation attending church, and then to come to the stair of the tolbooth, site of town government, to make his apology. In the year after the Reformation in Inverness, John Morison, who had slandered the minister, had to apologize twice: once at the market cross, perhaps because he had slandered him in the open street; and again on a Church holy day.[46] Some cases even involved disputes between officials. The Aberdeen case of 1528 involved Wat Saneray, a sergeand, insulting Duncan Mar, a bailie.

The early law on disobedience to the alderman cited above states that the defendant is to deny his slander "with open mouth," perhaps foreshadowing the later ritual rebuking of the tongue. Punishment of the tongue in this way fit into widespread medieval ideas about the sins of the tongue. From 1215 on, pastoral manuals and treatises proliferated to help priests deal with their parishioners' confessions by setting out the sins into which they could fall. "Sins of the tongue" were sometimes counted as part of the Seven Cardinal Sins, at other times given space of their own. Peraldus devoted twenty-four chapters of his *Summa de vitiis*, written in the 1230s, to specific sins of the tongue. Such works were known widely throughout Europe and influenced pastoral literature for three centuries;[47] the ideas they set forth were well-known to Scottish clergy. "Ratis Raving," a fifteenth-century advice poem in Scots that also discussed the seven sins, makes reference to such pastoral books,[48] although unfortunately few Scottish examples have survived. However, early inventories of Scottish libraries indicate that the works of Peraldus and others such as Angelus de Clavasio, Antoninus of Florence, John Mirk, and the anonymous author of the late fourteenth- or early fifteenth-century English *Manual for Parish Priests,* were to be found in several churchmen's collections of books.[49] In Scottish literature itself, the seven deadly sins were described in Ireland's treatise on penance and confession, in Dunbar's two confession poems, and also in his poem on the dance of the seven deadly sins.[50] By the late fourteenth and fifteenth centuries, the discourse on "sins of the tongue" had become popularized in sermon treatises, ballads, poetry, and illustrations. The mystery plays that flourished in England (and also in Scotland, although only brief mentions of such performances survive) from the late fourteenth century until the Reformation often included sins of the mouth.[51]

The importance of exercising control over the tongue was stressed in several Scots didactic works of the later Middle Ages. The author of "Ratis Raving" has quite a bit to say about the tongue and the need to control it: "Fore-thi, my sone, quhill [while] thow art zonge / With wordis of lawte [good faith] vs thi twnge." A marginal note in the manuscript, "nota de lingua," at the beginning of this discussion draws attention to the advice offered on the proper use of the tongue. The narrator of the fifteenth-century "Consail and Teiching at the Vys Man Gaif His Sone" warned "And ever be mastyr of thi twnge," while "A Dietary," a Scots translation thought to be based on a Lydgate poem, advised the reader to be "Closs of toung, of word nocht dissavable." A poem sometimes ascribed to James I (1394–1437), but probably of the later fifteenth century, included the advice "Sen word is thrall, and thocht is only fre / Thou dant [subdue] thy toung, that power hed and may."[52] An anonymous poem written before 1534 commented "quha [who] rewlis weill his toung he may be comptit wyiss."[53] In the middle of the sixteenth century, Richard Maitland counseled his son that if he wanted to do well in court, he should "to thy tung tak tent [pay heed]." If a poem of 1572, "Aganis sklandrous tovngis," is indeed by Chancellor John Maitland of Thirlestane, it appears that at least one of Maitland's sons paid attention to his father's advice.[54] The public ritual seemed designed to underline this lesson, by forcing the sinner to rebuke, and, thus, enforce his control over, his own tongue.

The idea of punishing the instrument that had caused the harm was echoed in another ritual of punishment imposed on those who had broken the peace of the community. Bloodshed often was punished with a fine, but sometimes with public penance. However, an extra element could be added. In 1492, Philip Whitehead of Aberdeen, who had "strubled" [troubled] Thomas Bard, was ordered to come to mass and bring his knife, drawn and carried by the point, and to offer it to his victim.[55] In some cases, the sword was then "to be put vp in ye tolbouth in ane yrne [iron] staple in example of otheris."[56] In this way, the sword or other weapon was brought under control and rendered incapable of doing further harm.

Could the same thing be done with the tongue, which was often described as or compared to a sword or other weapon in contemporary literature and proverbs?[57] Thomas Rolland in his translation of *The Seven Sages* (ca. 1560) cited a common saying, "The wyse man sayis thair toungis are schairp / As ony sword is wrocht with hand."[58] Robert Henryson, in "The Paddok and the Mouse" from his version of Aesop's fables, compared the tongue to an arrow: "Ane silkin toung, ane hart of crueltie, / Smytis more sore than ony schot of arrow." In his poem "Against Hasty Credence," speaking of the backbiter who hid "ane bludy tung," Henryson pointed out that "Thre personis several he slays with ane wowrd—/ him self, the heirar, and the man saiklace [innocent]."[59] Indeed, the tongue could be worse than the sword for its thrusts went to the soul; as another proverb pointed out, "Wordis more then swordis the inward heart do wound."[60]

But the tongue might be less easy to bring under control than the sword. In the thirteenth century, Peraldus had described the tongue as "a directionless organ driven to loquacity by its natural energy"; moreover, "it is moist and slippery and so falls easily." The difficulty of controlling it was emphasized in medieval writings, reflecting Scripture, especially James 3:7, 8: "the tongue no man can tame, an unquiet evil, full of poison."[61] In "Against Hasty Credence" Henryson accused the "wicket tung, sawand [sowing] dissentioun" of being "Moir perrellus than ony fell pusoun." Reflecting the influence of Psalms 140:3 ("They have sharpened their tongues like a serpent: the venom of asps is under their lips"—Douay), the tongue was sometimes compared to an eel, or to a serpent. Dunbar, in "The Flyting," criticized Kennedy's "serpentis tung." A Scottish proverb even applied this characterization to the owner of the lying tongue himself: "He that a grip of him hes halds a slidderie eill be the taill."[62] What was needed was for the individual to control the slippery eel and thus himself.

One way in which to try to enforce control of the tongue was to treat it as separate from the sinner.[63] In this way the sinner could be ordered to control it. When David Stewart spoke "curious words" (presumably insults) to the Dundee officers who accused him of unlawful trading in 1552, he was ordered to ask their forgiveness and "to refrane his twng fra sic sayingis in tyme cumming."[64] In Dumfries in 1523, two men who had insulted each other were ordered that neither of them were to make any provocation "by their tongues" under penalty of 8s. In Linlithgow in 1532 two cases of "troublance" were described as "troublance by his tongue." In Elgin, Cristian Sutherland was accused of abandoning her tongue "to lous renyeis [loose reins]," while Margaret Innes was ordered "that scho sall kepe hir townge clos from bakbytting slanderinge and flytting aganis ony within this toun."[65]

Moreover, the sinner did this through speech, thus emphasizing the fact that God honored humans by giving them a tongue for the use of speech. Speech was the organ of reason; by using it as such, the sinner was restoring the positive power of speech and returning the tongue to the use that God had intended for it.[66] As one late fifteenth-century Scottish poet put it, quoting Proverbs 18:21, "lyf and ded lyis in the twnge."[67] This proverb was glossed by one pastoral writer as "Death and life in the hands of the tongue: death because the tongue which lies slays the soul, life because by the mouth may come conversion to salvation."[68] A Scottish version of this proverb emphasized the first part: "The mouth that lyes, slayes the soul."[69] But the ritual of public penance, which imposed control over the tongue, could bring about salvation, both to the sinner and to the community where discord had been fomented by the slander.

The poet Kennedy's desire that his rival Dunbar flog himself reflects the penitential practice of self-flagellation, but towns might also impose other punishments on those guilty of defamation. In 1521 Janet Crag of Dundee, who had "mispersoned" Will Gibson's wife, was not only to pass to the market cross and "sa tong, scho leit" but also was to carry "the beads" about her neck and pass with them about the town. These "tolbooth beads" (as they were called in another case) were apparently a heavy chain that symbolized a rosary.[70] In 1545 Janet Blakadir of Stirling, who called Janet Bell "ane notable theiff and huir" and also accused her of assisting her husband in a theft, was ordered to stand in irons (probably the iron collar known as the jougs) and then to pass to the place where she said the "evil words," to kneel, to ask Janet Bell's forgiveness, and to say "tong, scho leid."[71]

In most cases where the formula was used, however, there was no additional corporal punishment. In this respect, rebuking the tongue that had committed the sin was perhaps a substitute for harsher physical penalties against the erring organ. The closest equivalent seems to be when Ewyn Talyeour of Inverness, who had insulted a bailie and two other officers, as well as hitting them, was ordered to say "Fals tong, yow led," *taking it in his hand.*[72] This more physical restraining of the tongue seems to have appealed to authorities in Reformation Scotland: in St. Andrews, both kirk and town authorities after 1560 sometimes ordered offenders to take themselves by the tongue.[73]

In a study of similar public rituals in Puritan New England, Jane Kamensky has argued that "One of the virtues of public apology, then, was that it created a perfect equilibrium between punishment and crime." Through a public apology, the offenders "could harness the power of words in the service of their victims, effectively undoing ungoverned speech by applying its opposite."[74] Indeed fifteenth- and early sixteenth-century Scottish town records ascribe this power of correcting sin to the tongue when they say that defendants admitted their guilt to the charge "by his (or her) own tongue grant."[75] Sins of the tongue were to be remedied by the tongue.

This remedy often included other words. One practice, which seems rather strange in modern eyes, was the practice of repeating the injurious words publicly, in effect "unsaying them." Thus Agnes Henderson of Stirling was ordered to pass to the church on Sunday with a wax candle and in front of her victims, a mother and daughter, to say to her tongue, "You leid that said Annapill Graheme wes ane freiris get [brat] and freiris yawde [jade] and ger [make] the moder cum to me and I sall tell hir how scho brynt hir faggald."[76] (To burn a faggot meant to recant heresy.) The tongue that had pronounced the words now was used to pull them back. It was also important to undo the effect of the words; as the Stirling authorities put it in 1545 when Patrick Lundy called Effame Douglas a "thief," he was to ask her forgiveness and "restore her to her fame."[77] In penance rituals where the "tongue, you lied" formula was not used, the offender often was required to say of the victim, "I know nothing of her/him but loyalty and honesty." In Elgin, for example, which appears not to have used the tongue formula at all, when Margaret Hay said that Margaret Balfour was a whore and a witch and that she rode widdershins (moving counter-clockwise in an attempt to bring misfortune) about men's houses wearing only her sark and her hair above her eyes for witchcraft, she was ordered to make a solemn oath "that she knows not but good & honesty to the said Margaret Balfour."[78] A study of post-Reformation kirk sessions shows that this formula was used in almost every parish. When the tongue ritual was taken over by kirk sessions after 1560, sometimes both formulae were used at once.[79]

This essay has traced some of the influences that contributed to the development of the "tongue, you lied" ritual in Scotland; one question still unanswered is why the ritual appeared when it did. Priscilla Bawcutt, commenting on the line "And thou sal lik thy lippis and suere thou leis" in "The Flyting" (l. 396), suggested it alluded to the use of the "tongue, you lied" formula in Scottish towns.[80] This implies that the practice was contemporary with the poem and would be well known to the audience. Because so many town records from before the sixteenth century have been lost, including those of Edinburgh with which Dunbar probably would have been most familiar, this suggestion certainly has merit. However, it is interesting that in the only run of urban records that survives in its entirety from the early fifteenth century, the first appearance of the ritual comes in 1509. Could there be a closer link here between literature and local legal practice?

In the town of Aberdeen, in April 1509, three fishermen were convicted of "great offence and troublance" to the burgess John Arthur. They all were sentenced to be put in the pillory and to remain there as long as Arthur willed. On the following Sunday they were to come to the church at the time of high mass—barefoot, bareheaded, and barelegged—and ask Arthur's forgiveness on their knees. And they were to say, "toung yai leid quhar [where] yai said he was ane theif. And allege & declair yt yai war drunkin." They were then to beseech the town magistrates, the provost, bailies, and council to make instance to Arthur to forgive them.[81] Could it be coincidence that Dunbar's "Flyting" was first published one year earlier, in April 1508? Dunbar's poems certainly were known in Aberdeen. Indeed, the earliest surviving manuscripts of two of his poems are preserved, probably by a notary, in the Aberdeen Burgh Sasine Register, a register of property transactions, of 1503–07.[82] Moreover, the Chepman and Myller print, which circulated from 1508, is incomplete, with the poem starting from line 316, so the relevant lines (325–29, 393–96) are near the beginning of the poem.[83] If the earlier part of the poem is consulted, the phrase "lik thy lippis," coming after the threat to cause Dunbar to defecate, might be seen as a response to Dunbar's earlier insult to Kennedy: that any sounds he makes come not through "goldin lippis" but from his "giltin hippis."[84] However, standing apart from the earlier flyting, could the phrase perhaps have suggested a new form of apology that could be put to use by the Aberdeen authorities?

Whatever its origins, however, the ritual never became well-established. In many towns it does not appear at all in the surviving records from this period. In those towns where it was used, it seems to have enjoyed short bursts of popularity with the authorities, then to have faded from view. In Dundee it was used in the early 1520s, in Stirling and Perth in the 1540s, in Inverness in the late 1550s. In Linlithgow it was apparently used only once, when a royal official was insulted, while in Aberdeen it was used only sporadically. By the mid-sixteenth century, even as the ritual was still in use in certain towns, secular authorities, both central and local, were looking for new ways to control the tongue. In 1546 Marion Ray of Stirling was in trouble for slandering not only Agnes Henderson but also her husband and her reputed lover. She was ordered to kneel before Agnes and the alleged lover and to ask their forgiveness and say "Toung, you leid on thaim"; then she was to remain in the tolbooth until the "clasps and cavill of iron devised before" were ready and could be locked on her for twenty-four hours.[85] The "clasps of iron" appears to be the first recorded reference to the branks or scold's bridle, an iron cage that was placed around the head. The council earlier had considered having such an instrument made, but this was the first time that it was to be used. The connection between the ritual and the branks was made even clearer in Perth on 4 July 1549. Margaret Randy and Christine Galloway were convicted of injuring Thomas Tuly and his wife with "mony inurious wourdis" and were ordered to kneel down in the place where the words had been said and ask forgiveness of Thomas's wife. Margaret was to say "toung, she leid." If they committed such a fault again, they were to pass about the town with the branks in their mouths.[86] In the later sixteenth century, the branks would become increasingly common as a punishment for both women and men for sins of the tongue.[87]

In "The Flyting," Kennedy had threatened Dunbar that he would order the tip of his tongue cut off. This may have reflected popular beliefs about the punishments suffered in purgatory—a common image of purgatory was of a place where tongues and lips of backbiters and liars were sliced away. Lines 315–20 of the poem refer directly to purgatory and the masses to be said for the soul to shorten one's time there.[88] There is no evidence for mutilation of the tongue in medieval Scotland, although corporal punishment could include the mutilation of other parts of the body: for example, ears were clipped or nailed to the public weighbeam so their owners had to rip them free, shoulders and cheeks might be branded with hot irons, hands of thieves and corrupt notaries were sometimes struck through. Often the mutilation was appropriate to the crime: for example, there are at least three examples from the period of men who had forged signatures or documents having their right hands struck off.[89]

In the early sixteenth century, the town authorities were content with merely having the guilty party chastise his or her tongue. This began to change, however, in the mid-sixteenth century. While the branks began to be used in local courts, there was also a move at the highest levels of the justice system towards more rigorous punishments of this erring member. Perhaps as a result of the rising religious and political tensions of the 1550s as Scotland was torn between French and English and Catholic and Protestant factions, the authorities increasingly became concerned about wrongful speech. This concern was noted by contemporaries such as David

Lindsay. When Pauper, a character in David Lindsay's play *Ane Satyre of the Thrie Estaitis* (first performed in 1552), speaks ill of a priest, he is warned "Hald thy toung, man, . . . Speak thou of preists, but [without] doubt thou will be hangit!"[90] In 1555 Parliament passed an act that decreed that those guilty of bearing false witness should be punished "be peirsing of thair toungis."[91] Although such a punishment was rarely inflicted, the fact that such legislation was enacted was a sign of increasing concern at the highest levels with the sins of the tongue.

NOTES

1. Dunbar, *Poems,* ed. Bawcutt, 1:200–18, lines 325–29, 393–96. See discussion of the date of this poem in ibid, 2:429.

2. Dunbar, *Poems,* ed. Bawcutt, 2:429. Dunbar also wrote an entire poem on "The Maner of Passying to Confessioun." See below for discussion of this work.

3. Bawcutt, "Art of Flyting," 9.

4. Maitland, "Of the Malyce of Poyetis," in *Maitland Folio Manuscript,* ed. Craigie, 1:325–26, line 23. Also cited in Bawcutt, "Art of Flyting," 9.

5. Dundee, Book of the Church, fol. 39v. Despite the title of this manuscript, it is mainly a record of the proceedings of the Dundee town court.

6. Aberdeen, Aberdeen Council Registers, 12:448.

7. For example, *Register of the Ministers of St. Andrews,* ed. Fleming, 1:441 (1579); *Selections from the Kirk Session of Aberdeen,* ed. Stuart, 70–73 (1609). See discussion in Todd, *Culture of Protestantism,* 251.

8. *Aberdeen Style Book, 1722,* ed. Meston and Forte, no. 182: "Ane sumonds for injures." This borrowing is a good example of the type of interaction that has been found for sixteenth-century England by Helmholz, *Canon Law,* 8–11.

9. Spargo, *Juridical Folklore,* 78–84.

10. *Borough Customs,* ed. Bataeson, 1:78. For the sexual symbolism of the nose, see Groebner, "Losing Face, Saving Face."

11. *Deutsche Rechtsaltertumer,* ed. Grimm, 2:301–02.

12. Mansfield, *Humiliation of Sinners,* 52.

13. *Statutes of the Scottish Church,* ed. Patrick, 4, 6, 74.

14. Aberdeen Council Registers, 8:949–50. Earlier public penance rituals include Aberdeen Council Registers, 5:364 (1459), 5:485 (1463).

15. Fitch, "Religious Community," 115–16.

16. *Early Records of Aberdeen,* ed. Dickinson, 8.

17. Braswell, *Medieval Sinner,* 33–34; Mansfield, *Humiliation of Sinners,* 99–100, 130.

18. Ireland, "Treatise on Penance," in *Asloan Manuscript,* ed. Craigie, 1:9,19. Such stress on more frequent confession was common in late medieval Europe (Duffy, *Stripping of the Altars,* 60).

19. Mansfield, *Humiliation of Sinners,* 41–42, 90.

20. Tentler, *Sin and Confession,* 31–32, 39, 342.

21. *Perth Hammermen Book,* 62.

22. Saldanha, "The Thewis of Gudwomen," 288–91.

23. MacDonald, "Catholic Devotion," 69–74.

24. "The Answer quhilk Schir David Lyndesay maid to the Kingis Flyting," in David Lindsay, *Poetical Works,* ed. Laing, 1:105–07, line 20; "The Flyting of Montgomerie and Polwart," in *Poems of Montgomerie,* ed. Parkinson, 1, no. 99, line 11.

25. Van Buren, "John Asloan," 15–24. I am grateful to Priscilla Bawcutt for her insights on Scottish notaries and their role in late medieval literature.

26. Mansfield, *Humiliation of Sinners,* 262. For images of penitents kneeling, see Duffy, *Stripping of the Altars,* plates 19, 20.

27. Schmitt, "Rationale of Gestures," 60–64. For the continuation of the importance of gesture after the Reformation, see Todd, *Culture of Protestantism,* 251–53.

28. For example, Dundee, Book of the Church, fol. 157r. Such a gown from the seventeenth century can be seen in the National Museum of Scotland (Johnston, "Jonet Gothskirk," 89–94).

29. *Records of Inverness,* ed. MacKay and Boyd, 1:40.

30. *Extracts from Stirling,* ed. Renwick, 1:47–48, 40–41.

31. Aberdeen Council Registers, 14:32.

32. Todd, *Culture of Protestantism,* 250.

33. "The Maner of Passyng," in Dunbar, *Poems,* ed. Bawcutt, 1:136–38, line 50. See Bawcutt's discussion in ibid., 2:374–75.

34. *Select Cases on Defamation,* ed. Helmholz, xxv–vi, xl.

35. Stirling, B66/15/2, fol. 12v (10 July 1545).

36. Maitland, "Of the Malyce of Poyetis," in *Maitland Folio Manuscript,* ed. Craigie.

37. *Ancient Laws and Customs,* ed. Innes. The laws are ascribed to David I (1124–53), but many are later than this. Copies were included in many town court books, and they were translated into Scots from the mid-fifteenth century onwards.

38. *Leges Burgorum,* no. 63, and *Fragmenta Collecta,* no. 39, in *Ancient Laws and Customs,* ed. Innes.

39. *Early Records of Aberdeen,* ed. Dickinson, 217.

40. Dunbar, "Flyting," in Dunbar, *Poems,* ed. Bawcutt, 1:200–18, lines 397–98; *Summa* as cited in Craun, *Lies,* 59.

41. *Leges Burgorum,* no. 100, in *Ancient Laws and Customs,* ed. Innes.

42. Bardsley, "Sin, Speech and Scolding," 145–64.

43. Fletcher, "Honour, Reputation and Local Officeholding," 92.

44. *Articuli Inquirendi,* nos. 8, 26, and *Iter Camerarii,* no. 28, both in *Ancient Laws and Customs,* ed. Innes.

45. Dundee, Dundee Burgh Court, 3:186v.

46. *Records of Inverness,* ed. MacKay and Boyd, 1:43, 58–59.

47. Craun, *Lies,* 10–22. For the influence of such works in the early sixteenth century, see Tentler, *Sin and Confession,* ch. 2; and Duffy, *Stripping of the Altars,* 54–59.

48. "Ratis Raving," in *Ratis Raving,* ed. Girvan, lines 1568–81. The poet suggests reading the "buk of confessione" to learn about the seven deadly sins.

49. Durkan and Ross, *Early Scottish Libraries,* lists several of the works discussed in Tentler, *Sin and Confession,* ch. 2. This work only includes printed books, however. Probably many more existed in manuscript. See Bawcutt, 'English Books and Scottish Readers" 1–4, which discusses survivals of works by John Mirk and *Speculum Vitae.*

50. "Off Februar the fyiftene nycht," in Dunbar, *Poems,* ed. Bawcutt, 1:149–56. See discussion in ibid., 2:385–88.

51. Bardsley, "Sin, Speech and Scolding," 146–49; McIntosh, *Controlling Misbehavior,* 196–97; Forest-Hill, "Sins of the Mouth," 11–13.

52. "Ratis Raving," lines 1046–72, 1072–73, and 1046, and "Consail and Teiching," line 3336, both in *Ratis Raving,* ed. Girvan, 66–79; "A Dietary," in *The Bruce,* ed. Skeat, 2:215–18, line 23; "Balade Attributed to James I of Scotland," in *Ratis Raving,* ed. Girvan, 176, lines 15–16.

53. Whiting, "Proverbs, Part Two," 143.

54. "The Laird of Lethingtounis Counsale to His Sone Beand in the Court," in *Maitland Folio Manuscript,* ed. Craigie, 1:21, line 4. For discussion of authorship of "Aganis sklandrous tovngis" see Mapstone, "Introduction," n. 39.

55. *Extracts from Council Register of Aberdeen,* ed. Stuart, 1:421–22. See also Dundee, Book of the Church, fol. 76r.

56. Dundee, Dundee Burgh Court, 3:82v (1551).

57. Sheneman, "Tongue as a Sword," 396–98.

58. Cited in Whiting, "Proverbs, Part Two," 137.

59. Henryson, "Aesop's Tales," in *Poems,* ed. Fox, 108, lines 2922–23; Henryson, "Against Hasty Credence," in *Poems,* ed. Fox, 165. See discussion by Denton Fox in Henryson, *Poems,* ed. Fox, 333–449.

60. *Fergusson's Scottish Proverbs,* ed. Beveridge, 123. This collection was compiled in the second half of the sixteenth century, ibid., ix–x.

61. Cited in Craun, *Lies,* 49, 26–27.

62. Henryson, "Against Hasty Credence," in *Poems,* ed. Fox, lines 41, 43; Dunbar, "Flyting," in Dunbar, *Poems,* ed. Bawcutt, 1:200–18, line 75; *Fergusson's Scottish Proverbs,* ed. Beveridge, 56.

63. Penitential practice would often prescribe punishment of the erring member of the body (Bawcutt, *Dunbar the Makar,* 224).

64. Dundee, Dundee Burgh Court, 3:186v.

65. Dumfries, Dumfries Burgh Court, 1:50v; Edinburgh, Linlithgow Burgh Court, B48/7/1, 69, 72; *Records of Elgin,* ed. Cramond, 2:24, 10.

66. Craun, *Lies,* 28–29, 50. Reason is discussed immediately after a section on the mastery of the tongue in "Consail and Teiching," in *Ratis Raving,* ed. Girvan, lines 3534–48.

67. "Consail and Teiching," line 3434.

68. Cited in Craun, *Lies*, 72.

69. *Ferguson's Scottish Proverbs*, ed. Beveridge, 96.

70. Dundee, Book of the Church, fol. 44r. Maxwell, *Old Dundee*, 346. For English examples of "rosaries," see *Select Cases on Defamation*, ed. Helmholz, nos. 24, 29.

71. *Extracts from Stirling*, ed. Renwick, 1:39.

72. *Records of Inverness*, ed. MacKay and Boyd, 1:43.

73. *Register of the Minister of St. Andrews*, ed. Fleming, 1:441 (1579); St. Andrews, B65/18/1 (3 June 1589).

74. Kamensky, *Governing the Tongue*, 132, 128. Mansfield argues, however, that rituals of public penance, by imposing public humiliation on the offender, were less restorative to the community than some historians have suggested (Mansfield, *Humiliation of Sinners*, 11, 265–66, 290).

75. For example, Aberdeen Council Registers, 12:98, 438.

76. *Extracts from Stirling*, ed. Renwick, 1:41–42.

77. Stirling, B66/15/2, fol. 12v (10 July 1545).

78. *Records of Elgin*, ed. Cramond, 1:84.

79. Todd, *Culture of Protestantism*, 251. The 1722 Aberdeen Commissary Court ritual used both phrases.

80. Bawcutt, *Dunbar the Makar*, 224.

81. Aberdeen Council Registers, 8:949–50.

82. Dunbar, *Poems*, ed. Bawcutt, 1:5, 2:320, 410.

83. Van Buren, "Chepman and Myllar Texts of Dunbar," 27.

84. Dunbar, "Flyting," in Dunbar, *Poems*, ed. Bawcutt, 1:200–18, lines 97, 99; see discussion of this insult in Fisher, "Contemporary Humour," 12.

85. *Extracts from Stirling*, ed. Renwick, 1:43.

86. Perth, B59/12/3, fol. 167r. I am indebted to Mary Verschuur for this reference.

87. Harrison, "Women and the Branks in Stirling," 114–31.

88. Dunbar, *Poems*, ed. Bawcutt, 2:440. For images of purgatory, see Duffy, *Stripping of the Altars*, 339.

89. Walker, *Legal History of Scotland*, 441.

90. Lindsay, *Ane Satyre*, ed. Lyall, lines 2035–36.

91. *Acts of Parliaments of Scotland*, ed. Thomson, 2:497, c 22.

Works Cited

Manuscript Sources

Aberdeen, Aberdeen City Archives, Aberdeen Council Registers (microfilm, University of Guelph Library).

Dumfries, Dumfries City Archives, Dumfries Burgh Court Books (microfilm, University of Guelph Library).

Dundee, Dundee City Archives, Book of the Church, Dundee Burgh Court Books.

Edinburgh, Linlithgow Burgh Court, National Archives of Scotland, B48/71/2.
Perth, Perth Museum and Library, B59/12/3.
St. Andrews, St. Andrews University Library, B65/18/1.
Stirling, Stirling Council Archives, B66/15/2.

PRIMARY SOURCES

The Aberdeen Style Book, 1722. Ed. M. C. Meston and A. D. M. Forte. Edinburgh:
    Stair Society, 2000.
Acts of the Parliaments of Scotland. Ed. T. Thomson et al. 11 vols. Edinburgh: HM
    General Register House, 1814–44.
Ancient Laws and Customs of the Burghs of Scotland 1124–1424. Ed. Cosmo Innes.
    Edinburgh: Scottish Burgh Records Society, 1868.
The Asloan Manuscript. Ed. W. A. Craigie. 2 vols. Edinburgh: Scottish Text Society,
    1923.
Borough Customs. Ed. Mary Bateson. 2 vols. London: Selden Society, 1904.
The Bruce. Ed. Walter W. Skeat. 2 vols. Edinburgh: Scottish Text Society, 1894.
Deutsche Rechtsaltertumer. Ed. Jacob Grimm. 2 vols. 1899; repr. Darmstadt: Wissen-
    schaftliche Buchgesellschaft, 1965.
Dunbar, William. *The Poems of William Dunbar.* Ed. Priscilla Bawcutt. 2 vols.
    Glasgow: Association for Scottish Literary Studies, 1998.
Early Records of Aberdeen. Ed. W. C. Dickinson. Edinburgh: Scottish History Society,
    1957.
Extracts from the Council Register of the Burgh of Aberdeen. Ed. John Stuart. 2 vols.
    Aberdeen: Spalding Club, 1844–48.
Extracts from the Records of the Royal Burgh of Stirling. Ed. R. Renwick. 2 vols. Edin-
    burgh: Scottish Burgh Records Society, 1887–89.
Fergusson's Scottish Proverbs from the Original Print of 1641. Ed. E. Beveridge.
    Edinburgh: Scottish Text Society, 1924.
Henryson, Robert. *Poems.* Ed. Denton Fox. Oxford: Clarendon, 1981.
Lindsay, David. *Ane Satyre of the Thrie Estaitis.* Ed. R. Lyall. Edinburgh: Canongate,
    1987.
———. *Poetical Works.* 3 vols. Ed. D. Laing. Edinburgh: William Paterson, 1879.
The Maitland Folio Manuscript. Ed. W. A. Craigie. 2 vols. Edinburgh: Scottish Text
    Society, 1919.
Montgomerie, Alexander. *The Poems of Montgomerie.* Ed. D. Parkinson. 2 vols.
    Edinburgh: Scottish Text Society, 2000.
The Perth Hammermen Book 1518 to 1568. Perth: Perth Hammermen Incorporation,
    1889.
Ratis Raving and Other Early Scots Poems on Morals. Ed. R. Girvan. Edinburgh:
    Scottish Text Society, 1939.
Records of Elgin. Ed. W. Cramond. 2 vols. Aberdeen: New Spalding Club, 1903–07.
Records of Inverness. Ed W. MacKay and H. C. Boyd. 2 vols. Aberdeen: New Spalding
    Club, 1911–24.

Register of the Minister, Elders and Deacons of the Christian Congregation of St. Andrews. Ed. D. Hay Fleming. 2 vols. Edinburgh: Scottish History Society, 1889–90.

Select Cases on Defamation to 1600. Ed. Richard Helmholz. London: Selden Society, 1985.

Selections from the Records of the Kirk Session, Presbytery and Synod of Aberdeen. Ed. John Stuart. Aberdeen: Spalding Club, 1848.

Statutes of the Scottish Church 1225–1559. Ed. D. Patrick. Edinburgh: Scottish History Society, 1907.

———. "Proverbs and Proverbial Sayings from Scottish Writings before 1600, Part Two, M-Y." *Mediaeval Studies* 13 (1951), 87–164.

Secondary Sources

Bardsley, Sandy. "Sin, Speech and Scolding in Later Medieval England." In *"Fama": The Politics of Talk and Reputation in Medieval Europe,* ed. Thelma Fenster and Daniel Smail, 145–64. Ithaca: Cornell University Press, 2003.

Bawcutt, P. "The Art of Flyting." *Scottish Literary Journal* 10/2 (1983), 5–24.

———. *Dunbar the Makar.* Oxford: Clarendon, 1992.

———. "English Books and Scottish Readers in the Fifteenth and Sixteenth Centuries." *Review of Scottish Culture* 14 (2001–02), 1–12.

Braswell, Mary Flowers. *The Medieval Sinner: Characterization and Confession in the Literature of the English Middle Ages.* London: Associated University Presses, 1983.

Craun, Edwin D. *Lies, Slander and Obscenity in Medieval English Literature.* Cambridge: Cambridge University Press, 1997.

Duffy, Eamon. *The Stripping of the Altars. Traditional Religion in England 1400–1580.* New Haven: Yale University Press, 1992.

Durkan, John and Ross, A. *Early Scottish Libraries.* Glasgow: J. S. Burns, 1961.

Fisher, Keely. "The Contemporary Humour in William Stewart's 'The Flytting betuis ye Sowtar and the Tailzour'." In *Literature, Letters and the Canonical in Early Modern Scotland,* ed. T. Van Hijnsbergen and N. Royan, 1–21. East Linton: Tuckwell, 2002.

Fitch, Audrey-Beth. "Religious Community in the North East at the Reformation." In *After Columba, After Calvin. Religious Communtiy in North-East Scotland,* ed. James Porter, 107–24. Aberdeen: The Elphinstone Institute, 1999.

Fletcher, A. J. "Honour, Reputation and Local Officeholding in Elizabethan and Stuart England." In *Order and Disorder in Early Modern England,* ed. A. Fletcher and J. Stevenson, 92–115. Cambridge: Cambridge University Press, 1985.

Forest-Hill, Lynn. "Sins of the Mouth: Signs of Subversion in Medieval English Cycle Plays." In *Subversion and Scurrility. Popular Discourse in Europe from 1500 to the Present,* ed. Dermot Cavanagh and Tim Kirk, 11–25. Aldershot: Ashgate, 2000.

Groebner, V. "Losing Face, Saving Face: Noses and Honour in the Late Medieval Town." *History Workshop Journal* 40 (Autumn, 1995), 1–15.

Harrison, John. G. "Women and the Branks in Stirling, c.1600 to c.1730." *Scottish Economic and Social History* 18/2 (1998), 114–31.

Helmholz, Richard. *Canon Law and the Law of England.* London: Hambledon, 1987.

Johnston, Flora. "Jonet Gothskirk and the Gown of Repentance." *Costume* 33 (1999), 89–94.

Kamensky, Jane. *Governing the Tongue. The Politics of Speech in Early New England.* Oxford: Oxford University Press, 1997.

MacDonald, Alasdair A. "Catholic Devotion into Protestant Lyric: The Case of the *Contemplacioun of Synnaris.*" *Innes Review* 35 (1984), 58–83.

Mansfield, Mary C. *The Humiliation of Sinners.* Ithaca: Cornell University Press, 1995.

Mapstone, Sally. "Introduction." In *A Palace in the Wild. Essays on Vernacular Culture and Humanism in Late Medieval and Renaissance Scotland,* ed. L. A. J. R. Houwen et al., vii–xviii. Leuven: Peeters, 2000.

Maxwell, Alexander. *Old Dundee: Ecclesiastical, Burghal and Social, Prior to the Reformation.* Edinburgh: D. Douglas, 1891.

McIntosh, Marjory. *Controlling Misbehavior in England 1370–1600.* Cambridge: Cambridge University Press, 1998.

Saldanha, Kathryn. "The Thewis of Gudwomen: Middle Scots Moral Advice with European Connections?" In *The European Sun,* ed. Graham Caie, 288–99. East Linton: Tuckwell, 2001.

Schmitt, Jean-Claude. "The Rationale of Gestures in the West: Third to Thirteenth Centuries." In *A Cultural History of Gesture,* ed. J. Bremmer and H. Roodenburg, 59–70. Ithaca: Cornell University Press, 1991.

Sheneman, Paul. "The Tongue as a Sword: Psalms 56 and 63 and the Pardoner." *The Chaucer Review* 27/4 (1993), 396–400.

Spargo, John Webster. *Juridical Folklore in England Illustrated by the Cucking-Stool.* Durham: Duke University Press, 1944.

Tentler, Thomas. *Sin and Confession on the Eve of the Reformation.* Princeton: Princeton University Press, 1977.

Todd, Margo. *The Culture of Protestantism in Early Modern Scotland.* New Haven: Yale University Press, 2002.

van Buren, Catharine. "John Asloan and his Manuscript. An Edinburgh Notary and Scribe in the Days of James III, IV and V (c.1470–c.1530)." In *Stewart Style 1513–1542,* ed. Janet Hadley Williams, 15–51. East Linton: Tuckwell, 1996.

———. "The Chepman and Myllar Texts of Dunbar." In *William Dunbar, 'The Nobill Poyet,'* ed. Sally Mapstone, 24–39. East Linton: Tuckwell, 2001.

Walker, David. *A Legal History of Scotland. Vol. III. The Sixteenth Century.* Edinburgh: W. Green & Son Ltd., 1995.

From Urban Myth to Didactic Image
The Warning to Swearers

Miriam Gill

A mural of the Virgin holding the horrifically mutilated body of her dead son and surrounded by a group of young men clutching dismembered body parts, such as hands and feet, was found sometime in or before the year 1849 at Broughton in Buckinghamshire (now subsumed within Milton Keynes).[1] Situated on the north wall of the aisleless parish church of St. Lawrence, this powerful image was the most striking of an extensive series of late medieval and post-Reformation wall paintings uncovered there in the nineteenth century. An early published account of the discovery conveys contemporary bafflement at this disturbing adaptation of the Pietà; the dismemberment of Christ, in variance to Scripture, drew particular comment.[2] Aesthetic, moral, or theological objections to their content led to the destruction of many of the medieval murals discovered in parish churches during the nineteenth century.[3] However, this unusual wall painting was retained and carefully retouched. The apparently faithful "restoration"—undertaken in ignorance of the mural's meaning—produced the easily legible, linear image visible today.[4]

A solution to this disturbing iconographic puzzle was established only more than seventy years later. M. R. James was the first to suggest that the Broughton painting was a visual expression of the late medieval polemic against blasphemy, in particular the use of "grete" oaths that mentioned parts of Christ's body.[5] James based this conclusion on a comparison between the mural and antiquarian records of a stained glass window from Heydon in Norfolk, which had shown the Pietà surrounded by young men and accompanied by a complex Middle English poem on the evils of swearing.[6] Polemic against blasphemy was explored further in Gerald Owst's work on the didactic themes of later medieval preaching in England.[7] Thus when a painting of youths accompanied by demons surrounding a Pietà was discovered in 1939 at Corby Glen in Lincolnshire, the initial publication of the mural was accompanied by a full review of the anti-swearing topos.[8] By 1955 this identification was so firmly established that Ernest Tristram and Monica Bardswell's monograph on fourteenth-century paintings confidently could describe the Broughton painting as "quite a straight-forward illustration of numerous passages" of anti-swearing polemic.[9]

The ideas expressed in these parochial images are part of a didactic tradition of opposition to swearing that can be found in a range of literature across medieval Europe. However, the visual polemic against swearing found in these parochial art works is unique to England. These paintings express objections to swearing by Christ's body. Their imagery relates closely to two specific insular literary traditions: a sermon illustration or *exemplum* and a complaint poem. The paintings and stained glass express themes and motifs found in these sources with a sophistication that belies the sometimes unimpressive artistic quality of the surviving images. The literary and visual rhetoric of this polemic indicates contemporary beliefs about the nature of swearing and the power of language. Investigation of all these areas serves to deepen understanding of the urgent concerns that generated such graphic and disturbing imagery and of the power of monumental representations to address these.

The young men in the stained glass window at Heydon in Norfolk were shown with their offending oaths coming from their mouths, almost like speech bubbles in a cartoon.[10] These included such exclamations as "Be the nie [knee] of God this was good ale / Be Godys feet me thwyt [I cut] it ryth smale."[11] It appears that the majority of blasphemous oaths condemned by this polemical tradition referred to Christ or part of his body, hence the common Latin label of swearing *per membra*.[12] However, oaths naming other saints and objects of devotion, such as the Holy Cross and the Virgin Mary, also are referred to by moralists such as Robert Mannyng.[13]

The chronology of the emergence of such swearing and the polemic against it is not easy to trace. However, Middle English complaints about swearing and didactic responses, including the *exemplum* discussed in this paper, can be dated to the period around the turn of the fourteenth century.[14] While the true incidence of such swearing cannot be ascertained from didactic writings, a material expression of the fashion is found in a mid-fifteenth-century gold ring said to have been discovered on the body of Richard Neville Earl of Warwick, "The Kingmaker," and inscribed "be goddis faire foote."[15]

Of the variety of medieval objections to blasphemy, this form of profane swearing was specifically condemned as an action that tore the body of

Christ.[16] The origins of this belief are not entirely clear, but it does represent the specific application of the idea that Christ is wounded by and continues to suffer as a consequence of human sin.[17] This belief was derived from Scripture and defended by the theological distinction between the impassible nature of God and the pain that Christ experienced as a consequence of his compassion for sinners.[18] Many English writers attributed the specific parallel between swearing and the wounding of Christ's body to St. Bernard of Clairvaux.[19] Certainly, the lament of Christ often attributed to Bernard has much in common with the theological objections to swearing *per membra*.[20] References to swearing *per membra* are included in late medieval poems of the complaint of Christ.[21] Interestingly, one such poem was painted on the cornice of the church of Almondbury in Yorkshire in 1522.[22]

The idea that swearing tears the body of Christ clearly became something of a commonplace in Middle English didactic writing. Probably the best known expression of the idea is Geoffrey Chaucer's The Pardoner's Tale, and a passage of anti-swearing polemic also is found in the mouth of Chaucer's Parson.[23] *The Canterbury Tales* was the source that confirmed M. R. James's identification of the Broughton painting.[24] The idea was expounded in sermon cycles such as Dan Michel's *Ayenbite of Inwyt* of ca. 1340: "Ac þise him tobrekeþ smaller: þanne me deþ þet zuyn [swine] ine bocherie [slaughter]."[25]

The English images of the Warning to Swearers are more than visual transcriptions of the general admonition that swearing tears the body of Christ. They relate to two specific expressions of this idea in a preaching *exemplum* and a poetic complaint. The *exemplum* of the swearer's vision was discussed by Gerald Owst in his section on blasphemy.[26] The poem was found in the Heydon window, and Rosemary Woolf identified a variant in the commonplace book of a merchant from Northampton.[27]

In the Middle Ages, monumental art sometimes was referred to as "muta predicatio" or "silent preaching."[28] English wall paintings often have been studied in relation to literary sources, particularly sermons.[29] Some devotional poetry was composed specifically in response to images or for display alongside them; ideas from such poetry certainly were intended to inform subsequent viewing of images.[30]

Although the didactic intention of many later medieval murals and stained glass windows is evident, the monumental representation of stories used as preaching *exempla* is rare. In the surviving corpus of English wall paintings, only the Warning to Gossips is represented more frequently than the Warning to Swearers.[31] Indeed, these are the only stories depicted more than once.

The existence of closely related literary sources is one of the most significant differences between the Warning to Swearers and the other "moralized"
image of the wounded Christ in English medieval wall painting. Found in at
least twenty-three church wall paintings in England and Wales, this other
subject comprises a standing Man of Sorrows surrounded by tools in order
to warn that work on feast days injures Christ's body.[32] This subject has a
variety of names, some of which date from the period before its meaning was
recognized, but the most recent, proposed by Athene Reiss, is the Sunday
Christ. This image has no identifiable literary source or analogue and can be
considered as fundamentally "visual" in origin and operation.[33] Thus the correct meaning of the painting was conclusively established only by a syste-
matic examination of its constituent visual motifs and, in some instances, its
context and the content of accompanying inscriptions.[34]

This subject and the rare related image of the Fastday Christ, which
shows a wrathful Christ menacing those who indulge on fast days, are found
in both England and Wales, and central Europe.[35] The earliest surviving examples of the Sunday Christ cluster in or near Switzerland, suggesting a Continental origin.[36] By contrast, the Warning to Swearers appears to be exclu-
sive to England in both literature and imagery.

The publication in 1989 of the full text and parallel translation of
Fasciculus morum, an anonymous preaching resource on the Seven Deadly
Sins dated to shortly after 1300, placed in the public domain what appears
to be the earliest written version of the *exemplum* from which this anti-swearing tradition derives.[37] Not only does this version of the story pre-date
all the others currently identified but also, in contrast to later variants, it
gives the narrative a very specific, near contemporary setting.

The author of the *Fasciculus* clearly was aware of the shocking impact of
the swearer *exemplum.* He deploys the tale as a warning at the end of a discussion of perjury, specifically in business transactions: "Lo, what happened
in London."[38] Unusually for the *Fasciculus*, this tale is attributed not to a
literary source but to a personal one—"Hugo de Lorgo," a "Lombard" merchant, recently deceased and buried among the Dominicans in London. This
tale is presented as arising from events surrounding the death of his squire.
This squire, "whenever he spoke," swore profane oaths *per membra* so "that
it was awful to hear him." As he lay ill, he had a vision of a lovely lady
entering his room and carrying a beautiful but wounded child in her arms.
On learning it was her son, the squire exclaimed that the assailant was "worthy of the greatest punishment." She replied, "You, wretch, are the one who
have thus torn my child with your oaths, which often were even false. And

now he will be your judge who has said to you, 'May it happen to you as you have said.'"[39] The vision ended and the young man recounted the tale to bystanders before dying. His last words were "I shall go to the devils."

The use of tales from contemporary life—urban myths we might call them—was characteristic of mendicant preaching. Although no historical de Lorgo has been identified yet, the details seem intended to give an impression of verisimilitude. A Dominican house had been established in London in 1250. Although originally it had been forbidden to receive burials, after 1274 this was modified to a ban on the "encouragement" of burials.[40] Lombard ("Lumbardus") seems to have been a common description of Italian merchants in London, particularly the community from Lucca.[41] The possibility that this *exemplum* originated in an English preaching resource that claimed to recount a specific dramatic incident from late thirteenth-century London may help explain why this story, and the related narrative and visual traditions, seems to have been confined to England.[42]

In the fourteenth and fifteenth centuries the story of the swearer's vision, or the "bloody child" as Frederic Tubach calls it, became popular in English didactic literature and circulated in numerous variants, with different settings and conclusions.[43] No subsequent versions of this story include the specific details of the *Fasciculus morum* tale or even repeat the London context. These narratives, a significant selection of which will be considered briefly in chronological order here, come from a range of different genres— poetry and prose, sermons, didactic instruction, and miracle stories. They include a range of additional motifs, and some of them have a happy ending. Given the differences among them and the absence of any simple, linear pattern of development, it seems likely that the surviving variants represent a small proportion of the circulating versions of this story.

A version of the tale is included in Robert Mannyng of Brunne's *Handlyng Synne*, which is dated sometime between 1303 and 1330.[44] This is a Middle English verse translation and augmentation of the Anglo-Norman *Manuel des pechiez*. The story of the swearer is not in the *Manuel*, but represents one of the most extensive and dramatic narrative additions made by the translator.[45] Mannyng does not give his tale a setting; he simply describes the protagonist as a rich man who was, thus, accustomed to swearing. However, he does ascribe the story to a mendicant source: "A lytyl tale y shal yow telle, / That y herde onys a frere spelle [friar tell]."[46] The words of condemnation he puts in the mouth of the Virgin are intriguingly close to those in the *Fasciculus*: "'Thou,' she seyd, 'hast hym so shent [shamed], / And with thy othys al torent [rent in pieces].'"[47] This accusation introduces a long complaint by the Virgin. The swearer responds with penitence and the resolve to forsake swearing and admonish others who swear.[48] Mary, in turn, assures the swearer that she will intercede for him with her son. Thus the tale has a "happy ending" and one that fits well with the encouraging tone of this pastoral work. Mannyng's version of the tale was clearly the source for that in *Peter Idley's Instructions* (ca. 1438–59).[49]

A further version of the story is recounted in John Mirk's *Festial* of ca. 1382–90 and retained in the fifteenth-century revisions of this vernacular sermon cycle for feast days.[50] The story is embellished and complicated by the introduction of a legal setting: the swearer is a justice, and his crime is the enforcement of judicial oaths. When presented with the wounded child, he judges himself and is damned. While this detail provides Mirk with a natural context for the Virgin's invitation for the swearer to unwittingly sentence himself, it introduces a potential problem, since judicial oaths were considered legitimate by the Church and were condemned only by the Lollards.[51] Mirk, who was staunchly orthodox, therefore assures his readers that these were profane and unnecessary oaths and that the justice's example encouraged reckless swearing. Interestingly, Mirk attributes this story to the "Gestus of the Romayns."[52] The fifteenth-century manuscripts of the *Gesta* that contain this story recount a more typical version, suggesting either the interpolation of different variants into English versions of the *Gesta* or a degree of modification on the part of Mirk.

From the early fifteenth century, a *Middle English Treatise on the Ten Commandments* of ca. 1420–34 presents the story as a miracle of the Virgin.[53] The protagonist is a cleric whose foul language sits uneasily alongside his Marian devotion. His vision occurs at the instigation of the Virgin Mary while he is praying to her. The mutilation of the child is described in detail, including the horrific motifs of eyes hanging out onto the cheeks and the heart cut out. The indignant cleric unwittingly passes sentence on himself, but the Virgin tells him that she has interceded for him. As in the *Handlyng Synne* version, he repents and makes a good end.

Another fifteenth-century variant on the tale is interpolated into the English version of the late thirteenth-century *exempla* collection *Gesta Romanorum*.[54] This characterizes the swearer as a sinful man who refuses to ask for mercy until at last Christ turns on him in exasperation, throws a handful of blood in his face, and he is damned. This detail is derived from a separate *exempla* tradition warning against deathbed impenitence.[55]

The degree of variation among these *exempla*—most notably the different characterizations of the swearer and the different endings—suggests a

broad tradition from which only a fraction of the original number of versions survives. The different contexts in which the story is deployed also in-
flect its use, for example, the "happy ending" introduced in pastoral works
on penance or the presentation of the story as a Marian miracle. The story
also becomes "contaminated" with another apparently widely circulated
exemplum in which Christ throws blood into the face of a dying sinner.[56] In
this stark story, as in the swearing *exemplum*, the means of redemption—the
blood and wounds of Christ—are revealed as instruments of judgment
against the impenitent.

Nonetheless, the different versions of the stories retain several common
elements. In each a single male swearer is the recipient of the vision. In each
the Virgin Mary presents the wounded and mutilated body of Christ—a
motif that immediately recalls the devotional image of the Pietà.[57] In each,
the dialogue between the unsuspecting swearer and the Virgin serves to
underline the gravity and horror of speaking great oaths.

Although their rare relationship to the *exemplum* of the Swearer's vision
is of particular interest, the wall paintings of the Warning to Swearers bear
an even closer relationship to the poetic form of the story. One version of
this poem is preserved in a fifteenth-century manuscript in Trinity College,
Dublin, and another was inscribed in the stained glass window at Heydon.[58]
In contrast to the highly personal "vision" of the *exemplum*, this poem includes a host of male swearers with various oaths. However, the relationships between the *exemplum* and the poem, between the poem and the visual
traditions, indeed between the two versions of the poem themselves are hard
to trace, and problems of survival and dating serve to further obscure them.

The antiquarians Blomefield and Martin separately transcribed one version of the poem from Heydon in Norfolk.[59] No visual records of the intact
window survive, but the tracery of the window is Perpendicular, suggesting
a late-fourteenth or fifteenth-century date.[60] Descriptions of the glass suggest
that it presented a scene of swearers gathered round a Pietà, closely re-
sembling the composition found in the surviving wall paintings. The accompanying literary text consisted of two distinct passages. The first is a series
of couplets containing the oaths of the young men. The second is a lament
from the Virgin at the sufferings inflicted on her son by the swearers. The
window also included a scene of the damned in hell, for which no accompanying text is recorded.

The second version of this poem is found in a fifteenth-century commonplace book that belonged to a Northampton merchant. This begins with
the lament of the Virgin. The first four lines are closely comparable with the

Heydon poem, but the rest is different, focusing on the fate of swearers at Doomsday.[61] There follow six short poems ascribed to swearers of different degrees and occupations: a tapster and a yeoman (who dispute about ale), diceplayers, shitters, merchants, and tennis players.[62] These clearly take the form of angry dialogues in which swearing is part of a culture of deceit and violence. A third element of the poem describes the sufferings of the swearers in hell and their laments.[63] Some of these punishments relate specifically to the sins that motivated them or the oaths sworn. For example, one is tormented with burning for swearing in anger, while another is tormented with lead and brass (presumably molten) for swearing by the "nayles of god."[64]

The format of these two poems is very similar. The commonplace book's final section about the suffering of swearers in hell provides a close parallel for the image described at Heydon. However, with the exception of the first lines of the Virgin's lament, the text of the two poems is completely different, even when the format is identical. Moreover, it is not clear which version of the poem is earlier, or whether either version can be placed confidently earlier than the earliest surviving wall painting.

The small corpus of images of the Warning to Swearers is similarly diverse. With the exception of the Heydon window, described above, they each will be considered in chronological order. However, with such a small sample, there are no guarantees that this order represents the sequence of iconographic development. As with the narrative traditions, there are significant variations among the images, and evidence of cross-fertilization with other iconographic motifs.

The earliest representation of this subject is a mural on the north wall of the north aisle at Corby Glen in Lincolnshire.[65] This church contains extensive remains of a number of schemes of painting. Costume and stylistic evidence suggests that the Warning to Swearers dates from ca. 1400. The Corby Glen mural has a central image of the Pietà, with the Virgin in a pale green dress, surrounded by three tiers of young male figures, each accompanied by a demon. Although virtually none of the texts included in this painting can be deciphered, it appears that the swearers' oaths were contained in inscriptions above their heads (see Fig. 1).[66]

At first sight, the position of demons is reminiscent of an iconography of other morality subjects, especially the Seven Deadly Sins, in which demons are shown tempting and indeed compelling individuals to commit or continue to sin.[67] However, at Corby Glen the devils are shown not only inciting the young men to swear but also wounding them. Moreover, the position of these wounds indicates that they relate directly to the swearers'

Figure 1. Upper part of wall painting of the Warning to Swearers. Corby Glen, Lincolnshire (ca. 1400). (Photograph R. Stevenson)

oaths; the youth immediately to the left of Christ's side is stabbed in the side. The injuries of the swearers thus parody the saving wounds of Christ that they have scorned in their blasphemous speech.

The painting also includes an additional figure of a naked woman riding on a goat.[68] This motif probably derives from the presentation of the Seven Deadly Sins riding on animals, which developed in central Europe in the first half of the fourteenth century.[69] The presence of the seven devils led E. Clive Rouse to speculate that the painting might combine the Warning to Swearers with the Seven Deadly Sins.[70] However, the distinctions among the figures seem too subtle, and their characterization does not correspond to the common motifs found in vignettes of the individual sins.

The elaborate costume of the young swearers suggests that the mural at Broughton in Buckinghamshire was painted about a decade after that at Corby Glen.[71] The painting shows the Pietà group surrounded by nine young men. There are no text scrolls in this mural; instead, the swearers hold dismembered parts of Christ's body or the host or cross to indicate their oaths. The body of Christ is visibly mutilated. The link between this carnage and the oaths is dramatized by a figure of a swearer reaching over the body of

Christ to draw out his eyes and another holding a foot that clearly has been wrenched from the corpse. At the base of the Pietà, two figures are seated at either end of a gaming board. The one on the left brandishes a cross in his hand, while his companion strikes his head with a long knife or perhaps a sword (see Fig. 2).

The mural at Walsham-le-Willows in Suffolk is known from nineteenth-century photography.[72] It appears to have dated from ca. 1460–70. Interestingly, it seems to have combined the iconography of the Sunday Christ with the Warning to Swearers.[73] Like the former, it focused on Christ's body, rather than a Pietà, and showed a multiplicity of tools. However, the body of Christ, rather than simply being pierced, was shown dismembered to such an extent that it is difficult from the nineteenth-century photograph of the painting to gauge how much of it was depicted originally. This visual reference to the mutilation associated with swearing is confirmed by the presence of profane oaths in the fragmentary scrolls at the bottom of the painting.[74] Damaged as these are, Athene Reiss is surely right to remark on their general resemblance to the oaths recorded in the Heydon window and the Dublin poem.[75] These are interspersed with vignettes that show two young men apparently dancing while another looks on, and two wrestling, and a table set with food and a gaming board in the background.[76] These vignettes may represent an expansion of the moralizing motif of the quarreling gamblers found at Broughton. They also may relate to the tradition of accompanying the Sunday Christ with scenes of illicit activity, evident, for example, at Crngrob in Slovenia.[77]

The variety apparent in this small sample of images, surviving and extant, suggests an iconographically and regionally diverse and rapidly developing tradition of visual polemic. Just as motifs from other tales were absorbed into the *exemplum* tradition, so we can see elements from an innovative presentation of the Seven Deadly Sins being included in even the earliest surviving image.

The fragmentary nature of both the literary and visual traditions makes it hard to determine the exact nature of the relationship between them. In terms of format, the visual tradition clearly had more in common with the fifteenth-century poems than the earlier *exemplum,* since the poems describe a multiplicity of swearers. However, the paintings do also contain elements that strongly recall details in the *exemplum* tradition, from the green dress of Mary, described by Mirk[78] and depicted at Corby Glen, to the motif of the eyes drawn out, depicted at Broughton and related in versions of the tale including the *Decalogue Treatise.*[79] More subtly, for a viewer, the image of the

Figure 2. Wall painting of the Warning to Swearers, Broughton, Buckinghamshire (ca. 1410). (Photograph R. Stevenson)

Pietà and the crowd of swearers may be said to provide an artistic equivalent of the swearer's vision, a confrontational image of the harm caused by swearing.[80] The other *exemplum* found in monumental art, the Warning to Gossips, also condenses a complex and humorous narrative into a single, striking image of the hidden enormity of a particular sin.[81]

This examination of the interconnection of text and image also raises the intriguing question of the extent to which the form taken by the *exemplum* tradition was influenced by the iconography of the Pietà. The earliest known representations of this Marian image are found in southern Germany in about 1300 and are thus contemporary with the early *exempla*.[82] Probably the earliest image of the Pietà in England is found in the Taymouth Hours of ca. 1330–40.[83] The subject is found in English sculpture and wall painting from the late fourteenth century.[84] If the idea of the Virgin holding the wounded body of her son was suggested by the innovative imagery of the Pietà, then the *Fasciculus morum* tale may represent the earliest piece of evidence for its presence in England. The Sunday Christ appears to have developed from exclusively visual sources; visual sources may have been more important in the development of the polemic against swearing than is now apparent. Certainly, the combination of the themes of swearing and Sabbath breaking in the painting at Walsham-le-Willows suggests that the common theological and visual logic of these two subjects was recognized in the Middle Ages.

Both these images employ a distinctive didactic strategy. They take a highly emotive devotional image—the Man of Sorrows or the Pietà—and they accentuate and particularize the dual message of repentance and compassion implicit in the wounds of Christ.[85] Thus the pious feeling associated with the original image is harnessed to confront a particular fault. The polemic relies on a prior familiarity with Passion images and an awareness of the sort of pious responses they are intended to prompt.[86] The Almondbury poem condemning swearing *per membra* may have prompted the congregation to interpret the ubiquitous devotional image of Christ on the cross as a warning against blasphemy. The motif of the Warning to Swearers gains emotional impact by making a familiar devotional image grotesque, visually enacting the blasphemy it condemns. If Chaucer's Pardoner considered it "grisly" to hear oaths, the artist at Broughton certainly made it "grisly" to see their consequences.[87]

This final section will explore what this English anti-swearing polemic reveals about contemporary perceptions of swearing and why this sin was singled out for such dramatic visual treatment.

The visual images, and to a lesser extent the *exemplum* tradition, consistently characterize swearing as a male sin. In this respect it forms an interesting contrast with the Warning to Gossips, where the protagonists are predominantly or, in the case of the mural painting corpus, exclusively female.[88] Although the narratives do present a judge, a cleric, and a rich man as archetypal swearers, the mural representations follow the original tale in associating this sin with young men. Moreover, the outlandish costumes present these young men as fashionable. In this respect, the paintings follow polemical writers in associating swearing primarily with young dandies and regarding it as the first step on the road to irreligion and damnation. In ca. 1380, John Wycliffe characterized attendants on prelates as "raggid and fittrid [ornamented] squyers sweryng herte and bonys and nails and othere members of Christ."[89] Margery Kempe describes a remarkably similar group of foul-mouthed retainers in the hall at Lambeth Palace.[90]

In contrast to the work tools presented in the Sunday Christ, the figures in these paintings are shown engaging in leisure pursuits: gaming, dancing, and wrestling. Only at Walsham-le-Willows does the inclusion of a pair of scales accompanied by an inscription suggest a reference to traders who swore false oaths to cheat their customers, causing preachers to complain that "even for the sake of a penny they will take God's name in vain."[91] By contrast, both Broughton and Walsham-le-Willows include references to gaming, a pursuit described by Chaucer's Pardoner as "verray mooder of lesynges [lies] / And of deceite and cursed forswerynges / Blaspheme of Crist, manslaughtre."[92] The text recorded at Heydon suggests that the lost window showed figures drinking.[93] Although none of the paintings appear to include any images of buildings, to a medieval viewer the range of activities depicted probably would have recalled the "sins of the tavern."[94] This location was associated so strongly with sinful behavior that a preaching commonplace styled it the "chapel" or the "church" of the devil; the medieval viewer may have felt invited to draw a contrast between the place in which they stood and that "other church."[95]

As well as portraying an image of swearing that has strong gender and social characteristics and that was linked to specific activities, the images at Broughton and Walsham-le-Willows imply a progression from the verbal violence of great oaths to physical violence. A similar progression is implicit in Chaucer's The Pardoner's Tale.[96] The quarreling gambler at Broughton brandishes the cross by which he swears like a weapon, while his opponent deals a blow. At Walsham-le-Willows the young men wrestle against a backdrop of broken limbs.[97]

This tendency to violence is extended in the iconography of the swearers wounded by devils at Corby Glen. This representation of the supernatural punishment of swearing is reminiscent of a genre of *exempla* stories about swearers who die sudden and horribly appropriate deaths. This genre may derive from an *exemplum* of the sudden death of a five-year-old swearer recounted by Gregory the Great.[98] In the illustration of this story in a copy of the *Manuel des pechiez* (ca. 1280), two devils are shown attacking the boy with knives.[99] The fact that great oaths specifically referred to parts of Christ's holy body can only have strengthened such accounts of divine punishment. Guillelmus Peraldus in his *Summa de vitiis* offers a brief *exemplum* of a gaming knight who swore by the eyes of God and who was punished by his eye falling out on the dice.[100] The thirteenth-century Dominican preacher Etienne de Bourbon recounts several such cases, including that of a swearer whose body shrinks and whose eyes liquefy.[101] At the end of the version of this story in the *Fasciculus morum*, the devils kill the tormented swearer by tearing out his eyes.[102] Thomas Gascoigne alleged that many people in England had died with blood coming out of their mouths, eyes, and other parts of their bodies as a judgment on the types of great oaths that they had sworn.[103] The physicality of these punishments recalls both the violence of the great oaths and the mutilating punishments prescribed for profane swearing in the civil law of the France of St. Louis.[104]

The activities of the devils at Corby Glen recall the statement in the *Dialogues* of Gregory the Great that those who swear give themselves over to the devils.[105] They also may prefigure the sufferings of the swearers in hell, where, preachers taught, every vice would be punished in an appropriate way.[106] The lost glass at Heydon included a scene of "hell and such sinners as those in its flames."[107] The Dublin complaint poem describes those who have sworn certain types of oaths receiving appropriate punishment. By contrast, the poem against swearing inscribed on the cornice of the 1522 wooden roof at Almondbury in Yorkshire ends, like the story in *Handlyng Synne*, on an optimistic note, promising heaven to all who stop swearing.[108] Athene Reiss's description of the Sunday Christ as both devotional and coercive in its appeal could serve equally well as a description of the Warning to Swearers.[109]

The violence and vehemence of this tradition of anti-swearing polemic reveals a culture in which the spoken word was considered very powerful. The association of great oaths with the mutilation of one of the most moving and significant images of late medieval devotional culture indicates the depth of concern at this offensive behavior. Distaste at swearing is perhaps one of the more important indications of the popular acceptance of the cult of the Passion. The images of swearers grasping dismembered limbs contrasted with the development of devotional imagery in which isolated elements such as the wounds of Christ or the sacred heart were presented for pious contemplation.[110] Moreover, in a culture in which—in the miracle of the mass—holy words made Christ present and made the saving grace of his redeeming sacrifice available, profane swearing presented almost an inversion of transubstantiation that amplified Christ's sufferings and wounded the speaker. In the visual tradition, the eucharistic resonance of the Pietà may have hinted at this inversion.[111]

However, the threat of judgment was tempered with hints of mercy. Some *exempla* gave this story a happy ending, and the distorted image of the Pietà retains its power to move the viewer to repentance. As the Pardoner says, "for the love of Christ, that for us dyde / Lete [Abandon] youre othes, bothe grete and smale."[112] Interestingly, forgiveness for oaths sworn was one of the merits of the mass as listed in a 1375 sermon by Bishop Brinton of Rochester.[113]

The cultural significance of the theme does not explain why this topic was selected for monumental representation in parish churches. All public parochial art represents outlay by individuals or communities. However, in the case of most wall paintings and, to a lesser extent, stained glass, neither written nor visual records of patronage have survived. Of the four images of the Warning to Swearers, only that at Corby Glen may have an identifiable patron. The mural is clearly by the same workshop as a painting of the Weighing of Souls further west on the north wall. This painting includes a kneeling clerical donor figure with a scroll requesting prayers, possibly the priest of the parish.[114] However, in general, it is difficult to judge whether English depictions of the Warning to Swearers were chosen and financed by pious parishioners or exasperated clergy, although Visitation records demonstrate that swearing, like Sabbath-breaking, fell under clerical jurisdiction.[115]

It is perhaps more profitable to set this subject in the context of the didactic culture of the later medieval church. The responsibility for lay education established by the Fourth Lateran Council of 1215 was expressed in syllabi of *pastoralia* on which the laity were to receive regular instruction. Both the Seven Deadly Sins and Ten Commandments commonly were included in such syllabuses. However, in visual instruction, the incidence of the Seven Deadly Sins greatly exceeds that of the Ten Commandments.

Reiss is dubious that the image of the Sunday Christ should be seen in relation to the meager tradition of representing the Ten Commandments.[116] Certainly, neither subject can be identified as belonging to a scheme of the Ten Commandments.[117] However, the relationship there and in the case of the Warning to Swearers may be a negative one. In contrast to covetousness, adultery, or murder, profane swearing did not fit easily into the more commonly represented pattern of the Seven Deadly Sins. This is evident in the fact that polemicists and preachers attempted to categorize it variously as an example of Avarice, Wrath, or Gluttony.[118] The earliest version of the *exemplum* of the swearer's vision is included in a section on the sin of Envy.[119]

As in the case of Sabbath-breaking, it was perhaps the apparent triviality of swearing that inspired those seeking to counter it to resort to such violent and brutal images. Many preachers reported common assumptions that swearing was too minor a sin to incur God's wrath or that such constant references to God were a form of piety.[120] However, there is evidence that visual and polemical campaigns may have made some of the laity sensitive to swearing. In the early sixteenth-century episcopal Visitation of Oxfordshire, the villagers of Bampton complained of a great swearer who would not amend, while those of Iffley stated that two of their fellow villagers always were swearing.[121] Such incidents may testify to the power of the anti-swearing narratives and images. As Athene Reiss suggests in her work on the Sunday Christ, perhaps we should think of these anti-swearing stories and pictures as affirming and consolidating established communal values, rather than conveying novel moral messages or representing historical evidence of widespread noncompliance.[122] It is also possible that the decision to depict swearing and related sins of gambling, fighting, and dancing in parochial art was intended to reinforce the contrast between that sacred space and the tavern as the "church of the devil."

CONCLUSION

The literary and visual tradition explored in this paper represents a uniquely English expression of an international polemic against profane oaths. The insularity of this subject may be connected to its alleged origins as an "urban myth" from late thirteenth-century London recorded in an English preaching resource. The tale proved both flexible and enduring. A later poetic tradition and a closely related range of visual images developed the essence of the swearer's vision into a dramatic indictment of swearing *per membra*. The parochial images are a very rare instance of the depiction of themes from an *exemplum* in monumental art. These images were intended to be interpreted and informed by an established range of devotional subjects. Indeed, the novel image of the Pietà may have played a part in the emergence of the original *exemplum*. These paintings expressed and perpetuated apparently common assumptions about those prone to swear *per membra*, particularly idle young men. They threatened the viewer with the possibility of temporal violence and eternal punishment. Above all, these graphic images harnessed the pious emotion inspired by devotional art for a specific moral purpose. While the didactic texts and the painting at Corby Glen suggest clerical promotion of this polemic, there is evidence of lay response to the campaign against swearing. Seen in the context of lay education, the paintings appear to be an expression of a campaign to teach aspects of the Ten Commandments that were not readily covered by the standard admonitory subject of the Seven Deadly Sins. Above all they demonstrate the ability of medieval preachers and painters to draw on a range of sources and strategies to develop a disturbing visual polemic against the specific sin of swearing *per membra*.

NOTES

1. Tristram and Bardswell, *English Wall Painting*, 144–45.

2. Anon., "Proceedings at the Meeting," 176.

3. See, for example, Edwards, "Some," 81–98.

4. Park, "Warning to Swearers," in *Gothic*, ed. Marks and Williamson, 409.

5. James, "Iconography," 288–89.

6. This window is no longer *in situ*. Although it generally is believed lost, Marks, *Stained Glass*, 80, suggests that a figure of a dice player now at Swannington Court in Norfolk may be a surviving fragment of this window.

7. Owst, *Literature*, 414–25.

8. Rouse, "Wall Paintings," 156–64.

9. Tristram and Bardswell, *English Wall Painting*, 104.

10. Woodforde, *The Norwich School*, 183.

11. Woodforde, *The Norwich School*, 184.

12. Craun, "'Inordinata Locutio'," 149.

13. Mannyng, *Handlyng Synne*, ed. Furnivall, lines 759–800.

14. *Mittelenglische*, ed. Bortanek, 106.

15. Cherry, "Ring with Bear and Ragged Staff," in *Gothic*, ed. Marks and Williamson, 232.

16. Craun, "'Inordinata Locutio'," 149, n. 150.

17. Reiss, *Sunday Christ*, 25; *Mittelenglische*, ed. Bortanek, 104.

18. *Mittelenglische*, ed. Bortanek, 105.

19. This appeal is attributed to Bernard: "Leve hensforwarde to synne, so synfully sweryng. For the wounde of this synne grevyth me more than the wounde of my syde" (*Speculum*, ed. Holmstedt, 21). See also *Mittelenglische*, ed. Bortanek, 105.

20. Reiss, *Sunday Christ*, 140, nn. 155 and 156.

21. Woolf, *The English Religioius Lyric*, 398–400.

22. Palmer, "An Iconography," 9–16.

23. Chaucer, *The Canterbury Tales*, 6.472–6 and 631–60, 10.587–99, in *The Riverside Chaucer*, ed. Benson et al. All references to *The Canterbury Tales* are to this edition.

24. James, "Iconography," 288–89.

25. *Mittelenglische*, ed. Bortanek, 107. For the text see *Dan Michel's Ayenbite*, ed. Morris, 64.

26. Owst, *Literature*, 424–25.

27. Woolf, *The English Religious Lyric*, 387. The text of this variant is printed in *Mittelenglische*, ed. Bortanek, 99–102.

28. Woolf, *Art and Doctrine*, 57.

29. The most extended classic treatment of this theme is Bardswell and Tristram, *English Wall Painting*, 108–12. See also Gill, "Preaching and Image," 155–80.

30. Woolf, *The English Religious Lyric*, 208–09.

31. Gill, "Preaching and Image," 169.

32. Reiss, *Sunday Christ*, 5.

33. Reiss, *Sunday Christ*, 58.

34. Reiss, *Sunday Christ*, 7–11, recounts this process; her own carefully argued assent to this conclusion is contained in chapter 4.

35. Reiss, *Sunday Christ*, 13, map ii. For Fastday Christ see Jaritz, "Bildquellen," 211.

36. Reiss, *Sunday Christ*, 14, 26.

37. *Fasciculus*, ed. Wenzel, 167.

38. This and subsequent quotations of the English translation of this tale are from *Fasciculus*, ed. Wenzel, 167.

39. *Fasciculus*, ed. Wenzel, 167.

40. Formoy, *Dominican*, 36–37.

41. Thrupp, *Merchant Class*, 221 n. 50.

42. D'Avray, *Preaching*, 198.

43. Tubach, *Index*, no. 5103. The most extensive published catalogues of the variants are *The Myracles*, ed. Whiteford, 110, 112, 117, 118, 123, 127.

44. Mannyng, *Handlyng Synne*, ed. Furnivall, lines 664–758. See also Robertson, "The Cultural Tradition," 162–85.

45. Kemmler, *Exempla*, 141–42.

46. Mannyng, *Handlyng Synne*, ed. Furnivall, lines 687–88.

47. Mannyng, *Handlyng Synne*, ed. Furnivall, lines 711–12. Compare with *Fasciculus*, ed. Wenzel, 166: "'Tu, inquit, maledicte, es ille qui sic filium meum per iuramenta tua [eciam] quamplura falsa dilacerasti.'"

48. Mannyng, *Handlyng Synne*, ed. Furnivall, lines 740–46.

49. *The Myracles*, ed. Whiteford, 117.

50. Mirk, *Festial*, ed. Erbe, 113–14. For the date of the *Festial*, see Fletcher, "John Mirk," 218.

51. *Knighton's Chronicle*, ed. Martin, 437.

52. Mirk, *Festial*, ed. Erbe, 113.

53. "A Middle English Treatise," ed. Royster, 18–19. The mercy of Virgin for the undeserving and her desire to protect her devotees was an important aspect of her cult (Gill, "The Wall Paintings," 184–85).

54. *The Early English*, ed. Herrtage, 409–10.

55. There are several English *exempla* that contain the motif of blood flung in the face of a dying man, but no reference to swearing (Herbert, *Catalogue*, 3, 130–31, 225, 261). This is an independent tale in *Fasciculus* (ed. Wenzel, 491).

56. Tubach, *Index*, 232.

57. Wenzel, *Macaronic Sermons*, 291–93, records a variant of this story in which the swearer is confronted by a cross.

58. *Mittelenglische*, ed. Bortanek, 99–115.

59. Woodforde, *The Norwich School*, 183–85.

60. Pevsner, *North East Norfolk*, 163.

61. This observation was first made by Woolf, *The English Religious Lyric*, 397.

62. *Mittelenglische*, ed. Bortanek, 99–100.

63. *Mittelenglische*, ed. Bortanek, 100–02.

64. *Mittelenglische*, ed. Bortanek, 101.

65. Rouse, "Wall Paintings," 157–63, pl. vii; Tristram and Bardswell, *English Wall Painting*, 104–05.

66. Rouse, "Wall Paintings," 160.

67. Tristram and Bardswell, *English Wall Painting*, 101–06.

68. Rouse, "Wall Paintings," 162.

69. Norman, *Metamorphoses*, 198–99.

70. Rouse, "Wall Paintings," 160.

71. The most recent discussion of this painting can be found in Park, "Warning to Swearers," 409, and Marks, "Viewing," 112.

72. Reiss, *The Sunday Christ*, 50, 106–07.

73. Woodforde, *The Norwich School*, 185–86. This date is based on the elongated and elegant style of the figures and their angular drapery as well as their fashionable costume. The male figures have shoes or boots with pointed toes and short tunics with pleated skirts. See, for comparison, Scott, *Visual History*, 92–93, 99–100.

74. These are transcribed in Woodforde, *The Norwich School*, 185.

75. Reiss, *The Sunday Christ*, 26–27.

76. Woodforde, *The Norwich School*, 185–86.

77. Balazic, *Gotik in Slowenien*, 257.

78. Mirk, *Festial*, ed. Erbe, 114.

79. "A Middle English Treatise," ed. Royster, 19.

80. Gill, "Preaching," 171.

81. Gill, "Preaching," 171–72.

82. Marks, "Viewing," 101.

83. Morgan, "Texts," 54.

84. Marks, "Viewing," 102. See also Gill, "Late Medieval Wall Painting," 330–32.

85. Reiss, *Sunday Christ*, 26.

86. For this consideration in relation to the Sunday Christ, see Reiss, *Sunday Christ*, 53.

87. Chaucer, *Tales*, 6.472–73.

88. Gill, "Female Piety and Impiety," 108–09.

89. Wycliffe, *The English Works*, ed. Matthew, 60.

90. *The Book of Margery Kempe,* ed. Meech and Allen, 36.

91. Owst, *Literature,* 419. The Dublin poem also refers to merchants; see *Mittelenglische,* ed. Bortanek, 100.

92. Chaucer, *Tales,* 6.591–3. Gamblers are mentioned in the Dublin poem; see *Mittelenglische,* ed. Bortanek, 100; Owst, *Literature,* 418.

93. Woodforde, *The Norwich School,* 186.

94. I am grateful to the MIP reader for drawing my attention to the implicit presence of 'tavern sins,' for which see Owst, *Literature,* 434–47.

95. I am grateful to the MIP reader for this helpful insight. For the formula of the tavern as the devil's church, see Owst, *Literature,* 438–39.

96. Chaucer, *Tales,* 6.463–968.

97. The Dublin complaint poem lists "ffyghters" among its malefactors (*Mittelenglische,* ed. Bortanek, 100).

98. Arnould, *Le Manuel,* 147; Craun, "'Inordinata Locutio'," 158.

99. Bennett, "A Book," 174.

100. Guillelmus Peraldus, *Summa,* fol. F3r.

101. *Anecdotes historiques,* ed. Lecoy de la Marche, 388.

102. *Fasciculus,* ed. Wenzel, 293.

103. Maddern, *Violence,* 82.

104. Owst, *Literature,* 421.

105. *Fasciculus,* ed. Wenzel, 388.

106. *Decalogue* describes a swearer who is tormented in hell by being pierced with a spear; see "A Middle English Treatise," ed. Royster, 19.

107. Woodforde, *The Norwich School,* 183.

108. Palmer, "An Iconography," 9–16.

109. Reiss, *Sunday Christ,* 57–58.

110. Hamburger, *The Rothschild Canticles,* 75.

111. For the eucharistic significance of the Pietà see Marks, "Viewing," 113.

112. Chaucer, *Tales,* 6.658–59.

113. Rubin, *Corpus Christi,* 63.

114. Rouse, "Wall Paintings," 153–54.

115. Anon., "Churchwardens,'" 211.

116. Reiss, *Sunday Christ,* 28.

117. Reiss, *Sunday Christ,* 27–28.

118. Early attempts to make such connections are discussed in Craun, "'Inordinata Locutio'," 186. The problem is also discussed in Tupper, "Chaucer," 95.

119. *Fasciculus,* ed. Wenzel, 167.

120. Owst, *Literature,* 419.

121. Anon., "Churchwardens,'" 101, 112.

122. Reiss, *Sunday Christ,* 58–59.

Works Cited

Abbreviations

EETS   Early English Text Society. London: Early English Text Society, 1864–.

Primary Sources

Anecdotes historiques, légendes et apologues tirés du recueil inédit d'Étienne de Bourbon. Ed. Albert Lecoy de la Marche. Paris: Librairie Renouard, H. Loones, successeur, 1877.

Anon. "Churchwardens' Presentments 1520." *Oxfordshire Archaeological Society* 70 (1925), 75–117.

The Book of Margery Kempe. Ed. Sandford Meech and Hope Emily Allen. EETS o.s. 212. London: Oxford University Press, 1940.

Chaucer, Geoffrey. *The Riverside Chaucer.* Ed. Larry D. Benson et al. Oxford: Oxford University Press, 1988.

Cherry, John. "Ring with Bear and Ragged Staff." In *Gothic: Art for England 1400–1547,* ed. Richard Marks and Paul Williamson (assisted by Eleanor Townsend), 232. London: V and A Publications, 2003.

Dan Michel's Ayenbite of Inwyt, or, Remorse of Conscience: In the Kentish Dialect, 1340. Ed. Richard Morris. EETS o.s. 23. London: Trübner, 1866.

Early English Versions of the Gesta Romanorum. Ed. Sidney J. H. Herrtage. EETS e.s. 33. London: Trübner, 1879.

Fasciculus Morum: A Fourteenth-Century Preacher's Handbook. Ed. Siegfried Wenzel. Philadelphia: Pennsylvania State University Press, 1989.

Guillelmus Peraldus. *Summa de viciis.* Cologne: Quentel, 1479.

Knighton's Chronicle 1337–1396. Ed. Geoffrey Haward Martin. Oxford: Oxford University Press and Clarendon, 1995.

Mannyng, Robert. *Robert of Brunne's, 'Handlyng Synne,' AD 1303, with those parts of the Anglo-French treatise on which it was based, William of Wadington's 'Manuel des Pechiez.'* Ed. Frederick J. Furnivall. EETS o.s. 119. London: Kegan Paul, Trench, Trübner, 1901.

"A Middle English Treatise on the Ten Commandments from St. John's College, Oxford MS 94." Ed. James F. Royster. *Studies in Philology* 6 (1910), 3–39.

Mirk, John. *Mirk's Festial: A Collection of Homilies.* Ed. Theodore Erbe. EETS e.s. 96. London: Kegan Paul, Trench, Trübner, 1905.

Mittelenglische Dichtungen. Ed. Rudolf Bortanek. Halle: M. Niemeyer, 1940.

The Myracles of Oure Lady Edited from Wynkyn de Worde's Edition. Ed. Peter Whiteford. Heidelberg: Winter, 1990.

Park, David. "Warning to Swearers." In *Gothic: Art for England 1400–1547,* ed. Richard Marks and Paul Williamson (assisted by Eleanor Townsend), 409. London: V and A Publications, 2003.

Speculum Christiani. Ed. Gustaf Holmstedt. EETS o.s. 182. London: Oxford University Press, 1933.

Wycliffe, John. *The English Works of Wyclif*. Ed. F. D. Matthew. EETS o.s. 212. 1880; London: Oxford University Press, 1940.

Secondary Sources

Anon. "Proceedings at the Meetings of the Archaeological Institute." *Archaeological Journal* 6 (1849), 176.

Arnould, Émile Jules François, ed. *Le Manuel des Péchés: Études de littérature religieuse Anglo-Normande (XIIIme siècle)*. Paris: Droz, 1940.

Balazic, Janez. *Gotik in Slowenien. Ljubljana 1 Juni bis 1 October 1995*. Ljubljana: Narodna galerija Ljubljana, 1995.

Bennett, A. "A Book Designed for a Noblewoman: An Illustrated *Manuel des Péches* of the Thirteenth Century." In *Medieval Book Production: Assessing the Evidence*, ed. Linda L. Brownrigg, 163–81. Los Altos Hills, CA: Anderson-Lovelace, 1990.

Craun, Edwin D. "'Inordinata Locutio': Blasphemy in Pastoral Literature, 1200–1500." *Traditio* 39 (1983), 135–62.

D'Avray, David L. *The Preaching of the Friars: Sermons Diffused from Paris before 1300*. Oxford: Oxford University Press, 1985.

Edwards, John. "Some Lost Medieval Wall-paintings." *Oxoniensia* 55 (1990), 81–98.

Fletcher, Alan John. "John Mirk and the Lollards." *Medium Aevum* 56 (1987), 217–24.

Formoy, Beryl E. R. *The Dominican Order in England before the Reformation*. London: S. C. K., 1925.

Gill, Miriam. "The Wall Paintings in Eton College Chapel: The Making of a Late Medieval Marian Cycle." In *Making Medieval Art*, ed. Phillip Lindley, 173–201. Donnington: Shaun Tyas, 2003.

———. "Preaching and Image: Sermons and Wall Paintings in Later Medieval England." In *Preacher, Sermon and Audience in the Middle Ages*, ed. Carolyn Muessig, 155–80. Leiden: Brill, 2002.

———. "Female Piety and Impiety: Selected Images of Women in Wall Paintings in England after 1300." In *Gender and Holiness: Men, Women and Saints in Late Medieval Europe*, ed. Samantha J. E. Riches and Sarah Salih, 101–20. London and New York: Routledge, 2002.

———. "Late Medieval Wall Painting in England: Content and Context, 1330–1530." Ph.D. thesis, Courtauld Institute of Art, 2002.

Gray, Douglas. *Themes and Images in the Medieval English Religious Lyric*. London: Routledge and Kegan Paul, 1972.

Hamburger, Jeffrey F. *The Rothschild Canticles: Art and Mysticism in Flanders and the Rhineland c1300*. New Haven and London: Yale University Press, 1991.

Herbert, John A., ed. *Catalogue of the Romances in the Department of Manuscripts in the British Museum*. Vol. 3. London: British Museum, 1910.

James, Montagu Rhodes. "The Iconography of Buckinghamshire." *Records of Buckinghamshire* 12 (1932), 281–98.

Jaritz, Gerhard. "Bildquellen zur mittelalterliche Volksfrömmigkeit." In *Volksreligion im hohen und späten Mittelalter. Quellen und Forschungen aus dem Gebiet der Geschichte,* ed. Paul Dinzelbacher and Dieter R. Bauer, 195–241. Paderborn: Schöningh, 1990.

Jennings, Margaret. "Tutivullus: The Literary Career of the Recording Demon." *Studies in Philology* 74 (1977), 1–95.

Kemmler, Fritz. *'Exempla' in Context: A Historical and Critical Study of Robert Mannyng of Brunne's 'Handlyng Synne.'* Tübingen: Narr, 1984.

Maddern, Philippa C. *Violence and the Social Order: East Anglia, 1422–1442.* Oxford: Clarendon, 1992.

Marks, Richard. *Stained Glass in England during the Middle Ages.* Toronto: University of Toronto Press, 1993.

———. "Viewing Our Lady of Pity." In *Magistro et Amico amici discipulique. Lechowi Kalinowskiemu w osiemdziesięciolecie urodzin,* ed. Jerzy Gadomski, 101–21. Cracow: Wydawn, 2002.

Morgan, Nigel. "Texts and Images of Marian Devotion in Fourteenth-Century England." In *England in the Fourteenth Century: Proceedings of the 1991 Harlaxton Symposium,* ed. Nicholas Rogers, 34–57. Stamford: Paul Watkins, 1993.

Norman, Joanne S. *Metamorphoses of an Allegory: The Iconography of the Psychomachia in Medieval Art.* New York: Peter Lang, 1988.

Owst, Gerald Robert. *Literature and the Pulpit in Medieval England: A Neglected Chapter in the History of English Letters and of the English People.* Cambridge: Cambridge University Press, 1933.

Palmer, Barbara D. "An Iconography for Swearers: The Almondbury Passion Poem." *EDAM Review* 12 no. 1 (1989), 9–16.

Pevsner, Nikolaus. *North East Norfolk and Norwich.* Harmondsworth: Penguin, 1962.

Reiss, Athene. *The Sunday Christ: Sabbatarianism in English Medieval Wall Painting.* British Archaeological Reports, Series 292. Oxford: Archaeopress, 2000.

Robertson, Durant Waite. "The Cultural Tradition of 'Handlyng Synne.'" *Speculum* 22 (1947), 162–85.

Rouse, E. Clive. "Wall Paintings in the Church of St. John the Evangelist, Corby, Lincolnshire." *Archaeological Journal* 100 (1943), 150–76.

Rubin, Miri. *Corpus Christi.* Cambridge: Cambridge University Press, 1991.

Scott, Margaret. *A Visual History of Costume: The Fourteenth and Fifteenth Centuries.* London: Batsford, 1986.

Thrupp, Sylvia L. *The Merchant Class of Medieval London, 1300–1500.* Chicago: University of Chicago Press, 1948.

Tristram, Ernest William, and Monica Bardswell. *English Wall Painting of the Fourteenth Century.* London: Routledge and Kegan Paul, 1955.

Tubach, Frederic C. *Index Exemplorum.* Helsinki: Suomalainen Tiedeakatemia, 1961.

Tupper, Frederick C. "Chaucer and the Seven Deadly Sins." *Publications of the Modern Language Association* 29 (1914), 93–128.

Wenzel, Siegfried. *Macaronic Sermons: Bilingualism and Preaching in late Medieval England.* Ann Arbor: University of Michigan Press, 1994.

Woodforde, Christopher. *The Norwich School of Glass-Painting in the Fifteenth Century*. London and New York: Oxford University Press, 1950.

Woolf, Rosemary. *Art and Doctrine: Essays on Medieval Literature*. Ed. Heather O'Donaghue. London: Hambledon, 1986.

———. *The English Religious Lyric in the Middle Ages*. Oxford: Clarendon, 1968.

DEVIANT SPEECH AND GENDER

Men's Voices in Late Medieval England

Sandy Bardsley

"[Where] wymmen arn," claimed a fifteenth-century playwright, "are many wordys."[1] Such aphorisms were commonplace in late medieval and early modern England: the 1542 poem *The School House of Women* commented that "where be women, are many wordys," and the phrase, "many women many words," was already cited as an "old prouerbe" in a book of 1600.[2] Women, according to late medieval poets, playwrights, wall painters, and clerics, were inescapably linked with excessive and disruptive speech, and disruptive speech was in turn connected with women. The law courts emphasized the connection too: in most secular and ecclesiastical jurisdictions, women comprised between 80 and 95 per cent of those charged with "scolding," the offense of engaging in loud, public arguments. Yet associations between women and disruptive speech had major implications for men as well as women, as Derek Neal has shown elsewhere in this volume. Because women and speech were so closely associated, men accused of speaking in problematic ways risked being labeled as womanly. In an age when masculinity might be characterized, in the words of Vern Bullough, as "fragile," a man who was disruptive or excessive in speech risked his gender identity in a way that a woman did not.[3] Yet the risk of effeminacy was one that might be mitigated in particular circumstances. Certain types of problematic male speech escaped associations with womanliness by being constructed less as speech than as deeds or actions. Other types of problematic speech were prosecuted and condemned, but less emphasis was placed on their association with spoken words than on their rebellious and generally insubordinate nature. So although late medieval cultural connections between speech and women meant that illicit male speakers ran a risk of being considered womanly, it was a risk that some forms of speech and some speakers could transcend. In short, men's relationship to deviant speech in late medieval England was considerably more complicated than that of women.

MEN'S VOICES AND THE RISK OF EFFEMINACY

When John Skelton sought to berate men for speaking ill in his 1529 poem "Against Venomous Tongues," he referenced the traditionally feminine connotations of deviant speech in a particularly emasculating turn of phase:

> Sometime women were put in great blame,
> Men said they could not their tongues atame;
> But men take upon them now all the shame,
> With scolding and slandering make their tongues lame.[4]

Others, too, condemned the limp appendage of which scolding men should feel ashamed and pointed out the association between disruptive speech and womanliness. Erasmus's early sixteenth-century treatise "On the Tongue" similarly coded problematic speech as "womanish" and unmasculine.[5] But these sixteenth-century associations between speech and effeminacy had late medieval antecedents. A fourteenth-century poem that lamented the degeneracy and unmanliness of contemporary knights, for instance, compared them explicitly to scolds, collapsing both class and gender into the charge: "Thus is the ordre of kniht turned up-so-doun, / Also wel can a kniht chide as any skolde of a toun."[6] Scolding knights constituted one estate against whom the charge of effeminacy might be wielded.[7] Far more frequently charged as both womanly and garrulous, however, were the medieval clergy.[8] Theoretically celibate, the clergy attracted criticism both for their "scandalous lechery" and for being "too dainty in . . . appearance."[9] Some members of the Church attracted particular concern: a fifteenth-century song, for instance, warned men to protect "thi wyff or thi doughtour . . . [o]r thi sun" against the lecherous advances of friars.[10] While these texts are part of broader antifraternal and anticlerical traditions, their ambivalent representations of clerical sexuality nonetheless point to concerns about the masculinity of members of the Church. Feared as both voracious heterosexuals and predatory homosexuals, their manliness was decidedly dubious: indeed, some even have suggested that the medieval clergy represented a "third gender," neither fully male nor fully female.[11]

Ambivalence about the gender status of the clergy also is evident in the ways and frequency with which their voices were challenged. Priests, in particular, were hauled before ecclesiastical courts for gossiping about their parishioners' misdeeds. Just like women who could, in the words of the Wife of Bath, "no counseil hyde," gossiping priests (armed with the secrets of the confessional) had the power to destroy reputations and expose people to ridicule.[12] In 1397, for example, the parishioners of Garway (Herefordshire) complained to the bishop of Hereford that their priest, Thomas Folyot, frequented taverns "improperly and excessively to the great scandal of the clergy," and had revealed publicly the confession of Robert Scheppert, one of his parishioners. Parishioners elsewhere made similar complaints before the ecclesiastical courts: John, chaplain of the neighboring parish of St. Weonard (Herefordshire), was given to frequenting taverns and gossiping improperly; Stephen Froggesmere, rector of Bere Regis (Dorset) in 1405, publicized John Smyth's confession of theft; and John Springe, rector of Pettaugh (Suffolk) in 1499, was alleged to have "published abroad the confessions of his parishioners."[13] In addition to specific allegations of verbal indiscretion, gossiping priests occasionally found themselves charged with the "womanly" offense of scolding, in either Church or lay courts. John Scarle of London, for instance, was charged in the mayor's court in 1421 for multiple offenses, including scolding, barratry, disclosure of confessions, and blackmail, since he allegedly threatened to reveal the confessional secrets of his female parishioners unless they agreed to commit adultery with him.[14] Authors of moral treatises agreed that revelation of confessional secrets was a serious offense indeed: Robert Mannyng of Brunne's fourteenth-century translation of the *Manuel des pechiez* included several added verses on priests' responsibility to safeguard confessions. Priests who betrayed confessional secrets, he explained, could expect to rot in hell. On earth their tongues were to be drawn out, while in hell they would be forced to chew on their tongues for all eternity.[15] Clearly some parishioners—such as those of Garway, St. Weonard's, Bere Regis, and Pettaugh—hoped for more immediate solutions by forcing indiscreet priests to answer for their misdeeds before their bishops, shaming them publicly by associating them with behaviors that late medieval society coded as feminine.

Medieval parishioners' expectations of clerical voices went beyond expecting priests to keep secrets. It also was important that they stay remote from village politics and disputes in general, rather than stirring up trouble. Unpopular priests in trouble for other offenses often were cited as "quarrelsome" or for "disturb[ing] the peace among [their] parishioners" or "disparag[ing] [their] parishioners and mak[ing] trouble between them," just as women, as a category, were condemned for causing disputes among men.[16] In advice literature, husbands often were cautioned to be skeptical about the tales that women told them, since women were inclined to stir up conflict. Women's mouths could cause serious trouble for men, cautioned John of Trevisa's fourteenth-century translation of *De proprietatibus rerum*, and no man "has more woo [woe] than he that has an euyll wife, cryenge and janglynge, chydynge and skoldynge."[17] Priests who behaved in such womanly ways, quarreling and causing disputes among their parishioners, thus could expect to be humiliated before the Church courts, alongside those who gossiped indiscreetly.

Yet priests, too, employed strategically the discourse about speech's effeminacy. Priests and *inquisitores* (laymen of relatively high social status) presented those accused of certain verbal transgressions—such as scolding, defamation, and gossiping in church—before ecclesiastical courts. In addition, members of the clergy used their sermons to send messages about appropriate speech, particularly in the context of the church service. One common *exemplum* used to illustrate sermons told of a cleric, sometimes identified as the young St. Martin, St. Brice, or St. Augustine, who unexpectedly burst out laughing in the middle of a reading in church. When reprimanded by his superior after the service, the cleric explained what he had seen. Behind two chattering women lurked a demon (sometimes named as Tutivillus), writing every word they said on a piece of parchment.[18] These women were so loquacious, however, that the demon soon ran out of space on his scroll. In order to stretch the parchment, he tugged it with his teeth. But in doing so he knocked his head against the wall, prompting the cleric's mirth. In some versions of the tale the noise of the demon's head hitting the wall was heard throughout the church, and later examination found black demon-blood in the place that his head had struck. Variations of this *exemplum* appear from the twelfth century onwards, from as far afield as Iceland, Sweden, and Estonia. Although it did not originate in late medieval England, the story seems to have had significant cultural currency there: among English sermons, plays, and poems of the thirteenth to sixteenth centuries, it appears in more than forty surviving manuscripts.[19] But whereas some aspects of the story were unstable—the cleric might be identified as the young St. Brice, St. Martin, St. Augustine, or left unnamed; the demon might or might not shed blood after stretching his scroll to make more room for their words—one key detail remained the same: whenever the individuals caught chattering were given a gender, they were always female. An early fifteenth-century poem that made reference to this tale demonstrated both an assumption that the tale was known widely and an assumption that talking in church was an especially feminine vice:

Tutiuillus þe deuil of hell,
He wryteþ har [their] names soþe [truth] to tel,
ad missam garulantes [those gossiping in mass]
Better wer be at home for ay,
Þan her to serue þe deuil to pay,
sic vana famulantes [as those serving vanities]
Þe[s] women þat sittiþ þe church about,
Þai beþ al of þe deuilis rowte [band],
diuina impedientes [impeding the divine service].

The poem goes on to describe how Tutivillus will draw these chattering women to hell, concluding with a general exhortation to be silent in church and thus win admission to God's inn and the bliss of heaven.[20] The Tutivillus *exemplum* illustrates the extent to which excessive and inappropriate speech was identified as a feminine crime. When priests wanted to warn their parishioners against chattering in church, they automatically selected women as the transgressors, efficiently denigrating potential chatterers of both sexes.[21] "Womanly" was not a compliment for either women or men.

The connection between women and church-time chatterers was not lost on those who commissioned and executed wall paintings and wood-carvings in the churches. The theme of Tutivillus lurking behind gossiping women appears in more than a dozen surviving English wall paintings, in a number of small stone carvings on both the interiors and exteriors of parish churches, and on at least seven surviving misericords (carved wooden ledges underneath the seats in the choirs of cathedrals and larger parish churches).[22] There even survives at Stanford-on-Avon (Northamptonshire) a stained glass window of the early fourteenth century that shows two gossiping women, with another woman behind them, being tempted by three demons.[23] Artistic representations of Tutivillus survive from the second half of the thirteenth century through the fifteenth century, with a peak in the fourteenth century. They appear throughout England—from Yorkshire to Kent to Somerset.[24]

Yet whereas the Tutivillus *exemplum* and wall paintings made a forceful connection between women, words, and sin, men were much more likely than women to be hauled up before Church courts for disturbing services by their chatter. Cases of impeding divine services were less frequent than cases of defamation or scolding, yet they were not altogether rare, especially by the mid-fifteenth century, as Table 1 shows.

TABLE 1. CHURCH-TIME CHATTER, 1397–1519

Diocese	Women	Men
Hereford, 1397[1]	1	2
Salisbury, 1405–08[2]	0	2
Ely (Deanery of Wisbech), 1460–79[3]	6	30
Norwich (Archdeaconries of Suffolk & Sudbury), 1499[4]	2	6
Kent, 1511[5]	1	5
Lincoln, 1519[6]	1	14
Total	11 (16%)	59 (84%)

Note: The numbers presented here refer to allegations, not individuals, so some individuals are counted more than once.

Sources:

[1] Visitation of parishes by John Trefnant, Bishop of Hereford, 1397 (Hereford Cathedral Library typescript of MS Hereford Cathedral 1779).

[2] *The Register of John Chandler*, ed. Timmins.

[3] *Lower Ecclesiastical Jurisdiction in Late-Medieval England*, ed. Poos.

[4] *The Register of John Morton*, ed. Harper-Bill.

[5] *Kentish Visitations*, ed. Wood-Legh.

[6] *Visitations in the Diocese of Lincoln*, ed. Thompson.

Across six dioceses, among seventy allegations of talking in church and disturbing services, fifty-nine were laid against men, yet only eleven against women. Some men were charged repeatedly: Robert Pygge of the Wisbech parish of St. Peter, for instance, was cited in 1469 for failing to cease his gossiping, even after he had been admonished by the priest. Male chatterers often were presented in groups of up to three or four at once, suggesting that the intention was perhaps to make an example of a particularly loud or garrulous clique of friends.

The gap between representations and prosecutions of church-time chatterers is an interesting one. Did the association between church gossip and women make gossiping men more conspicuous? Did gossiping men pose more of a threat by setting a bad example for women? To both priests and *inquisitores*, gossip during services must have represented a flaunting of authority, a disorderly form of insubordination that ran contrary to the increasingly popular discourse of order and good governance. The apparent contradiction between literary and artistic constructions of church gossip and those presented before the courts, however, demonstrates the very resilience of gender norms about speech. Whereas the proportion of men charged as church gossips did not change significantly over time, the stereotype of women as disturbers of church services persisted. Inevitably, therefore, men who were charged with gossip must have experienced some association with things effeminate, compared as they were to the well-known depictions of gossiping women under the eye of the demon Tutivillus. Indeed, some of the words used to describe their speech were akin to those used for scolding, a crime associated overwhelmingly with women: Robert Pygge of Wisbech was described as a "garulator in ecclesia" while Bartholomew Edmund was cited "pro garulatione in ecclesia." John Mayson junior of Emneth was allegedly a "communis objurgator in ecclesia," whereas Robert Johnson of the same parish was accustomed to "litigare in ecclesia et cimiterio [churchyard]."[25] Each of these words (derived from the verbs *garrire, objurgare*, and *litigare*) also was used in both local and ecclesiastical courts to describe scolds. So although the context of their chatter was circumscribed, church gossips—mostly men—were almost scolds and quite likely were intended to feel shamed by their association with a womanly crime. The discourse on the effeminacy of speech was one that could be employed strategically by both clergy and laity.

Swearwords as Deeds

Yet while medieval men—clergy and laity alike—risked being charged with womanly behavior if they gossiped or spoke angrily, certain types of speech transcended this association. In particular, the crimes of swearing and blasphemy—which tended to be identified primarily with men—escaped a close connection with effeminacy. As Miriam Gill explains in her essay in this volume, medieval profanities often involved invoking parts of Christ's or God's body by swearing, for instance, "by the bones of Christ," and common late medieval *exempla* warned swearers that the physical body of Christ in heaven was harmed each time such an oath was uttered. Because of the harms they inflicted on Christ with their oaths, habitual swearers sometimes were punished in kind with comparable pains, either on earth or in the afterlife. But just as the Tutivillus story usually was told or depicted with women as the culprits of church-time gossip, *exempla* of swearing almost always featured men as the transgressors.[26] Indeed, gender seems more central to the *exemplum* than social status: one story told of a gentleman whose swearing "by God's blood" caused him to bleed to death in a spectacular manner, while another story attributed a similar fate to a London apprentice who swore "by the bones of God."[27] Swearers could come from any social class. Commentators lamented that the third commandment (to refrain from taking God's name in vain) was broken "a-monge lered and lewde, a-monge yeonge and old, a-monge ryche and pore, frome a litill yeonge chyld that can unnethe speke, to an olde berded man that age hath ny3 be-nome his ry3t speche," yet they conspicuously failed to state that swearing took place among both women and men.[28]

The male-associated nature of swearing was thrown into greater relief by stories and representations, discussed by Miriam Gill, in which Mary, as mother of Christ, laments her son's pain or intercedes on his behalf to halt his suffering. Stories, poems, wall paintings, and even a stained glass window depicted Mary holding Christ's broken body and condemning those who swore. While women occasionally were connected with swearing, as exemplified by the Wife of Bath, who claimed that "For half so boldly kan ther no man / Swere and lyen, as a womman kan," medieval tales, *exempla,* poems, and artistic representations overwhelmingly associated swearing and blasphemous speech with men.[29]

Yet men who swore somehow remained exempt from the charge of effeminacy leveled at complaining knights and indiscreet priests. The *exemplum* and representations showing the fate of the swearing men are both explicit and emphatic in their warnings about the evils of blasphemous speech, yet they do not claim such speech to be womanly. While poets and sermon authors were quick to imply womanliness in feeble knights or men whose dress was thought to be too modern or elaborate, it is noteworthy that they did not make similar charges against swearing or blasphemous men. How did medieval people reconcile the fact that troublesome speech in general was associated with women, while swearing in particular was associated with men? Part of the answer doubtless lies in the capacity of medieval culture, like modern culture, to incorporate contradictions and ambiguities. But part also, I suggest, lies in the ways in which swearing was constructed in late medieval England.

Exempla of men who swore by parts of Christ's body represent the crimes of the men less as speech than as acts or deeds. The oaths of the blasphemous men wreak physical, tangible results for Christ's body (and their own), in a way that women's gossip does not. Contemporary aphorisms and maxims suggest that an important distinction existed in late medieval and early modern England between words (typically gendered female) and deeds (associated primarily with men). "Words they are women, and deeds they are men," proclaimed a proverb first recorded in 1598 but probably dating from earlier.[30] By viewing the act of swearing as a deed, a physical attack on the body of Christ, the binaries of speech and deeds, women and men, could be maintained without disruption.

MALE SPEECH AS DEEDS IN THE COURTS

Speech could be constructed as a deed in the context of the courtroom, too. In 1315, Geoffrey Shepherd of Redgrave (Suffolk) was puzzled to find himself sued for defamation by Richard the Chaplain. Geoffrey explained that he did not use any force in his conflict with Richard and protested being sued not for committing any act but instead for "wind." The "wind" to which Geoffrey referred was that of spoken words.[31] Like Geoffrey—and like *exempla* and visual representations—medieval courts also distinguished between words that were "wind" and words that implied deeds.[32] Unlike Geoffrey, however, they took "wind"-like speech, speech dangerous in and of itself, just as seriously as speech that implied or promised action. Moreover, the distinction between words-as-words and words-as-deeds was heavily gendered, especially from the late fourteenth century onward.

On some occasions, words that accompanied assaults were punished in the courts, but they were constructed in different ways from the closely associated crime of scolding. Men were far more likely than women to be charged with assault and other types of violence, staples of medieval local court business; indeed, they outnumbered women in allegations of violent crimes by a ratio of more than 5:1.[33] Presumably, men did not fight in silence; however, verbal offenses that accompanied assaults are mentioned only seldom in the court records. One exception can be seen in the court records of Battle (Sussex), in which men often were cited for making "assaults with contumelious [insulting or outrageous] words," which may or may not have been accompanied by physical violence. Indeed, among surviving records from Battle between 1460 and 1470, men who made assaults with contumelious words numbered almost as many as scolds. Surviving courts from this decade list eight scolds—one man and seven women—whereas seven men are recorded as having made assaults with contumelious words (and many more for regular assaults). Yet the ways in which scolding and assaults with contumelious words were constructed in the court rolls are revealing. Those committing assaults with contumelious words were presented as having committed specific actions, described with verbs, rather than as people occupying a particular identity, that of "common scold," described with nouns. They also received slightly lower fines than scolds (an average of 3.29*d.* compared with an average of 3.75*d.*), suggesting that the court regarded the offense of assault with contumelious words as less problematic than that of scolding.[34] In other jurisdictions, men who were disorderly in their speech sometimes were charged with general disruptiveness rather than with scolding per se. When

John of Langham and Robert Porter of Leicester spoke "litigious words and threatening words" to Richard Gamson, bailiff of the lord Duke of Lancaster, on a market day in 1379, they were charged as disturbers of the peace rather than as scolds.[35] In the court records of Battle and Leicester, the distinction between doing and being, committing assaults and occupying the category of scold, thus was maintained quite explicitly.[36]

In addition to swearwords and "assaults with contumelious words," other types of problematic speech also managed to dodge the association with effeminacy. From the late fourteenth century onward, manorial and borough courts recorded particular concern about the verbal abuse of community officials and inappropriate speech in the courtroom, and these offenses were committed especially by men.

As Table 2 shows, those who allegedly abused bailiffs or constables or other local officials and those who muttered, gossiped, or created commotions in the courtroom were typically men. No women were named among the twenty-two charges of contempt and gossip in Methwold between 1368 and 1406. A couple of women were charged at Crowle for inappropriate speech in the courtroom, but these are the exceptions to the rule. Verbal insubordination in the courtroom was largely a male crime.

TABLE 2. ABUSE OF OFFICIALS AND DISRUPTION IN COURT, 1332–1406

Jurisdiction	Charges against Women	Charges against Men
Crowle (Lincolnshire)[1]	2	5
Methwold (Norfolk)[2]	0	22
Middlewich (Cheshire)[3]	1	5
Wakefield (Yorkshire)[4]	0	6
Total	3 (7%)	38 (93%)

Note: The numbers presented here refer to allegations, not individuals, so some individuals are counted more than once. These numbers do not include those cited for contempt of court unless the contempt is clearly verbal in nature. In some places, individuals could be cited for contempt if they arrived to court late or withdrew from the court before the session was completed. See, for example, *Court Rolls of the Manor of Wakefield from September 1348 to September 1350,* ed. Jewell, 23, 100, 101, 124, 200.
Sources:
[1] Lincolnshire Archive Office CM 1/22–/42.
[2] Public Record Office DL 30 104/1471–80.
[3] Public Record Office SC2 156/2.
[4] *The Court Rolls of the Manor of Wakefield from October 1331 to September 1333,* ed.

Walker; *The Court Rolls of the Manor of Wakefield from October 1338 to September 1340*, ed. Troup; *The Court Rolls of the Manor of Wakefield from September 1348 to September 1350*, ed. Jewell.

Part of the explanation for men's preponderance among rebels and courtroom mutterers is doubtless that men were far more likely to be actors in the courtroom context. Manorial courts required the attendance of the suitors—those who owed suit to the court—and these were generally the male heads of household. If a woman was engaged in conflict over debt or trespass, the case typically was brought by her husband or father (unless she was a widow or—in the rare instance—she was trading as a *femme sole*). Yet men were also more likely to be charged as rebels for abusing officials outside the courtroom itself. They threatened rent collectors, swore at constables, and bad-mouthed bailiffs. In some scenarios, one cannot help but wonder whether the same behavior coming from a woman might not have been described as scolding rather than rebelliousness. In 1349, for instance, William, son of Philip Sagher, confessed in the court of Wakefield to having threatened John, son of Henry Forester, while John was performing his duty as ale-taster. William was charged with contempt against the lord.[37] Women certainly were, occasionally, charged with rebellion against ale-tasters—Sherri Olson cites examples from the Huntingdonshire manors of Upwood and Ellington in 1403 and 1425—but other women who protested the authority of local officials might have found themselves charged as scolds instead.[38] Karen Jones and Michael Zell have suggested that rebellion against local authority was a recurring theme in scolding prosecutions and that women tended to be punished more harshly than men for insubordination.[39] Similarly, Maryanne Kowaleski's work on the scolds of Exeter has highlighted the threat they posed to members of the local elite.[40] In other words, similar behaviors performed by men and by women might have been interpreted and labeled differently by the manorial or town officials on whom they were visited. Women, once again, were associated with an identity based around words, whereas men carried out rebellious deeds or deeds merely accompanied by injurious or contumelious words.

Male Scolds

Even on the rare occasions when men were charged as scolds, they might have been able to escape the association with things womanly. The low number of male scolds makes it difficult to generalize about their characteristics, but among the small sample three main patterns stand out. First, men accused of scolding often were charged alongside their wives. Of twenty men accused in manorial and borough courts between 1373 and 1464, for instance, six were accused of scolding together with their wives, and a further two were accused in groups alongside women who shared the same surname (and hence may have been wives, sisters, or some other female relation).[41] A typical example is that of Hugh Welesson of Middlewich (Cheshire). In 1434, Hugh and his wife Isabel were involved in an argument with Helen, wife of Peter Bradwall. Helen, the court heard, scolded both Isabel and Hugh, calling Isabel a "child murderer" and Hugh a "skallet [wretched] knave." Isabel and Hugh in turn scolded Helen, calling her a "lying bletherer." Helen was fined 6d. for each scolding (that is, a total of 12d.), and Hugh and Isabel were assigned a joint fine of 6d. The record of the court proceedings reveals frustratingly little about the dynamics of this incident. How did it begin? Was Hugh perhaps drawn into the argument in an effort to support his wife? Was Isabel perhaps drawn in, in an effort to support her husband? Nor do we know how Hugh felt about his scolding conviction—whether he felt deeply shamed, sorely aggrieved, or unconcerned. It is possible, however, that he and other men charged as scolds alongside their wives might have regarded their charges as resulting from their support of their wives. In other words, even though they were charged as scolds, they garnered such charges as the result of performing typically masculine and husbandly tasks. Although charged with a crime with strongly feminine associations, these associations might have been mitigated by their performance of stereotypically manly behaviors, those of providing support and protection for wives and other female family members.

Second, in examining male scolds we also can see that—if they had substantial social and economic resources—the womanly associations that accompanied scolding charges were not necessarily sufficient to remove them from positions of power. Male scolds (like female scolds) came from a range of social and occupational backgrounds, although members of local elites perhaps were over-represented among the men. Of five male scolds from Middlewich, for example, three came from prominent local families, owned land and/or businesses, and regularly served in the relatively prestigious positions of juror or chamberlain. Moreover, scolding accusations did not necessarily spell an end to local prominence and public office-holding. In 1425, William Croucher was fined in the county court as a common litigator [scold] and "baratemaker" [troublemaker] among his neighbors in the town of Middlewich. Yet William continued to be chosen as juror, town chamberlain, and churchwarden throughout the 1420s, 1430s, and early 1440s, positions to which no local woman was ever appointed. Men who could draw on social and economic resources thus were able to "ride out" scolding charges and associations of effeminacy without losing access to local power.

Third, men accused of scolding were often in trouble for multiple other offenses. John Scarle, for example, a parson of London, was accused simultaneously in a civil court in 1421 as a fornicator, a scold, a barrator, a discloser of confessions, and a wrongful practitioner of the profession of surgeon. Richard Maynhard of Bridgwater (Somerset) faced multiple charges across the 1370s and 1380s as a raiser of unjust hues and a regrator of fish. And William Croucher of Middlewich was almost constantly in trouble during the 1410s and 1420s in the borough court, sheriff's tourn, and county court for assault, looting, rape, theft, and participation in plans for murder. William's punishment for scolding followed a year in which he had appeared in the county court on no fewer than thirteen occasions, both alone and with accomplices.[42] Ruth Karras has proposed that when women were charged with scolding alongside multiple other crimes, prosecutors might have been trying to send the message that "Here is a woman out of control."[43] Court records of male scolds suggest that, in the cases of at least some men, scolding convictions expressed the same sentiment as for women, whether or not they carried the same consequences. In such situations, scolding charges were typically only one of multiple ways in which local authorities attempted to discipline individuals regarded as unruly.

Men who appeared before the courts as alleged scolds indeed may have been regarded in their communities as womanly and emasculated. But the small sample of surviving cases in which men were charged suggests that some men may have been able to overcome such associations if prosecutions seemed to result from their support of family members, if they possessed substantial social and economic resources, or if their scolding presentments were overshadowed by other, more serious charges.

CONCLUSION

The relationship between men and speech in late medieval England was significantly more complicated than that between words and women. Because illicit speech was so emphatically coded a feminine failing, men who spoke too much or in inappropriate contexts risked the charge of effeminacy, of possessing "lame tongues," worn out by overuse. Indeed, the term "old woman," sometimes applied to gossipy men in modern society, demon-

strates one way in which masculinity can still be undermined by an association with excessive speech. Yet despite the general connection between
excessive or disruptive speech and effeminacy, certain types of illicit speech
and certain male speakers managed to dodge such connotations. Crimes
such as swearing, abusing community officials, and attacking others with
contumelious or injurious words often were constructed—in both literary
and artistic representations and in court records—as actions or deeds, as opposed to womanly words. The man who swore by "Christ's bones," muttered in the courtroom, or abused a bailiff was seen as committing a misdeed
rather than misspeaking. Reflecting a long-standing cultural binary that
connected women with words and men with deeds, the verbal crimes commonly committed by men were not represented as speech per se. Even on
the few occasions when individual men were prosecuted for the female-associated crime of scolding, they may have been able sometimes to escape the
connection with effeminacy by means of their social and economic resources or by constructing their alleged scolding as appropriate husbandly
support of their wives. Men perhaps had more to lose than women by being
disparaged as womanly, yet they also had more room to maneuver in avoiding such derision.

However, medieval men still had to negotiate one more twist to the
complex gendering of speech norms: just as excessive speech was effeminiz-
ing, so too—on occasion—was excessive silence. When, as Priscilla Martin
has pointed out, the Host in *The Canterbury Tales* tries to goad the Clerk
into telling a story, he casts the Clerk's silence as unmanly:

> Ye ryde as coy and stille as dooth a mayde
> Were newe spoused, sittynge at the bord;
> This day ne herde I of youre tonge a word.[44]

The Clerk is emasculated by his failure to contribute verbally to the entertainment of the pilgrims. Just as garrulous men made their tongues lame
with overuse, men who failed to use their tongues at all were seen as verbally impotent. Unwise silence, the last of twenty-four "sins of the tongue"
enumerated and explained by Guillelmus Peraldus in his thirteenth-century
treatise, was akin to cowardice. Quoting Ezekiel, Peraldus explained that
priests who held their tongues, hesitating to intervene to prevent sins, put
the souls of their parishioners in jeopardy and were as guilty as those who
failed to blow their horns to warn of an enemy's attack.[45] Failure to speak
could be just as unmanly as speaking too much.

Appropriate masculine speech in late medieval England thus occupied a middle ground between silence and garrulity; at either margin, men risked being seen as effeminate. While certain types of male speech were sheltered from an association with womanliness, the consequences for those who transgressed the boundaries could be humiliating. For late medieval English men, speech norms were both more fraught and more flexible than for their sisters and their wives.

Notes

1. From *The Castle of Perseverance*, in *The Macro Plays*, ed. Furnivall and Pollard, 156.

2. Apperson, *English Proverbs*, 705. See also Roberts, "'Words they are Women'."

3. Bullough, "On Being Male."

4. "Against Venomous Tongues," in John Skelton, *The Complete Poems*, ed. Henderson, 245–49 at 248.

5. Parker, "On the Tongue."

6. "The Simonie," in *Political Songs*, ed. Wright, 323–45.

7. For discussion of late medieval satirical and complaint literature on the subject of knights, see Owst, *Literature and Pulpit*, 331–38.

8. As Peter has discussed, the clergy faced attack in late medieval literature far more often than any other profession (*Complaint and Satire*, 80–84).

9. Both quotes are from synodal sermons preached at York in 1372 and 1373, quoted by Owst, *Literature and Pulpit*, 274. For a general discussion of attacks on the clergy, see Owst, 222–86.

10. "A Song Against the Friars," in *Reliquiæ Antiquæ*, ed. Wright and Halliwell, 2: 247.

11. Swanson, "Angels Incarnate."

12. Geoffrey Chaucer, *The Canterbury Tales*, in *The Riverside Chaucer*, ed. Benson et al., III.980. All references to *The Canterbury Tales* are to this edition. Similar complaints about wives' inability to keep secrets may be found, for example, in the mid-twelfth-century "*Proverbs of Alfred*," in *An Old English Miscellany*, ed. Morris, 118–22. At least six thirteenth- and fourteenth-century manuscripts containing these proverbs survive.

13. Visitation of parishes by John Trefnant, Bishop of Hereford, 1397 (typescript of MS Hereford Cathedral 1779 held at Hereford Cathedral Library); *The Register of John Chandler*, ed. Timmins, 25; *The Register of John Morton*, ed. Harper-Bill, 3: 201–02. In most cases, priests were able to find the requisite number of compurgators who would attest to their innocence, but the very necessity of appearing in front of one's bishop on such a charge must have proven humiliating.

14. *Calendar of Pleas and Memoranda Rolls,* ed. Thomas, 127. Barratry was a crime that originally involved wasteful litigation, or the pursuit of spurious court cases. By the time of Scarle's conviction, however, it had expanded to imply problematic speech in general.

15. Mannyng, *Handlyng Synne,* ed. Furnivall, 125–26.

16. See, for example, *The Register of John Waltham,* ed. Timmins, 122–23, 127; *The Register of John Chandler,* ed. Timmins, 25, 48, 74, 85–86, 93–94.

17. See, for example, "Great Cato, or Cato's Distichs," Bk. 1, in *The Minor Poems of the Vernon Manuscript,* ed. Furnivall, 564; Bartholomeus, *De proprietatibus rerum,* trans. John Trevisa, 197.

18. In early versions of the Tutivillus tale the whole congregation sometimes was guilty of chattering, but whenever individual church-goers were mentioned, as in most thirteenth- to fifteenth-century versions of the tale, they were always women (Jennings, *Tutivillus,* 27).

19. For a complete list of English examples, see Jennings, *Tutivillus,* Appendix I. Jennings also has discussed Tutivillus's function as a demon who collected the words and phrases that priests skipped over or mumbled when they said mass; texts that give only this *exemplum* have not been included in my count.

20. "On Chattering in Church," in *Religious Lyrics of the Fifteenth Century,* ed. Brown, 277.

21. Associations between women and rumors had existed since biblical times: see 1 Tim. 5:13 for a warning about widows who "gad about" and gossip.

22. Miriam Gill identifies fifteen wall paintings, of which twelve are currently visible: Brook (Kent), Wissington (Suffolk), Colton (Norfolk), Little Melton (Norfolk), Peakirk (Northamptonshire), Grundisburgh (Suffolk), Lower Halstow (Kent), Slapton (Northamptonshire), Eaton (Norfolk), Nedging by Naughton (Suffolk), Crostwight (Norfolk), Melbourne (Derbyshire), Wiston (Suffolk), Stokesby (lost), Great Conrad (Suffolk). I am very grateful to Dr. Gill for giving me a copy of her dissertation. Misericords representing Tutivillus and the gossiping women survive at Ely, Enville (Staffordshire), Gayton (Northamptonshire), New College Chapel in Oxford, Minster-in-Thanet (Kent), and St. Katherine's Hospital of Stepney (London). An example of Tutivillus on a nave arcade stone carving may be seen at Sleaford (Lincolnshire) (see Sekules, "Women and Art," figure 13).

23. This window is reproduced in Marks, *Stained Glass,* 80–81; and in Alexander and Binski, eds., *Age of Chivalry,* 446.

24. Nearly all the wall paintings of Tutivillus, however, are found in the east of England—Norfolk, Suffolk, Northamptonshire, and Kent—which is the area where wall paintings most tend to survive.

25. *Lower Ecclesiastical Jurisdiction,* ed. Poos, 275, 318, 360, 388, 466.

26. Charges of such blasphemy do occasionally appear in ecclesiastical courts but are rare: John Wulrerd of Walberswick, for example, was charged in 1499 as a "common blasphemer by the body of Christ and His other limbs." John admitted the charge and was ordered to carry a candle worth 4*d.* to the altar on the following

Sunday and offer it to the honor of the body of Christ (*The Register of John Morton*, ed. Harper-Bill, 3: 184).

27. Owst, *Literature and Pulpit*, 424.

28. Owst, *Literature and Pulpit*, 416.

29. Chaucer, *Tales*, III. 227–28. Note also that John Wycliffe argued for a female-associated meaning of the word *blasphemy* when he suggested that it was derived from the words *blas* and *femina*, meaning a foolish and harmful woman (Lawton, *Blasphemy*, 105). For one mention of women swearing oaths, see *A Selection of Latin Stories*, ed. Wright, 61–62.

30. Roberts, "'Words they are Women'," 161, n. 1. See also *Oxford Dictionary of English Proverbs*, 175. The Latin proverb "Where there is a breast, there is a swelling; facts are masculine, words are feminine" began Erasmus's 1525 treatise "On the Tongue" (Parker, "On the Tongue," esp. 460, n. 6).

31. *Select Cases*, ed. Helmholz, 33. Richard might have retorted that Geoffrey's "wind" had tangible consequences indeed. Allegedly, Geoffrey told others that Richard had assaulted another man, drawing blood, and Richard was indicted at the sheriff's tourn and fined 40*d.*

32. Linguists and theorists recently have considered distinctions between speech that is mere "wind" and speech that performs some action by its very utterance. Austin's work on performative speech, *How to Do Things with Words*, in which he identified particular words and phrases as ones that performed actions by their very utterance (for example, spoken in the right circumstances, "I thee wed" performs the action of marrying someone) has inspired work on "performance theory." Recent scholars have sought to extend the notion of performance to a wide variety of social categories. Best-known to historians of women, perhaps, is Butler's work on the performance of gender, in which she argues that gender identity is constituted by performances or expressions of gender (*Gender Trouble*). Butler's more recent book, *Excitable Speech*, considers the violence that can be performed through hate speech and negative labels. For an example of a medievalist's application of Austin's speech-act theory, see Little, *Benedictine Maledictions.*

33. In Brigstock (Northamptonshire), women were charged with 17 per cent of 175 assaults, threatened assaults, and *hamsokens* [housebreakings] between 1287 and 1348 (Bennett, *Women*, 39). In the manor court of Wakefield, they accounted for 11 per cent of 632 assaults. They also were charged with 7 per cent of 2696 homicides among gaol delivery rolls from Norfolk, Yorkshire, and Northamptonshire between 1300 and 1348 (Hanawalt, "The Female Felon," 258, 268).

34. Henry E. Huntington Library, BA 546–648.

35. *Records of the Borough of Leicester,* ed. Bateson, 2: 183.

36. Olson notes that—before the plague—women in Upwood and Ellington tended to be cited for contempt of officials whereas men were more likely to be cited for rebellion against officials (*A Chronicle*, 112).

37. *Court Rolls of the Manor of Wakefield*, ed. Jewell, 92, 104, 126, 133, 139.

38. Olson, *A Chronicle*, 217.

39. Jones and Zell, "Bad Conversation?"

40. Kowaleski, "Gossip, Gender, and the Economy."

41. The sample of twenty men that I am using here consists of five men from Middlewich, Cheshire (Public Record Office SC2 156/2–7), three from London (*Calendar of Pleas and Memoranda Rolls*, ed. Thomas), five from Nottingham (*Records of the Borough of Nottingham*, ed. Sevenson et al., vol. 2), one from Bridgwater, Somerset (*Bridgwater Borough Archives*, ed. Dilks, vol. 2), two from Colchester (*Court Rolls of the Borough of Colchester*, ed. and trans. Jeayes and Benham, vol. 3), two from East Merrington, Durham (*Halmota Prioratus Dunelmensis*, ed. Booth), one from Chedzoy, Somerset (Public Record Office SC2 198/19), and one from Battle (Henry E. Huntington Library BA 610).

42. *Calendar of Pleas and Memoranda Rolls*, ed. Thomas, 127; *Bridgwater Borough Archives*, ed. Dilks, vol. 2; PRO CHES 25/12.

43. Karras, *Common Women*, 139.

44. Geoffrey Chaucer, *Tales*, IV. 2–4; Martin, *Chaucer's Women*, 222–24.

45. *Book*, ed. Diekstra, 532.

WORKS CITED

ABBREVIATIONS

EETS   Early English Text Society. London: Early English Text Society, 1864–.

MANUSCRIPT SOURCES

Hereford, Hereford Cathedral Library, Visitation of parishes by John Trefnant, Bishop of Hereford, 1397 (typescript of MS Hereford Cathedral 1779).

Lincoln, Lincolnshire Archive Office, CM 1/22–1/42.

London, Public Record Office, PRO CHES 25/12; DL 30 104/1471–1480; SC2 156/2–7; SC2 198/19.

San Marino, Henry E. Huntington Library, BA 546–648.

PRIMARY SOURCES

Bartholomeus. *De proprietatibus rerum.* Trans. John Trevisa. N.p., 1495.

Book for a Simple & Devout Woman: A Late Middle English Adaptation of Peraldus's Summa de Vitiis et Virtutibus *and Friar Laurent's* Somme le Roi, *Edited from British Library Mss Harley 6571 and Additional 30944.* Ed. F. N. M. Diekstra. Groningen: Forsten, 1998.

Bridgwater Borough Archives. Ed. Thomas Bruce Dilks. Vol. 2. Somerset Record Society Publications, vol. 53 (1938).

Calendar of Pleas and Memoranda Rolls Preserved among the Archives of the Corporation of the City of London at the Guild-hall. Vol. 4: *1413–37.* Ed. A. H. Thomas. Cambridge: Cambridge University Press, 1943.

Chaucer, Geoffrey. *The Riverside Chaucer*. Ed. Larry D. Benson et al. 3rd ed. Boston: Houghton Mifflin, 1987.

Court Rolls of the Borough of Colchester. Ed. and trans. Isaac Herbert Jeayes and W. Gurney Benham. Vol. 1. Colchester: s.n., 1941.

The Court Rolls of the Manor of Wakefield from September 1348 to September 1350. Ed. Helen M. Jewell. The Wakefield Court Rolls Series of the Yorkshire Archaeological Society. 2nd series, vol. 2 (1981).

The Court Rolls of the Manor of Wakefield from October 1331 to September 1333. Ed. Sue Sheridan Walker. The Wakefield Court Rolls Series of the Yorkshire Archaeological Society, vol. 3 (1982).

The Court Rolls of the Manor of Wakefield from October 1338 to September 1340. Ed. K. M. Troup. The Wakefield Court Rolls Series of the Yorkshire Archaeological Society, vol. 12 (1999).

Halmota Prioratus Dunelmensis, Containing extracts from the halmote court or manor rolls of the prior and convent of Durham 1296–1384. Ed. John Booth. Surtees Society Publications, vol. 82 (1886).

Kentish Visitations of Archbishop William Warham and His Deputies, 1511–12. Ed. K. L. Wood-Legh. Kent Records Publications, vol. 24 (1984).

Lower Ecclesiastical Jurisdiction in Late-Medieval England: The Courts of the Dean and Chapter of Lincoln, 1336–1349, and the Deanery of Wisbech, 1458–1484. Ed. L .R. Poos. Oxford: Oxford University Press, 2001.

The Macro Plays. Ed. F. J. Furnivall and Alfred W. Pollard. EETS e.s. 91 (1904).

Mannyng, Robert. *Robert of Brunne's, 'Handlyng Synne,' AD 1303, with those parts of the Anglo-French treatise on which it was based, William of Wadington's 'Manuel des Pechiez.'* Ed. Frederick J. Furnivall. EETS o.s. 119. London: Kegan Paul, Trench, Trübner, 1901.

The Political Songs of England. Ed. Thomas Wright. Camden Society Publications, vol. 6 (London, 1839).

The Proverbs of Alfred. In *An Old English Miscellany*, ed. Richard Morris, 102–38. EETS o.s. 49. London: N. Trübner & Co., 1872.

Records of the Borough of Leicester. Ed. Mary Bateson. Vol. 2: *1327–1509*. London C. J. Clay and Sons, 1901.

Records of the Borough of Nottingham. Ed. W. H. Stevenson, et al. Vols. 1–3. London: B. Quaritch, 1882–85.

The Register of John Morton, Archbishop of Canterbury 1486–1500. Ed. Christopher Harper-Bill. Vol. 3: Norwich *Sede Vacante*, 1499. Canterbury and York Society Publications, vol. 89. Woodbridge, 2000.

The Register of John Chandler, Dean of Salisbury 1404–1417. Ed. T. C. B. Timmins. Wiltshire Record Society Publications, vol. 39 (1983).

The Register of John Waltham, Bishop of Salisbury 1388–1395. Ed. T. C. B. Timmins. Canterbury and York Society Publications, vol. 80 (1994).

Religious Lyrics of the Fifteenth Century. Ed. Carleton Brown. Oxford: Clarendon, 1939.

Reliquiæ Antiquæ: Scraps from Ancient Manuscripts, Illustrating Chiefly Early English Literature and the English Language. 2 vols. Ed. Thomas Wright and James Orchard Halliwell-Phillips. London: J. R. Smith, 1845.

Select Cases on Defamation to 1600. Ed. R. H. Helmholz. London: Seldon Society, 1985.

A Selection of Latin Stories from Manuscripts of the Thirteenth and Fourteenth Centuries. Ed. Thomas Wright. Percy Society Publications, vol. 8 (1843).

Skelton, John. *The Complete Poems of John Skelton, Laureate.* Ed. Philip Henderson. 4th ed. London: J. M. Dent, 1959.

Visitations in the Diocese of Lincoln, 1517–1531. Ed. A. Hamilton Thompson. Vol. 1. Lincoln Record Society Publications, vol. 33 (1940).

SECONDARY SOURCES

Alexander, Jonathan, and Paul Binski, eds. *Age of Chivalry: Art in Plantagenet England 1200–1400.* London: Royal Academy of Arts, with Weidenfeld and Nicolson, 1987.

Apperson, G. L. *English Proverbs and Proverbial Phrases: A Historical Dictionary.* London: J. M. Dent and Sons, 1929.

Austin, J. L. *How to Do Things with Words.* 2nd ed. Cambridge, MA: Harvard University Press, 1975.

Bennett, Judith M. *Women in the Medieval English Countryside: Gender and Household in Brigstock before the Plague.* New York: Oxford University Press, 1987.

Bullough, Vern L. "On Being Male in the Middle Ages." In *Medieval Masculinities: Regarding Men in the Middle Ages,* ed. Clare A. Lees, 31–46. Minneapolis: University of Minnesota Press, 1994.

Butler, Judith. *Gender Trouble: Feminism and the Subversion of Identity.* New York: Routledge, 1990.

———. *Excitable Speech: A Politics of the Performative.* New York: Routledge, 1997.

Gill, Miriam. "Late Medieval Wall Painting in England: Content and Context (c. 1350–c. 1530)." PhD. diss., Courtauld Institute of Art, University of London, 2002.

Hanawalt, Barbara. "The Female Felon in Fourteenth-Century England." *Viator* 5 (1974), 253–68.

Jennings, Margaret. "Tutivillus: The Literary Career of the Recording Demon." *Studies in Philology* 74 (1977), 1–95.

Jones, Karen, and Michael Zell. "Bad Conversation? Gender and Social Control in a Kentish Borough, c. 1450–c. 1570." *Continuity and Change* 13 (1998), 11–31.

Karras, Ruth Mazo. *Common Women: Prostitution and Sexuality in Medieval England.* Oxford: Oxford University Press, 1996.

Kowaleski, Maryanne. "Gossip, Gender, and the Economy: The Origins of Scolding Indictments in Medieval England," forthcoming.

Lawton, David. *Blasphemy.* Philadelphia: University of Pennsylvania Press, 1993.

Little, Lester K. *Benedictine Maledictions: Liturgical Cursing in Romanesque France.* Ithaca: Cornell University Press, 1993.

Marks, Richard. *Stained Glass in England During the Middle Ages.* Toronto: University of Toronto Press, 1993.

Martin, Priscilla. *Chaucer's Women: Nuns, Wives and Amazons.* Iowa City: University of Iowa Press, 1990.

Olson, Sherri. *A Chronicle of All that Happens: Voices from the Village Court in Medieval England.* Toronto: Pontifical Institute of Mediaeval Studies, 1996.

Owst, G. R. *Literature and Pulpit in Medieval England: A Neglected Chapter in the History of English Letters and of the English People.* Cambridge: Cambridge University Press, 1933.

Parker, Patricia. "On the Tongue: Cross Gendering, Effeminacy, and the Art of Words." *Style* 23 (1989), 445–65.

Peter, John. *Complaint and Satire in Early English Literature.* Oxford: Clarendon, 1956.

Roberts, Michael. "'Words they are Women, and Deeds they are Men': Images of Work and Gender in Early Modern England." In *Women and Work in Pre-Industrial England,* ed. Lindsay Charles and Lorna Duffin, 122–80. London: Croom Helm, 1985.

Sekules, Veronica. "Women and Art in England in the Thirteenth and Fourteenth Centuries." In *Age of Chivalry: Art in Plantagenet England 1200–1400,* ed. Jonathan Alexander and Paul Binski. London: Royal Academy of Arts, with Weidenfeld and Nicolson, 1987.

Smith, William George, and F. P. Wilson. *Oxford Dictionary of English Proverbs.* 3rd ed. Oxford: Oxford University Press, 1970.

Swanson, R. N. "Angels Incarnate: Clergy and Masculinity from Gregorian Reform to Reformation." In *Masculinity in Medieval Europe,* ed. D. M. Hadley, 160–77. London: Longman, 1999.

Husbands and Priests
Masculinity, Sexuality, and Defamation in Late Medieval England

Derek Neal

"Alas womman, hold y[ou]r tong, you will undo us both." These words of William Palmer to his wife Margaret serve well to introduce my theme. It was 1474, in a village near Hull; friends were gathered in someone's house; and Margaret had, in front of everyone, alleged a sexual relationship between a priest and a local woman. The danger of being undone—the real, humiliating, expensive consequences that could follow on words in fifteenth-century England—dogged both speaker and object, and this couple was well on their way. We know this because our record of these words is testimony in the defamation suit Margaret found herself facing.[1]

Even in these sketchy outlines, the Palmer case illustrates, in several ways, how speech could be a gendered concern. William's first exclamatory sentence evokes some powerful medieval commonplaces: a woman's proverbially unruled and scandalous tongue, and a husband's anxiety to control it. The gendering of speech affected both men and women. Household governance, including the proper governance of a wife, reflected greatly on a premodern masculine identity. A husband's legal or customary responsibility for his wife's behavior was one of many faces of masculinity in this society; gender, then, is vital to understanding speech as a historical subject. The reverse is also true: speech is crucial to the historical understanding of gender. We best understand gender as a set of meanings about sexual difference, meanings sustained in discourse. And the importance of oral discourse for medieval society, especially among non-elite strata, hardly needs to be underlined here. So speech takes us to the heart of gender.

A more practical reason is that transgressive or offensive speech left discernible traces among the documentary records of late medieval England. Margaret Palmer's predicament arose during an intensely speech-conscious

185

era, which we could call the "very long fifteenth century." English itself was in motion: vowels shifting, dialects modulating, meanings recombining, as a written culture, entrenched and replicating within expanding bureaucracies, conversed with an older oral culture. Contemporaries may not have been aware of such subtle changes, but there were more tangible developments also: English institutions (Parliament, Church, borough) became increasingly concerned with regulating, monitoring, censoring, indeed criminalizing speech.[2] So the records of injurious speech in England are, for medieval records, rich. One class of these records, private suits of defamation in the ecclesiastical courts, provides the evidence for this essay.

Defamation has obvious links to the social face of gender, as a defamation suit sought to defend, or repair, a reputation held among peers. Because the social demands on men, indeed the meaning of being male in society, differed from the meaning of femaleness, reputation and gender identity are inextricably linked. Moreover, men and women tended to take different slanders to court; women were far more likely to sue over allegations of sexual misbehavior. Much has been written about these patterns after the mid-sixteenth century, when documentation is better. In England, in the fourteenth and fifteenth centuries, most people suing for defamation were men, and most of them sued other men. And most of the time, the words initiating the suit involved accusations or insinuations of dishonesty, especially of theft. I have argued elsewhere that the words that brought men to court in late medieval England operated in terms of a deep-laid association of masculinity with openness and transparent honesty, and hence of falseness and trickery as the unmasculine opposite, signified by the slanderous designation "thief."[3]

While originally these suits may have been motivated by fear of the consequences should such an accusation be taken seriously by the authorities, changes in practice beginning in the late fifteenth century meant that general slurs, far vaguer insults, with no real danger of the victim's prosecution, could land the speaker in court.[4] In such a context, words only make sense as injurious if they are understood as signifying a whole set of other associations. The possibilities for *private* reactions to offensive speech were changing, and this suggests a changing understanding of injury, possibly a modified concept of reputation itself (unintentional as these changes surely were). This more subjective concept of injury had always existed, more or less explicitly, in the canon law that governed defamation, but English practice, reading the authorities rather narrowly, had tended to exclude it, focusing on imputations of actual crimes.[5] Increasingly, words could be taken to injure people's honor not only because of their literal meaning, as signifying illicit *acts,* but because of the reaction they provoked in the individual; defamation could be signaled by the degree to which someone *felt* defamed.

In effect, the interior level of insult was becoming more visible. Hints of such a shift toward individual reactions or perspectives (and at this stage I can only speak in terms of "hints") are visible elsewhere within the Church court system. In 1512 a London defamation suit witness was asked what *he* would have said if he had been in the defendant's place.[6] The court's interest in what one man thought or perceived, how he assessed a situation, rather than what he heard, seems new at that stage. Whether new or not, it should remind us to keep in mind certain possibilities, certain subtleties, lurking unobserved in our historical subjects (and I use that last word in all its senses): possibilities of individuality, variation, dissent. This is not, of course, to disregard the crucial role of others—one's peers and neighbors—in judging the state of one's reputation and the extent of damage to it. Here there is definite continuity; one's social self was maintained through others, its profile or "size" largely a matter of the impression (here a particularly apt word) one was able to make by exerting pressure on them.

William Palmer's second sentence, "You will undo us both," reminds us that these were real people, especially once we note a bit of extra narrative detail: as he said those words, we are told, William left the room in tears. Were those tears spontaneous (fear or shame breaking through the surface), or affected (a bit of theatrics to disown emphatically his wife's slander)? Did they gain his friends' sympathy, or their surprise, or their contempt? Were they in fact shed at all, or did a witness invent them to make a point? Regardless of the answer, William's tears mean something, and no matter how we approach them, the meaning is a gendered one. They stand for a man's individual response—actual, idealized, or dramatized—which is inseparable from a masculine social and personal identity. Keeping in mind that gender has an interior dimension enriches our understanding of both gender and reputation in history; since gender is an aspect of identity, it could hardly be otherwise.

Ordinary medieval people did not leave behind volumes of confessional autobiography. But that does not mean that we must throw up our hands and abandon all hope of understanding them as something other than the pieces of a social whole. Language, which reaches us in specially charged form in defamation evidence, represents the link between social and interior aspects of individual experience and provides a key to something deeper and more varied than flat statements of social norms. In this article, I use defamation evidence to explore some basic questions about masculinity and reputation in medieval England. I do not claim to provide definitive answers, especially since the number of different cases I can discuss is necessarily restricted, but I hope through the exposure of the questions to show how complex and subtle interpretation of these issues should be. How important was sexuality in a masculine reputation, and what was its true place? And what does a negative example (clerics, those men who were not supposed to define themselves sexually) tell us about the whole?

Up to the Reformation era, sexual insults did not usually, in themselves, lead men to sue in court. In late medieval England, we see very few defamation suits brought over accusations of cuckoldry, and only one has ever been traced to an imputation of sodomy.[7] But we cannot assume that sexual aspersions had no power to offend men. On the contrary, perhaps they failed to surface in court because men dealt with them informally. It would be unwise to speculate about the specific means without the evidence. But we have to keep in mind the limitations of the evidence we do have. Suing for defamation is a formal treatment of speech offenses; these suits react to repeated, premeditated rumor, which according to canon law had to be intended to damage the victim's reputation. Words blurted out in anger were not *supposed* to form the basis of a suit.[8] As often happens with rules, this one seems to have been tested with some frequency. Nevertheless, defamation suits may largely exclude an entire species of masculine reactions to injurious words: the immediate defense against an insult. It stands to reason that sexual mockeries could fall into that group. We know from other times and places, including our own, that dishonor through words can lead to physical conflict between men. (That same London witness admitted that "one bad word calls for another.") So it would make sense to seek an answer among the records of petty assaults, including those which led to homicide. Unfortunately for the historian, English law was not favorable to those who committed violence and claimed provocation through verbal insult. So insults do not tend to surface among the limited surviving evidence of self-defense in the English criminal court records.

Occasionally we are granted glimpses of such conflicts, even in the Church courts. One example, to which I will return, originated in London in the summer of 1511. A priest named John Thorpe sued Edmund Wytton in the Church court for assault, claiming Wytton had thrown a drinking mug at his head and cut his face. While Wytton denied having hurt Thorpe, saying one of the witnesses had prevented him from throwing the "bowle" he had at hand, he did protest that he had been provoked: Thorpe, he said, had called him a cuckold. Wytton's witnesses disagreed; one claimed that Wytton had first insulted Thorpe as "lewd priest," and received "knave" as a response from the cleric. The fact that Thorpe felt it necessary to mention the provocation, even as he denied the assault, shows that answering a sexual insult, in the moment and in view of one's peers, had a certain basic value.[9]

For the most part, however, we are left with speech sued for its own sake. Defamation suits, at least those which follow the traditional rules, might therefore seem to reveal a stratum within masculine identities somewhat removed from impulse, from gut reaction, and perhaps from the most deeply held and guarded aspects of the self. Their relation instead to a more conscious and calculated protection of identity does not, however, diminish their value. Also, there was more than one possible way to respond to offensive speech through a defamation suit. One did not necessarily have to be the plaintiff. And, despite the rarity of suits directly or overtly concerned with sexual slander of men, defamation actions do have important things to tell us about the role of sexuality in premodern masculine identity.

That role was variable. Sexuality interacted with other aspects of masculine reputation and honor, and the relationship was often subtle. Most analyses of sexual masculinity in medieval history tend to reduce subtlety in their concern to produce clear general statements. Medievalists, like everyone else, have been influenced strongly (and often unwittingly) by Keith Thomas's formulation of the "double standard."[10] The obsessive premodern restriction of *female* sexual behavior established in subsequent scholarship leaves one to imagine, through easy, binary contrasts, a paradoxical cartoon vision of *male* sexuality: indulged with impunity and yet (or therefore?) in the larger picture strangely unimportant. Historians of medieval sexuality have not so much created this impression, as failed to supply any sustained corrective to it. Shannon McSheffrey's analysis of London court evidence, which suggests the possible negative consequences of his own adultery for a man's reputation, is the exception.[11] In complete contrast, sexual behavior elsewhere has been placed, in a very reductive way, squarely at the *center* of medieval masculine identity.[12] A similar dichotomy is apparent in the more numerous studies of early modern masculinity. Elizabeth Foyster, concentrating mostly on seventeenth-century evidence, strongly stresses sexual honor in defining masculine reputation. Foyster defines "cuckold" as the most damaging insult to men and conceives of a society in which control of women's sexuality within marriage was the central masculine concern, female adultery being the worst offense against masculine honor. Foyster also places male sexual prowess at the forefront of reputation, arguing, for example, that husbands who became cuckolds through neglecting their wives, or failing to satisfy their legitimate sexual needs, could expect rough treatment by their peers. Anthony Fletcher and Faramerz Dabhoiwala also foreground sexual potency and voracity as the early modern measure of a man. Laura Gowing, who studied defamation patterns in early modern London, has claimed that there was "no way of condemning [a man's] sexual promiscuity." Hence the domination of sexual slander suits by women; men could talk about their behavior without worrying about implicating themselves. Bernard Capp represents a contrary voice, arguing that men might be as concerned as women not to be known as adulterous or promiscuous, and that they could be at the mercy of women's threats to expose and prosecute sexual misconduct.[13]

Though they are not the only key to the puzzle, defamation patterns can help us to reconcile these ideas, to shape them into a nuanced whole. We begin in Canterbury. Which rumor offended John Adrian more: that he slept with a servant woman, or that he stole some doves belonging to Thomas Holweldyng, the man he sued? We simply have no way of judging Adrian's motivations from the evidence available to us. A lawsuit, of course, involved actors other than the disputing parties, and the Adrian case reminds us that we can seek clues about reputation through the traces left by these others: most importantly, lawyers who shaped questions and witnesses who answered them. As in civil law today, the ecclesiastical proctors worked out a formal statement of the points in question, providing a hint to their view of the case's priorities. As usual, these "positions" and "articles" have not survived for Adrian's case. Nevertheless, to judge by the format of the depositions here, the examiner asked first simply whether Adrian had been defamed, to which the witnesses (or at least the first one, John Byfeld) responded with the tale of the servant woman, Joan. The court asked about the allegation of theft separately, in the next question. The lawyers and/or the witnesses may have considered the fornication to be a grave matter, which *in itself* was sufficient to defame.

Thomas Fode, the second witness, claimed to have heard Holweldyng telling these stories often and in various places, including Fode's own house. When the court asked about the alleged theft, Fode responded that Holweldyng had spoken as much of one matter as of the other, that is, as much of adultery as of theft.[14] This sounds like emphasis, an insistence to put facts a different way than what the court wanted; Fode seems to have wished to stress the adultery. Given that he was a witness for Adrian, it is hard to see this as a strategy to downplay the sexual offense.

This was the second decade of the fifteenth century, when defamation still was supposed to relate directly to temporally punishable offenses. Adultery was liable only to ecclesiastical penalties, not criminal ones, but we should not underestimate those. Pure chance might determine whether a criminal or a church case got heard first. In addition, doves were petty theft; even had the case gone to trial, their value might well have been adjusted to keep Adrian out of the capital felony class.[15] While punishment for adultery did not physically threaten Adrian's life, it could bring considerable embarrassment and notoriety. This applied to both men and women, but most likely in different ways. Even if the men of Adrian's acquaintance thought it no great thing to sleep with a servant, and even if some of them were doing exactly that, a special kind of humiliation still would attach to being the one who got caught, the one who had, eventually, to parade around and through the church dressed only in his shirt, and then to make a public apology to lift the penalty of excommunication. Never mind one's immortal soul; one's mortal pride could be just as much worth protecting. We cannot assume a purely pragmatic motivation for the lawsuit.

The point here is that the informal results of defamation were probably as significant as the formal ones. Being seen to respond through the courts, whatever the real risk of the accusations themselves, might be worth the money spent in buttressing one's position in the world of men. The next two examples show how different men attempted to respond, in defense of their social selves, against attacks of different kinds.

The two related suits Richard Knapton brought against Joan Mudde and her husband Roger, in 1527, show how multilayered a dispute between men over speech could be. Against Joan, Knapton claimed she had accused him of having a child through an adulterous affair, and then of being implicated in the child's death. It was entirely typical that a slander alleging a man's sexual irregularity should come to court only when something else was involved: in this case, a "criminal accusation" was a direct consequence of the sexual misbehavior. Yet Knapton's positions in fact separate Joan's defamation into three separate groups. Vague slurs like "harlot" and "lollard," in the first position, carried minimal risk of legal sanction and, one would think, were the least substantial concerning credible injury to reputation. The bastardy allegation was alone in the second position, indicating perhaps that the sexual behavior (punishable by a Church court, but not incurring criminal penalties as infanticide would) was worth considering on its own. Last came the more serious, but more outlandish and perhaps less credible, accusation that Knapton had abandoned his bastard child for swine to tear apart.

So much for Joan. Knapton sued Roger Mudde for a different slander, which was not sexual. Unlike the positions against Joan, those against Roger claim *only* vague slurs with no supporting context: "false heretic," "lewd knave," "harlot," "Lowler." The witnesses had nothing specific to say about these, but testified to a more substantial verbal offense. Robert Cartwright had heard Mudde say to Knapton, "False carle, ye delyth falsely with my wyfe, but I shall qwhite the[e] and lay noo hands upon the[e]." The "false dealing" was not sexual. Rather, Cartwright said "that [Mudde] was provoked to call hym so because the said Knapton caused the wyfe of the said Roger Mudde to be suspended oute of the churche."[16]

In both cases, the Muddes were accusing Knapton of shifty underhanded dealing: concealing a bastard, trying to squirrel away the evidence of his misdeed, in the first; using his influence in the other. These were classic allegations of unmasculine falseness, guile, and trickery. Even if everyone knew the accusations to be untrue, showing he would not stand for them was still worth Knapton's while. The tenor of the suit against Roger suggests that Knapton was spinning Mudde's statement as a revenge slur, which itself, interestingly, involved falseness, in dealing with the law. Roger Mudde's own claim speaks to the rights of the husband concerning an injury to his wife. Contained in the supposed defamation, we see Mudde in turn defending *his* social self, of which his wife formed part. (The second witness, blurring the two, reported "wheder it [i.e., the false citation] was servyd of Roger Mudde or of his wyfe he can not tell, but he saith it was servyd of one of thame.") Roger's additional comment, "I shall qwhite the[e] and lay noo hands upon the[e]," pushes the tension higher and evokes a different masculine discourse. It meant "I'll take care of you without having to lay hands on you," demonstrating that Knapton's injury was *worth* personal attack, but that he had sufficient self-command to restrain himself. The kind of self-command seen here is a careful assessment of strengths and weaknesses, along with a face-saving posture of self-assertion: rational, sensible, protective.

The important thing was to leave no doubt that Mudde would answer an injury. Saying this in a public place, with "the more parte of the parish" present, Mudde could take the advantage of making public something that was technically private. Exposing hidden treachery (perhaps, in addition, by suggesting that Knapton had tried to strike at him through his wife rather than face to face), while presenting himself as open and fair in his "dealing," Mudde took the stance of the consummate man: responsible for his wife, prepared to respond, yet reasonable and rational. Unfortunately for the Muddes, whatever the community's opinion, the Church court sided with Knapton, and ordered both husband and wife to pay costs. The point, nonetheless, stands: both plaintiffs and defendants reveal gendered motivations in defamation suits. Where the gender in question was masculine, there was a wider choice of discourses from which to draw.

In the following Canterbury tale (from the nearby Kent village of Sturrey, actually) of 1415, conflict emerged between men even though the honor at stake was a woman's. Witnesses for Alice Yarewell claimed she was a virgin, who had been of blameless reputation until the day John Maldon declared, to some men gathered in John Mycham's house, that she was a common whore. Maldon said he knew of three men who had lain with her, of whom he named two. One of these was Maldon himself. The other, Richard Bokeland, was a witness in the suit. He testified that Maldon said that when *Bokeland* slept with Alice, the woman told Bokeland that he should go away and leave her in peace, because he did not know how to "do the deed." Maldon then boasted that, in contrast, Alice had lavished praise on *his* sexual technique, saying, "Benedicaris tu, quia tu scis bene facere facta tua" [you ought to be blessed, because you truly know well how to do your deeds].[17]

However much this story may have amused these men, I doubt that Alice was laughing. Her promising marital prospects evaporated once the rumor started going around, and witnesses were quite specific about her losses: Richard Bocher, a man worth forty pounds, dropped her, as did Bachelor Number Two, a fisherman who was "able to spend five marks per year." These were tragic but unsurprising results for a woman; no wonder she sued. Yet what does the unpleasant episode say about masculine honor, masculine reputation?

The gathering of men in that house was a little arena, or a little stage, where they could enact the mundane dramas of socially demonstrated masculinity. John Maldon scored a few points by bragging about a sexual conquest. By using the same story to belittle Richard Bokeland, he scored a few more. No great surprises here; there is no such thing as "just a joke," and the utility of humor, especially sexual humor, to enforce interpersonal hierarchies is well known. If these were young and subordinate males, such as students or apprentices, this coarse competition would seem understandable and somehow limited in its significance. Yet they were not youths; Bokeland was more than thirty, and the other witnesses were even older, which probably means that Maldon was also not very young. There seems at first to have been no shame or perceived danger even for these mature men in frankly discussing illicit sexual conduct.[18]

Even more intriguing is Richard Bokeland's response. The supposed incompetent would have had some legal grounds for a defamation suit of his own, since fornication was punishable by the Church courts. Further, John Maldon apparently kept telling the story all that summer (over which period it presumably lost much of its comic value). Bokeland did not sue, but this did not mean he was untouched. He made the deliberate decision to testify against Maldon. This strategy thus covered both an actionable slur and the non-actionable, but possibly more degrading, insinuation of a sexual failing. Speculation about the true nature of that suggested failing is probably not very worthwhile. The more important thing to take away may be the complexity of the response, where one motive enfolds another.

Testifying on behalf of Alice Yarewell meant supporting and defending a decent woman who had been credibly and materially injured; this was the *formal* part of Richard Bokeland's reaction. We need not bring "chivalry" or gallantry into the question to appreciate how important such a response could be to Bokeland's masculine social self. Not to come to Alice's aid might have offended far more ordinary group standards of solidarity and neighborliness in this small community. (Also, of course, Bokeland may have been connected in some way to Alice's kin or their interests, giving him a more tangible reason to speak up for her; this was technically supposed to disqualify him as a witness, but the Canterbury examiner's formulaic questions on the point were even more mushily phrased than usual.) Then, the formal and plainly acceptable route of testifying for Alice also allowed Bokeland to testify against John Maldon, providing a legal means to react to an injury that ordinarily would not have had formal redress. That injury could not be defined in the usual terms. It makes most sense as homosocial competition, in which being seen to have reacted, not to have let a challenge go unanswered, had value.

All these conflicts among laymen illustrate the equilibrium of pushing and pulling that characterized ordinary social relations between male peers, a dynamic that, despite medieval stereotypes about feminine gossip, depended just as much on the exchange of words as on any more formal, or more physical, kind of conflict. Clerics, despite their obvious markers of distinctiveness, were not exempt from the intra-masculine competition signaled by such verbal conflict. This is a point worth making because some recent studies have argued that the clergy experienced special difficulties in establishing, and sustaining, a masculine identity, because of their vow of celibacy. Placing sexual behavior at the center of gender identity, this theory maintains, in effect, that neither private nor social masculinity could be proven, to self or to peers, without sexual experience. Clerics, in this view, lived a defining and essential difference from laymen, which they could not practically bridge.[19]

The place of sexuality in gender identity certainly deserves attention, and the differences between clerics and laymen also shaped their social relations. Nevertheless, the argument for clerical masculinity as a problem, as insufficient, needs more careful qualification at several levels. Sexuality neither begins nor ends with sexual acts: wishes, fantasies, and desires (conscious, unconscious, and sublimated) form the broader texture of an individual sexuality throughout an individual life. Their influence is hardly restricted to the world of the psyche. John Maldon's sexual boasts, for example, are probably understandable as fantasies of self-enhancement, phallic both in their literal (sexual) and metaphoric (social) aspects, here given unusually unsubtle form. Yet the expression need not be even this manifest. Consider, for example, how aggression and excitement in competition (in sport or recreational fighting, to use only the bluntest examples), so important in male peer groups past and present, can serve to structure the social standing of males. Viewed on a continuum of pleasure, carnal and aggressive drives are not so far apart.

This broader conception is especially important because clerics in late medieval England very rarely were isolated from the secular world of men in any practical sense. The quarrel between John Thorpe and Edmund Wytton shows how extensively the clerical and lay worlds might interact. Wytton's claim of provocation assumes it was credible that a cleric would utter an insult, just as Thorpe's own witnesses have him answering one; conversely, if a priest talked like a layman, he could expect to take the same consequences. Nor was this probably considered unusual. As Sandy Bardsley remarked in her response to the original version of this essay, clerics "were often over-represented among *perpetrators* of speech-crimes as well as victims."[20]

Moreover, the quarrel took place amid a game of bowls in the garden of one witness, where John Thorpe was playing and drinking alongside the laymen. (One of these game-pieces was the "bowle" that Edmund Wytton claimed *not* to have thrown at Thorpe.)[21] Wytton also protested to the court that Thorpe had not been dressed as a priest in this gathering. We safely may discount, given this tiny London parish, Wytton's rather fishy argument that he therefore did not know Thorpe was a priest. Still, even Thorpe's witnesses admitted that Thorpe had been dressed down, only in jacket and tunic, for the purposes of the game. They did not report this with any sense of wrong. Alongside the reports, in sundry ecclesiastical records, of priests who misbehaved while fraternizing with lay people, we should keep in mind the many uneventful and unrecorded instances when such socializing caused no trouble at all: the priests who had a drink at the pub, or played football, and did not gossip, get drunk, get into fights, or make passes at women.

Nevertheless, clerics' interests in the masculine lay sphere extended far beyond recreation. Not only did clerics have to engage the structures and inhabitants of lay society but also their own clerical "world" shared many characteristics with the secular sphere. As soon as they took holy orders, clerics entered a world of masculine competition. All the evidence suggests that the career prospects for newly ordained priests in late medieval England were not a great deal more encouraging than those awaiting newly minted humanities Ph.D.s in twenty-first-century academia.[22] In such a climate, clerics needed to use their contacts with laymen to their own benefit, and to the disadvantage of their competitors. Once a cleric had a position, the nature of that homosocial engagement simply altered a little; it did not diminish. The better-off, the lucky beneficed clerics, just like their poorer unbeneficed brethren, depended on laymen, and not just in the large milestone moments of sponsorship for ordination or presentation to a benefice. In day-to-day life, "patronage" was a matter of many small practices, many short performances. This became explicit in a Norwich case of 1512, where according to a witness one priest said to another, "Yu art a false preste and a false flattering preste and a false tale teller, and yo hast mysinformyd my lorde Fitzwatre and [th]e Lady his modre of me, so that through yor synystre informacyon [th]ei be not contented with me."[23]

This subject could fill books, but it is indispensable here as we consider how clergy sought to maintain a masculine identity. With many of the same concerns at stake, with everyday existence depending not just on interacting with laymen but also on acting like them, clerics' celibacy can have affected only a restricted part of the masculine social identity they inevitably generated. No matter what the stereotypes, clerics shared more interests with lay males than they did with women.

Clerics themselves had household concerns; they might head a household, or they might serve in one. Their connections to secular households were widespread and often controversial. They might be a trusted friend or confessor to a master, or to his wife. Yet clerics' household connections might run counter to, or at least not in perfect consonance with, the masculine responsibilities of the lay head of the household. This had much to do with clerics' real or imagined contact with women. So the double bind for clerics, certainly at least for a more powerful minority of them, was not a sexual but a social one. In maintaining their own social interests and identity by means of their livelihood, which shaped a great part of their masculinity, they could easily find themselves in situations that compromised the interests of other men.

In the early 1360s, a young unmarried Yorkshirewoman named Margaret, the sole daughter of Thomas de Pikworth, became pregnant by her father's servant. On learning of this, Thomas dismissed the man from his household. Subsequently, one William de Bracebridge made some outrageous allegations about Thomas: most shockingly, that Thomas knew full well that the man who had got Margaret pregnant was not the servant, but Thomas' own priest, William de Saperton. Thomas was covering up this scandal by bribing the servant to take the blame. Everyone, Bracebridge alleged, knew what was going on.[24] Thomas and the priest sued Bracebridge together in 1363, though probably with different motives. For Thomas, public rumor of such a shameful affair would imply poor governance of his family and household. Since his daughter was undeniably pregnant, however, poor governance could not be ruled out, so the lawsuit's official version puts the best face on things by showing that Thomas administered discipline by firing the offender. Bribing a servant instead would have meant entering a relationship of trust and dependence with a social inferior, making his confidence dependent on payment. These are the classic and, in context, understandable concerns of a *paterfamilias*.

The threat to William de Saperton, the priest, seems cruder, less subtle, but it was not simple. Of course he possibly faced ecclesiastical penalties, but these in practice were much a matter of discretion. More immediately, he could have cleared himself through compurgation (bringing to court a specified number of respectable men to swear to his innocence). The defamation suit really served to restore trust damaged by the allegation that Saperton had abused another man's confidence in him, as well as abusing his property (i.e., Margaret Pikworth). Clearly, nothing actually did happen between Saperton and Margaret, but the defamer William de Bracebridge drew on a common expectation that a priest in the household (or even, in this case, merely coming to the household) meant sexual trouble. For clerics, this kind of sexual situation was especially complex because their self-command in celibacy bore directly on the respect for property expected of responsible husbands.

Because the meaning of sexual continence, self-restraint, for clerics and husbands in this respect was at root the same, it should not surprise us that their interests could coincide as easily as they might conflict. In 1510, a priest named William Kemp sued Thomas Castell for insinuating that he had had a sexual affair with a married woman, the wife of William Radley, of Orsett in Essex. Although in fact the husband himself was called merely as one of several witnesses for Kemp, it seems fair to allow him the primary voice in the story. On Good Friday, Radley related, Castell had confronted him in the parish churchyard and asked what Radley's wife had been doing in London on a recent Monday. Falling straight into the trap, Radley replied (in an unfortunate phrasing) that she was there taking care of some business. To this Castell replied, "I beshrew soche erands For she was shet in the parsons Master Kemp chamber at London and ther was alone with hym on the morow after." According to Radley, nobody had been present to overhear Castell, but somehow the story got out, because Radley went on to name several other people who had called him a cuckold. Another witness verified that Radley had been called cuckold "face to face" in Orsett parish.[25]

Despite being the one who brought the suit, William Kemp seems oddly absent from the text of the depositions, aside from the defamatory statements themselves. Everyone affirmed that they had heard the tale about Kemp and that his grievance was justified. But somehow the injury to William Radley, the husband, seems the more immediate and the more tangible to the people in his community; we do not hear what the after-effects for Kemp were said to be. (The equally slandered wife, we must note, retreats even further to the margins, the suit not admitting even her name into the record.) The situation resembles Robert Bokeland's experience in Kent a century earlier. Bokeland had used a woman's defamation suit to strike back at the man who insulted him; Radley rode the coattails of a defamed priest in order to avenge a similarly painful but also dubiously actionable slur. Perhaps, also, the actionability of the slanders was not the main determining factor. Kemp, the priest, seems to have been a man of some means. He is named "parson," and his tryst with Radley's wife was said to have happened in his chamber at the Charterhouse of London, while an "old bawd" named Rose walked about in "his" garden. A parish priest with a London *pied-à-terre*, Kemp might well have been better equipped to finance a lawsuit than Radley, who described himself only as a "husbandman." The investments of both cleric and layman in an honorable masculine reputation could work together.

The case of Margaret Palmer, with whom we began, hints at the power of speech to lay bare these fundamental masculine concerns for both clerics and laymen. We have already seen how Margaret's own husband was represented as anxious to limit the potential damage of his wife's incautious words. The witnesses against Margaret also invoked husbandly concerns in reporting her speech and their own. Emmet ("Emmota") Jenkynson claimed that Margaret had come to her while she lay in childbed and declared, "This is a foulle mater of Sir William Hochonson and Janet Johnson." Asked to explain, Margaret went on to allege the affair, claiming "that is evyn the comyn voce, and that h[e]ard of ij of the best husbands with in Cotyngham." Even in this current of speech among women, a rumor endorsed by men, the "best husbands," the most respectable household heads, could be imagined to have particular authority. Joan Cartwright reported that Margaret had said, "the same Sir William is huldyn the gretest hore master [in] Cotyngham suckyn." The "whoremaster" or "whoremonger," a generic conception of male sexual misconduct, evokes a perversion of responsible masculine husbandry, wherein failure adequately to rule oneself leads logically to the misrule of others, or the rule of the wrong others. Margaret herself tried to show that she had been concerned for the good name of both parties, knowing that a friendship between a priest and a married woman would cause talk. Her witness Peter Hogge said that William Palmer had told him:

> Sir, Margaret my wife, for the goode luff and favor that sho had to my sister Thomas Johnson wife and Sir William Hochenson, sho yode [went] unto Emmet Jenkynson and prayd here in secrete wyse that sho wolde meve my sister Johnson to withdrawe her fro the feliship of . . . Sr William, for to avoid the sclaunder and diffame that was lyke to rise and grew betwene them amonge the people of the parysshyn.[26]

Still, one suspects that regardless of whose side they took, everyone involved cared far more about Janet Johnson's good name than that of Huchenson. In fact nobody felt obliged to say a single good word of substance about him. (He had the resources to bring the suit, so perhaps on that account he was not considered pitiable.)

The sneak thief, the liar, and the whoring priest share a common defining flaw: they are all false, that most common insulting adjective. They inhabit and exploit spaces, literal or symbolic, under the visible surface of life. So, for that matter, does the father who covers up illicit sex in his household. These are not "true men." In the wider context of everyday clerical life amid laymen, with its highly gendered social roles, a cleric had more to lose, as a man, by breaking his vows of celibacy than by remaining chaste. Chastity cut him out of the subordinate discourse of masculine self-indulgence, that hypercharged embodiment prized by the young and unmarried. But sexual activity jeopardized his place in the far more important discourse of masculine maturity, manhood, where the ultimately higher stakes lay. Touching too many sensitive nerves, it threatened to spoil his vital connections to those other men among whom he must buy, sell, negotiate contracts, and angle for dinner invitations, and possibly, thereby, help to make a nice marriage for his sister or cousin, find a good position for his godchild, or act as respected mediator in some local dispute. Janet Johnson may have represented just such a link for William Huchenson, to her kin or her husband, apart from (but not precluded by) any other interest the priest may have had in her.

In her comments on an early oral version of this essay, Sandy Bardsley asked some fundamental questions about my interpretation: essentially, why the values I evoked should be considered aspects of masculinity. In her words:

> what makes such qualities as trust and reliability about "masculinity" rather than about "being a decent person," about being a "true *man*" rather than being a "*true* man" [or woman, for that matter]? What is it about preserving celibacy that we should consider it an element of masculinity, rather than a gendered form of goodness or true-ness, in the same sense that other varieties of piety often took gendered forms?[27]

The points are well taken. One thing I hear Bardsley saying behind all this is that trust and reliability could be praiseworthy in women as well as men and that preserving celibacy also certainly reflected well on women. But I think there are several important differences.

"Trust and reliability," as Bardsley put it, are not really the main point in true-ness, though they follow from it. True-ness, rather, is about open-ness and transparency, about not being "double": the absence of discrepancy between outward appearance and inner reality.[28] There are several main reasons why this ideal qualifies as masculine in premodern society. One is the proverbial attribution of trickery, guile, and falseness to women. So women who were noticeably honest, open, and trustworthy certainly would be approved, but I think they would be seen as having transcended the expected flaws of their sex, not as having displayed exemplary "woman-liness" or femininity.

Another reason is the different social roles incumbent on men and women. We now know a great deal (Bardsley certainly more than I) about women's contributions to the medieval economy, and know the danger of any imagined division between "masculine public" and "feminine private" spaces or (dare I say it) spheres. Women's work was everywhere, indispens-able. But just as in rural Africa or Albania in recent years, doing essential work did not translate into social visibility or personhood. In Natalie Zemon Davis' words: "[Women] had skills, of course, and it was recognized that they could make gold thread, or run a linen shop or a manor house well or badly, but their calling was to put those skills to use in whatever household they found themselves."[29] Trust among peers, what early modernists have lately begun to discuss as "credit," had a much more crucial and central role in masculine identities than in feminine ones.[30] Being a man, having a masculine-enough identity, meant having, as Gary Shaw has suggested, a social self that was more rounded, more multifaceted, and some-how larger than that of a woman.[31] To put it another way, a man who could not find and maintain a place uniquely his in a homosocial nexus was an incomplete or diminished man, an unmanly man. A woman who could not do the same was still (nothing more than) a woman.

On the second question, I think Sandy Bardsley is right that celibacy was "a gendered form of goodness or true-ness." But the fact that it was gendered, in a particular way, is the whole point. The origins of the celibate ideal relate (in a somewhat extreme and ironic way) to ancient values of self-command, or self-control, given perhaps their most memorably eloquent formulation by Cicero.[32] Again, all the advantages and honors of such a life strategy were masculine ones; it was for men among men that they mattered. The Christian application of this ethic in the monastic ideal was in some ways revolutionary, because it made celibacy, a very special form of self-command, equally honorable for men and women. But I do not believe that, culturally, celibacy as self-control ever lost its fundamentally masculine sig-nificance. From the earliest times, women (female religious, women saints) who maintained their celibacy in the face of severe temptation or brutal threat were praised as having overcome feminine weakness, as having taken on masculine virtues and strengths.[33] In the more ordinary world of late medieval England, several factors combined. Celibate men were in the world, to a degree very rarely achieved by celibate women. The secular involvements of male clerics were so significant that they had to maintain secular credit among laymen as well. Where celibacy was concerned, the masculine ethic twisted back on itself: failure to maintain a clerical ideal could diminish one's masculine social self in the lay world.

In that world, sexual reputation had a role in the stretching and compressing of social selves, feminine and masculine. For women, sexual honor was the linchpin, without which the entire structure collapsed. But men could not afford to ignore it either. Though unlikely by itself to ruin or salvage their lives, sexual honor could be useful, enough to turn a situation to advantage in the incessant jockeying for position that defined masculine social relations, especially in the small community. Speech was central to these struggles. Spoken words, like dynamite, might clear a space where one could build, or they might blow up in one's face. Skill in handling them made the difference.

Demonstrating that same skill, showing that one knew to treat speech with the proper respect, itself reflected on reputation; speech was not only a medium through which reputations could be made or unmade. This comes through clearly in the Palmer case, where the witnesses all seem to have been at pains to distance themselves from transgressive speech and to show that they took no pleasure in malicious gossip. Emmet Jenkynson responded to Margaret Palmer's story with "Pese, pese . . . for shame, and say no more . . . ye myght as wele have sayd so of my son and me as of tham twa." Emmet's husband John, to whom Margaret supposedly spoke the next night, reported that in his conversation with her, he first denied that his wife had repeated any of her conversation with Margaret; Emmet, the court was to note, was (unlike Margaret) not a chatterer. He then claimed that he had told Margaret, "I councel you hold your tong; ye will mak your self at doo and your husband . . . [ye] aght not to lose your guds and therefor I councell you hold your tong and hale your frends."[34] And as we have seen, Margaret's own witnesses tried to emphasize the helpful, rather than divisive, intent in the woman's speech.

My temporally latest example collects the issues I have discussed, and in addition seems to raise something both old and new; for those reasons, history being a narrative in time, the case is well suited to come at the end. In late 1532 the chantry priest Henry Taylor sued John Hole, of Aberford (near Leeds), who, he claimed, had alleged "that Sir Henry Tailior haith hadde two chylder with Margaret Feldhouse or one chyld at the lest."[35] Hole's response was to deny that he had said this, but to claim that Margaret had admitted to having three children by Taylor. Thus far the issues are not very interesting. More than one child by the same woman would imply a clerical concubinage of long standing, not a momentary passionate failing, and might have been more sternly regarded by the court.

But John Hole did not stop at defending himself. He made counter-allegations against Henry Taylor, asserting not only the existence of the bastard children but something even more serious: that Taylor "caused the same Margrett to dystroy them with drynks & other crafts." (This seems not to have been taken seriously by the court.) The offenses of which Hole accused Taylor were principally those of speech. Taylor had, Hole claimed, made more than one sexual boast: most memorably, "that he wold dyng the duyle furth of his breik at an hoirs ars letting for no man and then mygth he serve God the better all the Weik aftyr."[36] The scene Hole described that summed up the situation is worth quoting in its entirety:

> Sir Henry, in Estre weke last past, said . . . "John Hole, why dyd thou say that I have dystroyed a child?" And the said John answered and said, "No, I said nott so, bott I said that I herd Margrett Feldhows [your hore][37] confess to Lionell Roger that she by your Counsell had dystroyed [3] children with drynks." Then answering, the said Sir Henry, "Why, Hole, is there no mo hoyrs in this parish batt she? Yes, an evere hoire had a prike sett in hire nose, there shuld bott fewe go withowt in this parsch."

More was involved here than the punishable misbehavior, apparently unremorsefully committed and even boasted about, which John Hole alleged. Layer on layer of defamation, or possible defamation, or rather possible dangerous speech, emerges. Hole defamed Henry Taylor by saying he had fathered children, the only allegation dealt with by the court, according to Taylor's positions and articles. Certainly Hole wanted to paint Taylor as a man of unruled sexuality. But that lack of self-command found additional, and additionally offensive, expression in his speech, and not only its subject but its manner. Hole's quotations of Taylor are distinguished by their open, defiant vulgarity: "wich as we thogth was no gudly words for a prest to speke," in Hole's opinion. Here Hole displays a drawing-back and distancing from words or locutions that are not necessarily criminal or even defamatory (as in the Palmer case sixty years earlier), but distasteful, "dirty." Hole held at arm's length Taylor's remark about the parish "whores": "Wich hus thogth was a shamfull sayng of hym, and had beyn many of ther Gostly fathers a for tyms, and more he said, the wich I am ashamed to spek of it." The tenor of Hole's countersuit is, roughly, "He said that I said that he had destroyed a child, which I actually know he as well as did, because he told his 'whore' on whom he had fathered them to do so. But I never actually said he had murdered them. All I did was report what this woman herself confessed. And he reacted to this with shameful language. So he is not only a licentious priest and one who covers up his sins through murder but also a slanderer of the women of this parish and a man of unruled language. I, in contrast, am no slanderer but an honest man who reports what is already common knowledge, and who knows how priests ought to conduct themselves."

It is very difficult to get a clear sense of what was commonly considered foul or vulgar language in this period, one we do not imagine as given to euphemism. The sense that priests ought to be held to a higher standard in governing their speech had been articulated long before in pastoral discourse, which condemned loose and salacious talk in general as sinful.[38] The Hole case suggests that this was becoming a standard maintained by the "we" of the lay community, whose attitudes are harder to discern than those of literate clerical authors. The almost prudish reaction to the language ("I am ashamed to speak of it") seems a new thing for the court to have bothered to record. It was now in a litigant's interest to present himself as respectable and clean of speech and manner, because the court was (or might be) willing to take that into account. (In this case, it was not enough; John Hole's side of the story was taken as a "confession" of defamation.) So perhaps it is not too old-fashioned to detect in this quarrel a hint of a changed climate, of the altered world to which the new religion, in 1532 just beginning its ascent in England with royal help, would lead over the succeeding decades. Where speech was concerned, there were puritanical people well before there were Puritans.

The expectation of self-governance by clerics that emerges in this late case reflects, however, a much older social norm. While excessive or incautious speech had dangers for both sexes, the self-command that kept the tongue in check was especially meaningful in a masculine social identity. Governance of sexuality formed part of the same masculine ethic, which bore on the reputation of clerics and laymen alike. For both groups, it meant that they could be trusted to respect the property (including the women) and, by extension, the symbolic territory or social space of their peers. That trust counted as credit in all the transactions and exchanges, by no means only commercial ones, comprising the homosocial networks within which masculinity had its public meaning. In turn, this social belonging enabled a man, lay or cleric, to define and build upon a place, a social self, he could identify as his own.

Notes

1. York, Borthwick Institute of Historical Research (hereafter BIHR), MS CP.F.256. Pages within this file are not individually numbered.

2. Green provocatively discusses the cultural impact of the shift from oral to written discourse in the justice system, in *A Crisis of Truth*. McIntosh, *Controlling Misbehavior*, includes the treatment of speech offenses in a thorough analysis of social regulation.

3. Neal, "Suits Make the Man," esp. 7–12.

4. *Select Cases*, ed. Helmholz, xxvi–xxx. Wunderli, *London Church Courts*, 67–68, dates the change to 1512 in the London consistory court.

5. *Select Cases*, ed. Helmholz, xiv–xxiv.

6. London Metropolitan Archives (hereafter LMA), MS DL/C/206, fol. 326r.

7. The sodomy example comes from Wunderli, *London Church Courts*, 83–84. The relative absence of cuckoldry insults is a marked contrast to the findings of Gowing, *Domestic Dangers*, and of Foyster, *Manhood in Early Modern England*, on which much of her work on seventeenth-century England depends; see also n. 13 below.

8. *Select Cases*, ed. Helmholz, xxvii, xxxii–xxxiii.

9. LMA MS DL/C/206, fol. 80r.

10. Thomas, "The Double Standard." Karras, "Two Models, Two Standards," compares ideal and reality, with more attention given to prescriptive literature.

11. McSheffrey, "Men and Masculinity," at 257–58.

12. Both Bullough, "On Being a Male," and McNamara, "The *Herrenfrage*," are problematic statements of this kind, to be read very cautiously.

13. Foyster, *Manhood in Early Modern England*, esp. 67–72, 104–17; Fletcher, *Gender, Sex and Subordination*, 92–97; Dabhoiwala, "Construction of Honour"; Gowing, *Domestic Dangers*, 63, 74; Capp, "Double Standard Revisited," passim.

14. Canterbury Cathedral Archives (hereafter CCA), MS X.10.1., fol. 124v.

15. Maddern, *Violence and Social Order*, 130.

16. Both suits in BIHR, MS CP.G.193.

17. CCA, MS X.10.1, fols. 92r–v.

18. Roper has shown how competing discourses of youthful (subordinate) and mature masculinity might both conflict and reinforce each other; see her "Blood and Codpieces."

19. McNamara, "The *Herrenfrage*," Swanson, "Angels Incarnate," and Cullum, "Clergy," all rely on this idea in making their respective arguments.

20. Bardsley, "Response," 2.

21. LMA, MS DL/C/206, fol. 80r.

22. Davis, "Preparation," esp. 50–51.

23. *Norwich Depositions*, ed. Hardy and Stone, no. 167.

24. BIHR, MS CP.E.249.

25. LMA, MS DL/C/206, fols. 25v–26v.

26. BIHR, MS CP.F.256.

27. Bardsley, "Response," 3.

28. Neal, "Suits Make the Man," 16.

29. Davis, "Boundaries," 61.

30. Shepard, "Manhood," passim, with reference to the late sixteenth and early seventeenth centuries.

31. Shaw, *Necessary Conjunctions*, 35–36, 38–39, 83–84.

32. Cicero, *On Duties*, I.88–136.

33. "This idea, that a virtuous woman could overcome the weakness of her sex though her virile soul, is a traditional description of female holiness . . ." (Newman, "Real Men and Imaginary Women," 1199–1200). Newman, "What Did It Mean to Say 'I Saw'?," 38, referring to Birgitta of Sweden, describes the idea that "Birgitta's 'manly' spirit had exalted her above feminine frailty" as an argument "long familiar in women's hagiography."

34. BIHR, MS CP.F.256.

35. BIHR, MS CP.G.166.

36. The first part of this remarkable utterance is so obscure that for comprehension's sake I must provide a modernization, though that rather spoils its flavor. "Duyle," or "dool," is northern and Scots dialect for "dowel" [rod]. The modern rendering most faithful to the sense would seem to be, "that he would strike (or thrust) forth the 'rod' from his trousers at a whore's arse, not letting any man stand in his way." Prof. George Clark's suggestion (personal communication, February 13, 2003) that "duyle" may also mean "devil" is, I think, quite compatible with this reading, in more ways than one. I thank Profs. Clark (Queen's University, Kingston) and Andrew Taylor (University of Ottawa) for their help in interpreting this text.

37. Interlineated in MS.

38. Craun, *Lies*, 158–62, 173.

WORKS CITED

MANUSCRIPT SOURCES

Borthwick Institute of Historical Research (BIHR), York, Cause Papers (fourteenth century), MS CP.E 249; Cause Papers (fifteenth century), MS CP.F 256; Cause Papers (sixteenth century), MSS CP.G 166, CP.G 193.

Canterbury Cathedral Archives (CCA), Consistory court deposition book, 1410–17, MS X.10.1.

London Metropolitan Archives (LMA), Consistory court deposition book, 1510–16, MS DL/C/206.

PRIMARY SOURCES

Cicero, [Marcus Tullius]. *On Duties*. Trans. M. T. Griffin and E. M. Atkins. Cambridge: Cambridge University Press, 1991.

Norwich Consistory Court Depositions, 1499–1512 and 1518–1530. Ed. Basil Cozens-Hardy and Edward Darley Stone. London, Fakenham, and Reading: Wyman & Sons Ltd., 1938.

Select Cases on Defamation to 1600. Ed. R. H. Helmholz. London: The Selden Society, 1985.

SECONDARY SOURCES

Bardsley, Sandy. "Response to Session 128: Sins of the Tongue/Transgressive Speech II." Unpaginated. 36th International Congress on Medieval Studies, Kalamazoo, MI, 2001. (Inquiries about this unpublished comment may be directed to Sandy Bardsley at sandybardsley@moravian.edu.)

Bullough, Vern. "On Being a Male in the Middle Ages." In *Medieval Masculinities: Regarding Men in the Middle Ages,* ed. Clare A. Lees, 31–43. Minneapolis: University of Minnesota Press, 1994.

Capp, Bernard. "The Double Standard Revisited: Plebeian Women and Male Sexual Reputation in Early Modern England." *Past and Present* 162 (1999), 70–100.

Craun, Edwin D. *Lies, Slander and Obscenity in Medieval English Literature: Pastoral Rhetoric and the Deviant Speaker.* Cambridge: Cambridge University Press, 1997.

Cullum, P. H. "Clergy, Masculinity and Transgression in Late Medieval England." In *Masculinity in Medieval Europe,* ed. D. M. Hadley, 178–96. London: Longman, 1999.

Dabhoiwala, Faramerz. "The Construction of Honour, Reputation and Status in Late Seventeenth- and Early Eighteenth-Century England." *Transactions of the Royal Historical Society,* 6th series VI (1996), 201–13.

Davis, Natalie Zemon. "Boundaries and the Sense of Self in Sixteenth-Century France." In *Reconstructing Individualism: Autonomy, Individuality and the Self in Western Thought,* ed. Thomas C. Heller, Morton Sosna, and David E. Wellerby, 53–63. Stanford: Stanford University Press, 1986.

Davis, Virginia. "Preparation for Service in the Late Medieval English Church." In *Concepts and Patterns of Service in the Later Middle Ages,* ed. by A. Curry and E. Matthew, 38–51. Woodbridge, U.K.: Boydell, 2000.

Fletcher, Anthony. *Gender, Sex, and Subordination in England, 1500–1800.* New Haven: Yale University Press, 1995.

Foyster, Elizabeth A. *Manhood in Early Modern England: Honour, Sex and Marriage.* London: Longman, 2000.

Gowing, Laura. *Domestic Dangers: Women, Words, and Sex in Early Modern London.* Oxford: Clarendon, 1996.

Green, Richard Firth. *A Crisis of Truth: Literature and Law in Ricardian England.* Philadelphia: University of Pennsylvania Press, 1999.

Karras, Ruth Mazo. "Two Models, Two Standards: Moral Teaching and Sexual Mores." In *Bodies and Disciplines: Intersections of Literature and History in Fifteenth-Century England,* ed. Barbara A. Hanawalt and David Wallace, 123–37. Minneapolis: University of Minnesota Press, 1996.

Maddern, Philippa C. *Violence and Social Order: East Anglia 1422–1442.* Oxford: Clarendon, 1992.

McIntosh, Marjorie Keniston. *Controlling Misbehavior in England, 1370–1600.* Cambridge: Cambridge University Press, 1998.

McNamara, JoAnn. "The *Herrenfrage:* The Restructuring of the Gender System, 1050–1150." In *Medieval Masculinities: Regarding Men in the Middle Ages,* ed. Clare A. Lees, 3–30. Minneapolis: University of Minnesota Press, 1994.

McSheffrey, Shannon. "Men and Masculinity in Late Medieval London Civic Culture: Governance, Patriarchy, and Reputation." In *Conflicted Identities and Multiple Masculinities: Men in the Medieval West,* ed. Jacqueline Murray, 243–67. New York: Garland, 1999.

Neal, Derek. "Suits Make the Man: Masculinity in Two English Law Courts, c. 1500." *Canadian Journal of History* 37 (2002), 1–22.

Newman, Barbara. "What Did It Mean to Say 'I Saw'? The Clash between Theory and Practice in Medieval Visionary Culture." *Speculum* 80 (2005), 1–43.

Newman, Martha G. "Real Men and Imaginary Women: Engelhard of Langheim Considers a Woman in Disguise." *Speculum* 78 (2003), 1184–1213.

Roper, Lyndal. "Blood and Codpieces: Masculinity in the Early Modern German Town." In Roper, *Oedipus and the Devil,* 107–24. London: Routledge, 1994.

Shaw, David Gary. *Necessary Conjunctions: The Social Self in Medieval England.* New York: Palgrave Macmillan, 2005.

Shepard, Alexandra. "Manhood, Credit and Patriarchy in Early Modern England c. 1580–1640." *Past and Present* 167 (2000), 75–106.

Swanson, R. N. "Angels Incarnate: Clergy and Masculinity from Gregorian Reform to Reformation." In *Masculinity in Medieval Europe,* ed. D. M. Hadley, 160–77. London: Longman, 1999.

Thomas, Keith. "The Double Standard." *Journal of the History of Ideas* 20 (1959), 195–216.

Wunderli, Richard M. *London Church Courts and Society on the Eve of the Reformation.* Cambridge: Medieval Academy of America, 1981.

Contributors

Sandy Bardsley, Associate Professor of History at Moravian College, is the author of *Venomous Tongues: Speech and Gender in Late Medieval England* (University of Pennsylvania Press, 2006). Her essay on women's wages appeared in *Past and Present* while essays on speech crimes have been included in several collections.

Scott G. Bruce is Assistant Professor of History at the University of Colorado at Boulder. Cambridge University Press has just published his *Silence and Sign Language in Medieval Monasticism: The Cluniac Tradition (c. 900–1200)*.

Edwin D. Craun is the Henry S. Fox, Jr., Professor of English at Washington and Lee University. He is the author of *Lying, Slander, and Obscenity: Pastoral Discourse and the Deviant Speaker* (Cambridge University Press, 1997); his essays on blasphemy, lying, slander, and excuses for sin have appeared in *Traditio, Studies in Philology*, *"Fama": The Politics of Talk and Reputation in Medieval Europe* (Cornell University Press, 2003), and *In the Garden of Evil: The Vices and Culture in the Middle Ages* (Pontifical Institute of Mediaeval Studies, 2005).

Elizabeth Ewan is University Research Chair in History / Scottish Studies at the University of Guelph. She has written extensively on women, urban life, governmental authority, and crime in medieval and early modern Scotland since her *Town Life in Fourteenth-Century Scotland* (Edinburgh University Press, 1990). She has co-edited *Women in Scotland c. 1100–c.1750* (Tuckwell, 1999) and *The Biographical Dictionary of Scottish Women* (Edinburgh University Press, 2006).

Miriam Gill teaches and is Slide Curator in the Department of the History of Art and Film, the University of Leicester. She has published extensively

209

on English mural cycles in relation to preaching, gender, monastic education, and the cult of the saints. She has worked recently on the Christianity and Culture Project: Images of Salvation.

DEREK NEAL's book *The Masculine Self: Men in Late Medieval England* is forthcoming from the University of Chicago Press. He has authored several articles on masculinity, including one on masculine identity in late medieval England in *Writing Medieval History* (Hodder Arnold, 2005); he teaches history at Nipissing University.

SUSAN PHILLIPS, Assistant Professor of English at Northwestern University, is the author of *Transforming Talk: The Problem with Gossip in Late Medieval England* (Penn State Press, 2007). Also forthcoming is "Gossip and (Un)official Writing" in *21st Century Approaches to Literature* (Oxford University Press, 2007).

PETER SCHROEDER is Professor of English, Emeritus, California State University at San Bernardino. His articles on Malory have appeared in *PMLA* and *Arthuriana*; he has also written on Old English poetry and Hrotsvita's plays.

Index

Typeset in 10 pt. LTC Goudy Oldstyle
with LTC Ornaments Three and
LTC Goudy Oldstyle Small Caps display

Designed by Linda K. Judy
Composed by Juleen Audrey Eichinger
Manufactured by Sheridan Books, Inc.

Medieval Institute Publications
College of Arts and Sciences
Western Michigan University
1903 W. Michigan Avenue
Kalamazoo, MI 49008-5432
http://www.wmich.edu/medieval/mip

 WESTERN MICHIGAN UNIVERSITY